THE PARTISAN
SPIRIT

PATRICIA WATLINGTON

THE PARTISAN SPIRIT

KENTUCKY POLITICS, 1779-1792

*Published for the Institute of Early American
History and Culture at Williamsburg, Virginia*

ATHENEUM

New York

1972

The Institute of Early American History and Culture
is sponsored jointly by the College of William and Mary
and the Colonial Williamsburg Foundation.

FOR

J. R. W.

AND

C. P. W.

FOREWORD

At the end of each school year, the very day I finish correcting exams and submitting grades, I reread Kingsley Amis's *Lucky Jim*. It has become a ritual to which I look forward, and knowing the book almost by heart now, I do not allow myself to read it at any other time of year. I sympathize with Jim Dixon's teaching and lecturing efforts, but most of all I muse on his effort at writing. "Let's see now; what's the exact title you've given it?" Welch asks Jim. "Let's see," Jim echoes Welch, "oh yes; *The economic influence of the developments in shipbuilding techniques, 1450 to 1485.* After all, that's what it's . . ." Jim is unable to finish the sentence. He is clear about the worth of his writing effort "from several points of view. From one of these, the thing's worth could be expressed in one short hyphenated indecency; from another, it was worth the amount of frenzied factgrubbing and fanatical boredom that had gone into it; from yet another, it was worthy of its aim, the removal of the 'bad impression' he'd so far made in the college and in his department."

A book on Kentucky politics from 1779 to 1792 perhaps

requires a similar apology. The thirteen years that it covers
are twenty-two fewer than Jim takes in, and the land area—
to say nothing of the population— is smaller. I think it as unlikely as Jim's article to redeem any "bad impression" I may
have made. As for the limited coverage, I shall say only that
it seemed to take this space to cover this material. As for
"frenzied fact-grubbing," I have certainly done that; but as
for "fanatical boredom," I have not experienced one moment
of it, with the sole exception of typing fair copies. The fact-
grubbing was always enjoyable, as was the travel that it took
to grub in facts (and grub it often was; some of the manuscripts had not been touched in years); and the writing was
always pleasurable. I look forward to more of it. Having
enjoyed it myself, I hope my readers will, too.

A host of people have contributed to the pleasure I have
found in researching and writing this volume. Not least are
the many librarians who facilitated my research, especially
Jacqueline Bull of the University of Kentucky. Several
friends have contributed to my work, including Julian P.
Boyd, Lowell H. Harrison, Jackson T. Main, Dwight Mikkelson, and particularly Joan W. Coward, who has for several
years offered me always helpful suggestions and corrections.
I am especially grateful to Stephen G. Kurtz, of the Institute
of Early American History and Culture, who rescued the
manuscript from the oblivion in which it languished at another press and offered to print it just as it stood (although I
did make some changes). Most particularly, I am indebted
to Edmund S. Morgan, who not only oversaw the development of this manuscript as a doctoral dissertation, but who
has also guided my professional growth since my graduation
from Yale. The Kentucky Historical Society and the Virginia
Historical Society have kindly given permission to reprint
material first published in their journals.

For any errors in the study I am, of course, alone responsible.

Quinnipiac College   PATRICIA WATLINGTON

CONTENTS

THE PARTISAN
SPIRIT

1

THE LAND

I PRIZE MY LIFE above Kentuckey lands—and shall take particular good care of myself upon all Occasions," [1] a young man wrote home in 1784. He was probably stretching the truth to comfort a worried mother. At that time few men traveled to Virginia's Kentucky district except to gain Kentucky land, and many established their holdings—as this young man did—only by risking their lives.

Virginia in the 1780s was a whale of a state, measuring nearly eight hundred miles from eye to tail. She suffered from the hump on her back, the Allegheny Mountains that lay in ridges from north to south, forming a series of barriers between Kentucky and Virginia proper. The man who called the mountains "divilish ruff" [2] was understating the case. They stood 3,000 feet tall, a forested, Indian-infested wilderness 250 miles across. Through the eastern ridges there were a few openings cut by rivers, but in the western-

1. William Breckinridge to Lettice Breckinridge, Dec. 22, 1784, Breckinridge Family Papers, I, Library of Congress.
2. Peter Byrns to John Preston, Nov. 6, 1790, Preston Family Papers (microfilm), Lib. of Congress.

most ridge—which extended from the Ohio River south to the Carolinas—there was only one break. That was Cumberland Gap, so narrow a wagon could not squeeze through it.[3]

Beyond these mountain barriers lay a new world. Even today the bluegrass region is beautiful; when it was virgin land it seemed "a garden where there was no forbidden fruit." [4] "A new sky and strange earth seemed to be presented to our view," wrote one pilgrim. "So rich a soil we had never seen before; covered with clover in full bloom, the woods were abounding with wild game—turkeys so numerous that it might be said they appeared but one flock, universally scattered in the woods." [5] Another recalled that "the face of this country was . . . delightful beyond conception. Nearly one-half of it was covered with cane, but between the brakes [of cane] there were spaces of open ground as if intended by nature for fields. The ground appeared extremely fertile and produced amazing quantities of weeds of various kinds, some wild grass, wild rye and clover. The . . . land appeared more level than at present, as the thickness of the growth prevented one from discovering the diversities." [6]

As for the vegetation, one observer wrote that the country was particularly rich with "cane, rye grass, and the native clover. The cane is a reed which grows to the height frequently of fifteen or sixteen feet, but more generally about ten or twelve feet, and is in thickness from the size of a goose quill, to that of two inches diameter; sometimes, yet seldom, it is larger. When it is slender, it never grows higher than from four to seven feet; it shoots up in one

3. Thomas Speed, *The Wilderness Road*, Filson Club Publications, No. 2 (Louisville, 1886), 29.

4. Samuel R. Walker, ed., *Memoirs of the Late the Hon. Felix Walker, of North Carolina* (New Orleans, 1877), 10.

5. *Ibid.*

6. "General Levi Todd's Narrative [1791]," in Willard Rouse Jillson, ed., *Tales of the Dark and Bloody Ground* . . . (Louisville, 1930), 73.

summer, but produces no leaves until the following year. It is an ever-green, and is, perhaps, the most nourishing food for cattle upon earth. No other milk or butter has such flavour and richness as that which is produced from cows which feed upon cane. . . . The rye grass, when it arrives to maturity, is from two feet and a half high to three and a half. . . . The clover is in no respect different from the clover in Europe, but as it is more coarse and luxuriant. There is a variety of other kinds of grass, which are found in different places." [7]

However picturesque the landscape and luxuriant the growth, it was the land itself that provoked the most frequent and eloquent descriptions. Men who had nursed crops out of Virginia's pale, tired sand or New England's rocky soil looked on the heavy loam of Kentucky as so many acres of black gold. "It is fine rich level land," [8] they said; "it is undubitably an immensely fertile soil." [9] Some were bankrupt for words: "Its fertility exceeds description"; [10] "the Land is so good that I cannot give it it's due Praise." [11] All were extravagant: "A richer and more Beautifull Cuntry than this I believe has never been seen in America yet. . . . [If my father] once sees the Cuntry he never will rest untill he gets in it to live." [12] Even Francis Asbury, who had been around enough to know, could offer

7. Gilbert Imlay, *A Description of the Western Territory of North America* . . . (Dublin, 1793), 41–42.

8. "Col. Christopher Gist's Journal," in J. Stoddard Johnston, ed., *First Explorations of Kentucky*, Filson Club Publications, No. 13 (Louisville, 1898), 122.

9. Peyton Short to Henry Skipwith, Feb. 1786, Short Family Papers, Lib. of Congress.

10. Peter Fontaine to Elizabeth Fontaine, Apr. 19, 1797, Shelby Family Papers, Samuel M. Wilson Collection, University of Kentucky, Lexington.

11. Journal of Thomas Hanson, July 8, 1774, copy in Commonplace Book, Campbell-Preston-Floyd Papers, Lib. of Congress.

12. George Rogers Clark to Jonathan Clark, July 6, 1775, in James Alton James, ed., *George Rogers Clark Papers, 1771–1781* (Illinois Historical Society, *Collections*, VIII [Springfield, Ill., 1912], Va. Ser., III), I, 9–10. Hereafter cited as James, ed., *Clark Papers*, I.

a superlative: "As to the land, it is the richest body of fertile soil I ever beheld." [13]

Except for the Indian danger, a man with an axe and a rifle could live in lazy comfort in Kentucky. Gilbert Imlay wrote, "That country produces [in addition to sugar maple] also all the pot-herbs which are common in Europe: several kinds of nuts grow in the forests, such as chesnuts, hickory, and black walnuts." The forests "abound in deer, wild turkeys, and a species of grouse which are called by the Americans promiscuously partridge or pheasant. There is an abundance of wild fowl," [14] all of them easy to kill and delectable to eat. The brakes of green cane, growing higher than a man's head, offered food to nourish a horse the year round. The water was pure, and nature had distributed salt licks across the country. Gigantic trees, amazing everyone by their size, offered material for a house and an apparently inexhaustible source of fuel—although the climate was reputedly so mild that one needed little firewood.

Above all there was the fertile soil; if the frontiersman chose to plant corn, it grew without cultivation. One early settler used to sit out in his cornfield at night just to listen and "thought he could hear the corn go tick, tick—it grew so fast." [15] Another claimed the corn sometimes grew six to eight inches in a twenty-four-hour period during wet or warm weather.[16] A third, asked about the land, replied,

13. *The Journals of the Rev. Francis Asbury* (New York, 1821), II, 74.

14. Imlay, *Description*, 89–90.

15. John D. Shane's interview with Patrick Scott, Lyman C. Draper Collection, Kentucky Papers, XI, 6, Wisconsin Historical Society, Madison. Draper's large and complex collection is divided into some 50 groups of papers, many of them running to dozens of volumes. Each group is given a letter designation, the Kentucky Papers being called "CC." It is conventional to cite first the volume of the grouping, then the letter designation, and finally the page within the volume. Thus this citation will hereafter be given as Draper Coll., 11 CC 6.

16. Harry Toulmin, *The Western Country in 1793; Reports on Kentucky and Virginia*, eds. Marion Tinling and Godfrey Davies

"Last summer, in walking through my field, I stuck my cane in the ground by a hill of corn to see how fast it (the corn) grew, and forgot it until gathering time, when we found that every stalk bore two ears of corn, while the cane had a nubbin on it."[17] "With moderate cultivation" corn yielded from sixty to eighty bushels an acre.[18] It is said that a frontier preacher concluding his sermon declared, "Heaven is . . . ," and then paused, lost for an image. No wonder he ended triumphantly, "Heaven is a Kentucky of a place!"[19]

The beauty of landscape, the fertility of soil, the ease of life, and above all else the emptiness of Kentucky made it a topic of the nation's conversation. "What a Buzzel is this amongst People about Kentuck?" a clergyman asked; "to hear people speak of it one would think it was a new found Paradise."[20] To many Americans "Kentucky" did mean something like "heaven,"[21] and it had the advantage of being attainable in this life, even though the gate was narrow, the way was hard, and there were relatively few who found it. More people spoke of going than actually went; John Rogers wrote that "one would think from the Discourse that is Generally heard among the People that half Virginia Intended to Kentucky."[22] Yet thousands did go, including one man who

(San Marino, Calif., 1948), 73. Hereafter cited as Toulmin, *Western Country*.

17. Leer Buckley, "Early Days of Kentucky's Government," *The Register of the Kentucky State Historical Society*, XL(1942), 406. Hereafter cited as *Register*.

18. Daniel Drake, *Pioneer Life in Kentucky*, Ohio Valley Historical Series, No. 6 (Cincinnati, 1870), 48. See also Imlay, *Description*, 93.

19. Arthur K. Moore, *The Frontier Mind: A Cultural Analysis of the Kentucky Frontiersman* (Lexington, 1957), 11. The preacher was Lewis Craig. Samuel Meredith to John Breckinridge, May 2, 1791, Breckinridge Family Papers, VII.

20. John Brown, Sr., to William Preston, May 5, 1775, Draper Coll., 4 QQ 15.

21. For a discussion of the concept of Kentucky as an earthly paradise see Moore, *Frontier Mind*, 11–43.

22. John Rogers to G. R. Clark, Oct. 17, 1779, James, ed., *Clark Papers*, I, 373.

had to spend eighteen years persuading his wife to make the move.[23]

Those who made the trip through the wilderness to Kentucky found that it took at least four perilous and tiresome weeks. It was sometimes as frightening to those who stayed at home as to the travelers themselves; "Pray my Dear Mr. Breckenridge," a wife would write, "be very caucious in comeing home especially in comeing through the Wilderness, As my whole happiness or Misery As to this life depends on your return."[24] People who made the journey carried food and spirits with them, and when supplies ran low they relied on game. Nights they slept on their baggage in tents or bark huts, keeping watch for Indians and thieves; days they rode their horses through the snow, forded creeks, and continued to watch for Indians. "[We] come to a turabel mountain that tried us all almost to death to get over it," one traveler recorded. "This morning there is ice at our camp half inch thick   we start Early and travel this Day along a verey Bad hilley way   cross one creek whear the horses almost got mired   Some fell in and all wet their loads   we . . . travell till late in the Night."[25]

To avoid the trip through the wilderness one could go down the Ohio River, but this alternate route was even longer and almost equally hazardous. The traveler went overland to Pittsburgh—or "Pitt," as it came to be called[26] —and waited there, perhaps for months, until the river was high enough to carry a boat. A lady would decline invitations to visit on shore because her traveling clothes were unfit for public view; she might serve wine and cheese to

23. Thomas Hart to William Blount, Dec. 23, 1793, Thomas J. Clay Papers, 1st Ser., II, Lib. of Congress.
24. Mary Breckinridge to John Breckinridge, Apr. 12, 1789, Breckinridge Family Papers, V.
25. Lewis H. Kilpatrick, ed., "The Journal of William Calk, Kentucky Pioneer," *Mississippi Valley Historical Review*, VII(1920–1921), 366–367.
26. David Meade to Ann Meade Randolph, Sept. 1, 1796, William Bolling Papers, Duke University, Durham, N.C.

guests in her cabin and be frightened by the militia gathered
on account of an Indian alarm.[27] But finally the river would
rise, and she would set off for Kentucky in a flatboat big
enough to carry a whole family with its cattle and household goods. One such boat "was fifty-five feet long, twelve
wide and six deep, drawing three feet of water. On its deck
had been built a low cabin, but very neat, divided into
several apartments, and on the forecastle, the cattle and
horses were kept as in a stable. It was loaded with bricks,
boards, planks, bars of iron, coal, instruments of husbandry,
dismounted wagons, anvils, billows, dry goods, brandy,
flour, biscuits, hams, lard and salt meat, etc." [28] Whether
she admired the beautiful Ohio or found the trip "the
fatiguinest time I ever saw," [29] the lady traveler was always
conscious of danger.

Both the wilderness route and the river route were
hazardous. One expected Indian encounters during the
wilderness trip, and many travelers actually were killed or
taken prisoner. The river route was somewhat safer, but
travelers seldom forgot the possibility of Indians lurking
behind those trees that lined the river. Even more distressing
than the Indians, perhaps, were the normal workings of
nature. A pregnant woman riding through the wilderness
dismounted to give birth and rested a few hours; then,
thanking the men who had constructed her buffalo-hide
shelter, she remounted her horse and rode on to Kentucky.[30]
A family traveling the river route, carrying supplies for
seven days, went eight weeks without bread when the river
froze, and a son lost part of his toes from frostbite.[31] Many

27. Mary Coburn Dewees, *Journal of a Trip from Philadelphia to
Lexington in Kentucky* . . . (Crawfordsville, Ind., 1936), 8–9.
28. Hector St. John de Crèvecoeur, "Sketch of the River Ohio and
of the Country of Kentucky," trans. from Vol. III of *Lettres d'un
Cultivateur Américain* . . . (Paris, 1787), in Durrett Collection,
University of Chicago.
29. Journal of Ichabod Benton Miller, Draper Coll., 13 CC 27.
30. John S. Goff, "Mr. Justice Trimble of the United States
Supreme Court," *Register*, LVIII(1960), 10.
31. "Unfinished Autobiography of John Rowan," in Jillson, ed.,
Tales, 93.

a man lost the accumulations of a lifetime when a heavily loaded boat struck a log and sank. Yet these and worse misfortunes were usually accepted quietly, for they were inherent in the journey. "Although we saw a great many of our things a swimming off," one victim of a sunken boat recalled, "their appeared to be not a murmur or regret but thankfull it was no worse than it was." [32]

Few people dared to travel alone. Usually they came through the wilderness in parties ranging in size from half a dozen to several hundred people. Almost every group included a variety of persons: men and women, cultured and crude, black and white, Scotch and Irish, Protestant and Catholic; a fat man wealthy enough to ride a fine horse; [33] a man who walked through the wilderness with his pantaloon legs rolled up and his feet bare, his wife beside him carrying a child; [34] a patriarch traveling with his three sons, four daughters, two daughters-in-law, five grandchildren, and forty Negroes; [35] "women and Children in the Month of December Travelling a Wilderness Through Ice and Snow passing large rivers and Creeks with out Shoe or Stocking, and barely as maney raggs as covers their Nakedness, with out money or provisions except what the Wilderness affords, the Situation of such can better be Imagined then discribed. To say they are poor is but faintly expressing their Situation,—life *What is it,* Or *What can it give,* to make Compensation for such accumulated Misery." [36]

"Ask these Pilgrims what they expect when they git to

32. Mememorandum [sic] made by me D Trabue in the year of 1827 of a Jurnal of events from memory and Tradition, Draper Coll., 57 J 131. Hereafter cited as Trabue narrative.
33. *Ibid.,* 39.
34. "Reverend John D. Shane's Interview with Pioneer William Clinkenbeard," *Filson Club History Quarterly,* II(1927–1928), 98.
35. "Reminiscences of James Bledsoe Tandy," *Register,* LIII(1955), 101–114.
36. "A Memorandum of M[oses] Austin's Journey . . . ," *American Historical Review,* V(1899–1900), 525. The people described in this quotation actually came in 1796, 20 years after some of the others in this paragraph.

Kentuckey. The Answer is Land."
   " 'Have you any?'
   " 'No, but I expect I can get it.'
   " 'Have you any thing to pay for land?'
   " 'No.'
   " 'Did you Ever see the Country?'
   " 'No but Every Body says its good land.'
"Can anything be more Absurd than the Conduct of man?"
the questioner wondered. "Here is hundreds Travelling
hundreds of Miles, they Know not for what nor Whither,
except its to Kentucky, passing land almost as good and
easy obtained, . . . but it will not do: its not Kentuckey,
its not the Promised land, its not the goodly inheritance, the
Land of Milk and Honey." [37]

"A goodly land I will allow," the traveler commented,
"but to them a forbidden land." [38] Actually Kentucky was
not a forbidden land to settlers, but neither was she the
"garden where there was no forbidden fruit" that an earlier
visitor had pictured. Even after the legal mechanics were
clearly defined, obtaining Kentucky land was not a simple
matter. Many of the settlers, even men nearly illiterate,
could take the uncertainty of land titles in their stride; day
by day they could live with it and find pleasure in discovering what moves would validate their own titles by depriving
their neighbors of land. Others were baffled by the confusion of claims. Too simple, too straightforward, or too
poor to press their cases, "exhausted and worn down with
distress and disappointment," they were "at last Obliged to
become hewers of wood and Drawers of water." [39]

In 1777, the year after Virginia asserted her claim over
Kentucky by establishing Kentucky County,[40] the legislature

   37. *Ibid.* I have edited the punctuation of this paragraph.
   38. *Ibid.*
   39. *Ibid.*
   40. William Waller Hening, ed., *The Statutes at Large; Being a
Collection of All the Laws of Virginia* . . . (Richmond, 1819–
1823), IX, 257. Hereafter cited as Hening, ed., *Statutes.*

resolved that titles to western lands would be given free to men who had settled there before June 1, 1776.[41] With its implicit promise of free land also for those who settled in Kentucky after 1776, this law was probably intended to stimulate migration to Kentucky, since western settlers would protect Virginia proper from Indian attacks. To insure that land claimants would be bona fide settlers the legislature specified that land would be given only to those who had made some improvement, such as raising a crop of corn or building a cabin. The "ancient cultivation law"—as it came to be known—did impel many people to go to Kentucky. Some, however, were inspired to go for the sole purpose of building a cabin there and so stayed only a few weeks,[42] and others hired a settler to build a cabin for them, without making even a brief trip to Kentucky.[43]

When in 1779 Virginia redefined the means of claiming Kentucky land, she fulfilled the promise of the ancient cultivation law by giving land to everyone who had built a cabin in Kentucky before 1778.[44] By that time, however, Virginia had on her hands a war for independence and an empty treasury, and it seemed as important to pay the soldiers and fill the coffers as to populate the frontier.[45] Consequently, she added to the settlement right two other types of claims on Kentucky land, military bounties and actual purchases. To each of her soldiers in the war she gave bounties ranging from fifty acres for privates to five

41. *Ibid.*, IX, 358.
42. Petition to Virginia, No. 8 in James Rood Robertson, ed., *Petitions of the Early Inhabitants of Kentucky to the General Assembly of Virginia, 1769–1792*, Filson Club Publications, No. 27 (Louisville, 1914), 47.
43. Petition of William Lytle, No. 22, *ibid.*, 74–75; Charles Gano Talbert, *Benjamin Logan, Kentucky Frontiersman* (Lexington, 1962), 89.
44. Hening, ed., *Statutes*, X, 35–50.
45. For a more precise discussion of factors involved in the passage of the 1779 land laws, see Thomas Perkins Abernethy, *Western Lands and the American Revolution* (New York, 1937), especially 217–229.

thousand for field officers.[46] Then she opened a land office
for the sale of western lands at forty pounds per hundred
acres, in depreciated paper currency.[47]

The most certain, and the least common, of these land
claims was the one based on settlement. A man who had
settled in Kentucky before January 1, 1778, was entitled to
the four hundred acres on which he lived. If he had made
any improvement on the land, he could preempt and
purchase a thousand acres adjoining his four hundred. A
man who had settled in Kentucky between January 1, 1778,
and January 1, 1779, received no settlement grant, but he
was allowed to preempt four hundred acres at the state
price of forty pounds per hundred. Virginia sent a court of
land commissioners to Kentucky to rule on these settlement
and preemption claims, which were prior to any other claim.
When a man had convinced the commissioners that he had
settled on his land before 1778 and had paid their fee, he
was given a certificate. He could get a land warrant by
taking the commissioners' certificate to the land office, if he
paid the land office fee and performed all these tasks in the
allotted time.[48]

To all her soldiers in the French and Indian War [49] and
in the Revolution [50] Virginia granted land bounties; thus
claims based on military rights were far more common than
those based on settlement. To get his military land warrant
a veteran had to obtain a certificate from his commanding
officer stating that he had served faithfully. He had then to
present the certificate to any Virginia court of record and
take an oath or show evidence of the truth of the certificate; finally, he took the certificate—now signed by a
clerk of the court of record—to the register of the Virginia

46. Hening, ed., *Statutes*, X, 23–27, 159–162.
47. *Ibid.*, 50–65.
48. *Ibid.*, 35–50.
49. *Ibid.*, VIII, 663–669.
50. *Ibid.*, X, 23–27, 159–162.

land office in Richmond.[51] The warrant that he was then granted was similar to a settlement warrant in that it entitled him to claim land in Virginia. Unlike the settlement warrant, it specified no particular location for the claim.

Whether he held a treasury warrant that he had purchased or a military or settlement warrant obtained by several complex steps, a warrant owner still had to establish title to his land. If he had a military or treasury warrant, he had to "locate" it or hire someone to locate it; that is, he had to decide what land he wanted to claim. Then every warrant owner had to "enter" the land; this meant notifying the county surveyor of his wish to claim that particular area. When the time for surveying came, he had to provide and pay for chain carriers and a person to mark the lines. Finally, he had to deliver to the land office the plat and certificate that the surveyor would give him. After all this, if he had paid the fees imposed at almost every step, he would be issued a patent for his land.[52]

As if these procedures were not complicated enough, the Virginia legislature made matters even more difficult by imposing a time limitation at almost every point along the way and then changing these limitations frequently.[53] If any step were not completed within the allotted time, a claim might be invalid. The land would once again become "waste and unappropriated," and the original claimant or someone else could enter it again.[54] Extensions in the time limitations were designed to make the laws operate more equitably, but their results were so erratic that Kentucky settlers finally begged the legislature to desist. "We wish no new laws to pass or amendments to be made until you know the sentiments of a majority of our District," they

51. *Ibid.*, 50–65.
52. *Ibid.*, 35–50, XI, 353–359.
53. *Ibid.*, X, 237–241, 354, 403, 431, 484–487, XI, 91–92, 149–150, 296.
54. Unsigned paper in the hand of George Nicholas's amanuensis, [1792?], Isaac Shelby Papers, VIII, #2690–2692, Lib. of Congress.

petitioned, "because frequent alterations in the Laws are very inconvenient to our remote corner of the State." [55]

The Virginia legislature insisted that entries be made with sufficient precision that the land entered could be found again,[56] but in a country covered with forest and devoid of any landmarks except rivers and creeks, that was not always easy to do. A typical entry reads, "Edward Hall, enters six hundred and twenty-two acres of land, upon a treasury warrant, on Eagle creek, a branch of Kentucky [River]; beginning at a small beech, marked thus, I.N. on the north side of a small drain, then east 320 poles, then north at right angles for [the] quantity [of land allowed by the warrant]." [57] The description may seem specific enough until one stops to consider, as one surveyor did, that "Eagle creek is fifty miles in length—has a thousand drains—and a million beech trees." Then it was plain that "I.N. being cut on any one of them, left it still destitute of *notoriety*." [58] When entries were that imprecise, it was possible for half a dozen men to enter the same land, never knowing that their claims overlaid one another.

Even surveys could overlap, though they were the last step before the patent was finally issued. "Surveyed 21st day of May 1785 for Alexander Dudgeon 4348 1/2 Acres of land," a plat might read, "lying on Licking Creek . . . Beginning at a hickory and three white oaks standing on the East side of a small drain." [59] Or, "Surveyed for William Kennedy 650 Acres of Land in Campbell County on the NE side of Licking Beginning at 2 sugars and 2 ash

55. Petition from Lincoln County to Virginia General Assembly, No. 17 in Robertson, ed., *Petitions*, 69.
56. Hening, ed., *Statutes*, X, 50–65.
57. Humphrey Marshall, *The History of Kentucky. Exhibiting an account of the Modern Discovery; Settlement; Progressive Improvement; Civil and Military Transactions; and the Present State of the Country*, 2d ed. (Frankfort, Ky., 1824), I, 151. This entry Marshall undoubtedly copied from an old surveyor's book, probably from his own or possibly from that of his father-in-law, Thomas Marshall.
58. *Ibid*.
59. Survey in Breckinridge Family Papers, II.

and white oak trees. . . ." [60] If it happened, as it sometimes did, that a hickory and three white oaks on Licking Creek stood near two sugars, two ashes, and two white oaks, one survey might easily lie atop the other. The only law governing the shape and placement of surveys was one providing that they should be at least one-third as wide as they were long,[61] so virtually nothing except the limit of his imagination could confine a surveyor who wanted to cover the largest possible amount of good land. Surveys were usually in the shape of a rectangle, but sometimes they took forms unknown to the geometrician.[62]

Thus it happened that almost every inch of Kentucky land was disputed. The Virginia legislature did, thoughtfully enough, provide a legal means by which a claim could be challenged. To throw the whole matter into the courts, one had only to file at the land office a caveat against someone else's claim.[63] In this way Virginia laid the foundation for a series of lawsuits that would clog the Kentucky courts for years. "The variety of different kinds of Claims, the Vagueness of their Location, and the very great number of Warrants granted by the State," said one surveyor, had made it impossible for anyone holding several warrants "to Locate them . . . to advantage without involving himself in disputes." [64] The litigation that resulted lasted nearly a century and a half.

The overlapping of land claims in Kentucky has been likened to the overlapping of shingles on a roof. Actually no competent roofer would ever have laid shingles so crookedly. Because there were three different kinds of claims and because entries and even surveys might overlap

60. Survey, *ibid.*, III.
61. Hening, ed., *Statutes*, X, 50–65.
62. An example is the memorable survey made for Evan Shelby on Beaver Creek (now West Virginia), Jan. 4, 1775, Shelby Papers, I, Lib. of Congress.
63. Hening, ed., *Statutes*, X, 50–65.
64. John May to Samuel Meredith and George Clymer, Aug. 5, 1789, T. J. Clay Papers, 2d Ser., I, Lib. of Congress.

within each type of claim, there might be six or more claimants for any given field. On the other hand, an entry so quickly became invalid if the claimant failed to provide for a survey, and so many people delayed the surveys from inability or unwillingness to pay the surveyor's fee,[65] that occasionally there was no claim at all to an exceptionally promising piece of land.[66] It was a situation to intrigue the brilliant and baffle the dull, to enrich the lucky and impoverish the unfortunate.

When Virginia passed the land laws of 1779, it had not yet been clearly established that she owned Kentucky. The wealth that presumably lay in Kentucky's fertile emptiness intrigued many people, including the members of several companies expressly organized to gain control of western lands. Although Kentucky was apparently included in Virginia's 1609 charter, the land companies with claims in that area were attempting to show that the king had never granted it to Virginia. They argued that from him it had fallen to the nation as a whole and that it thus belonged under the jurisdiction of the Continental Congress. Most of the land companies were operating out of Philadelphia and could not profit from the Virginia claim, but a congressional claim would mean they might cash in on their purchases of the land from Indians. They evidently hoped to receive congressional land grants and then to sell the land in small parcels at high prices.[67]

The land laws of 1779 were Virginia's answer to the land companies. She cemented the interest of settlers to her claim by giving them land under it and urged a host of soldiers to take up lands under the Virginia claim and become settlers.

65. Hening, ed., *Statutes*, XI, 441.
66. Humphrey Marshall found such a field, now the site of the capital of Kentucky. Willard Rouse Jillson, *Early Frankfort and Franklin County, Kentucky* (Louisville, 1936), 31.
67. Abernethy, *Western Lands*, especially 230–241.

More important, she invited speculators to join her. The act establishing the land office provided specifically that a man might buy as much land as his heart desired and his pocketbook permitted without any requirement that he cultivate it or even that he ever see it.[68] In case a man's heart was willing, but his pocketbook weak, Virginia even permitted investors to buy Kentucky land on credit.[69]

Many speculators took the bait. The day the land office opened, October 15, 1779, a crowd was there to buy Kentucky land,[70] and many more brought warrants later. *"People are Running Mad for Kentucky Hereabouts,"* [71] one Virginian wrote. Hundreds of thousands of acres were sold; land was dispensed in staggering quantities. A single man acquired treasury warrants for a million and a half acres, and another gained a million acres.[72] Kentucky became a place "where principalities are acquired, and real Lords of the creation will arise." [73] There was hardly a statesman of Virginia or a statesman-to-be of Kentucky who did not own a few thousand acres at least.

When the land office in Kentucky opened on May 1, 1780, and the surveyor of Kentucky County began to take entries on treasury warrants, it became obvious that Virginia had sold or had given away far too much land.[74] States ought "to be *just,* before they are *generous,"* [75] a speculator said later. Virginia had delayed the opening of the Kentucky land office a year to give settlers and soldiers time to enter their claims before any treasury warrants were

68. Hening, ed., *Statutes,* X, 50–65.
69. *Ibid.,* 177–182.
70. John Rogers to G. R. Clark, Oct. 17, 1779, James, ed., *Clark Papers,* I, 373.
71. Joseph Herndon to Jonathan Clark, Oct. 23, 1779, Draper Coll., 1 L 71.
72. Abernethy, *Western Lands,* 228.
73. John Taylor to George Nicholas, June 23, 1790, Henry Clay Papers, I, Lib. of Congress.
74. See Paul W. Gates, "Tenants of the Log Cabin," *Miss. Valley Hist. Rev.,* XLIX(1962–1963), 4.
75. Marshall, *Kentucky,* I, 153.

entered, and it seemed that the military warrants alone would cover most of Kentucky's good land.[76] Yet treasury warrants for 1,600,000 acres were lodged in the surveyor's office before May 1,[77] and when the office opened so many people were waiting to enter treasury land that they finally cast lots to see who would go first.[78] The applicants that day were so numerous that it took the surveyor, John Floyd, and his two or three deputies several days to receive the treasury warrants, and people had to wait fifteen or twenty days more while he arranged the warrants before they could actually enter the land.[79] "The state [treasury] warrants of a late date I fear will be of little value," [80] Floyd wrote.

Eventually land warrants did depreciate wildly. "The Depretiation of Land Warrants being equal to that of the Paper Currency has become a Publick Notority," some settlers would complain in 1782; "the one Exchanges for the other without being in credit for scarcely any Commodity." [81] In 1779 and 1780, however, land warrants were a desirable commodity, as sought after in Kentucky as in Virginia. Sometimes warrants were sold several times before a title was established; a patent for treasury land might grant "unto Thomas Welsh, assignee of Jesse Cartwright, assignee of John Holden, assignee of L. Ship, who was assignee of James Winn a certain tract . . . of land." [82]

76. John Floyd to William Preston, May 5, 1780, Draper Coll., 17 CC 124–127.

77. *Ibid.*

78. Trabue narrative, *ibid.*, 57 J 51.

79. "Bradford's Notes on Kentucky," *Kentucky Gazette* (Lexington), Oct. 13, 1826.

80. Floyd to Wm. Preston, May 5, 1780, Draper Coll., 17 CC 124–127.

81. Petition to Virginia General Assembly, spring 1782 (read May 30, 1782), No. 15 in Robertson, ed., *Petitions,* 64 (original in Virginia State Library, Richmond).

82. Patent dated Sept. 20, 1786, J. T. Dorris, "Early Kentucky History in Madison County Circuit Court Records," *Register,* XLIII(1945), 83.

Military claims were as subject to speculation as treasury claims, and settlement and preemption rights were the most desirable of all. One man was offered six fine Virginia-born Negroes for his commissioners' certificate,[83] surely a handsome price for only fourteen hundred acres, even though it was the choicest of Kentucky land. "You never saw such keenness as is here about land," [84] he reported.

A warrant, of course, had no real value until it was laid on good land. Because it was impossible to locate land except by going to Kentucky, speculators often operated in pairs, one remaining in Virginia and the other moving west. They used a multitude of devices for acquiring choice locations. It was reported that "some fellows (a Craig and Broadehead) have a great scheme in contemplation which is to caveat the Lands surveyed on old Military Warrants granted by Lord Dunmore and which by a law of the May session of 1783 appear to be forfeited." [85] Another speculator made his entries on lands that had previously been entered but had never been surveyed.[86] Almost all of these men had friends in the Virginia legislature and in the Kentucky surveyors' offices. Some also had friends in Congress whom they found helpful.

"In case it should be in your power to procure any military Warrants," wrote one Kentucky speculator to his partner in Virginia, "I think you had better not get an assignment on the Warrant [from the original owner to yourself] but a power of attorney to the Surveyor to transfer the Plate which will be much less expence; the expence of entering in an assigned warrant is a dollar for every hundred [acres] which would amount to a very considerable sum to

83. Floyd to Wm. Preston, Oct. 30, 1779, Draper Coll., 17 CC 184–185.

84. *Ibid.*

85. James Preston to John Breckinridge, May 31, 1784, Breckinridge Family Papers, II.

86. John Fowler to Henry Lee, Aug. 14, 1784, Draper Coll., 13 CC 5.

enter a large Quantity and the cost of an assignment on a
Plate is but very trifling." [87] To men who thought in terms
of hundreds of thousands of acres, a dollar for each hundred
acres would have amounted to a very considerable sum
indeed. Consequently, the patents were granted in the
name of the warrant's original owner, and today it is impossible to know how much Kentucky land any Virginian
owned.

Unable to find choice locations for themselves, absentee
speculators and new migrants had to rely on settlers who
knew the Kentucky forest thoroughly, the woodsmen pioneers and the surveyors. The business of locating, or "land-
jobbing," became an important one in Kentucky. Locators
received a handsome price for their services. Sometimes they
were paid in cash, but more often they were given a part
of the land; this presumably stimulated them to find especially good tracts and to seek out land that would be free
from disputes. "The general rule is to give . . . one fourth
of the land clear of any expence to the person who located,"
one wrote home; "this I think is very reasonable." [88] Since
most locators took one-third and later some took one-half,
one-fourth of the land was indeed reasonable.[89]

The speculators and locators soon realized that the flow
of migration into Kentucky worked to their disadvantage.
The migrants were prone to build a cabin and settle on any
spot that seemed unoccupied, even if it had been surveyed
for someone else, and before 1779 they were often able
to establish a claim to it. "Weak *Kentucke*," a locator wrote,
"is distracted with the clashing Interests of Cabinning and
surveying. . . . How it may end Heaven Knows! I'm
afraid to loose sight of my House lest some Invader takes

87. James Breckinridge to John Breckinridge, Nov. 18, 1784,
Breckinridge Family Papers, II.
88. *Ibid.*
89. Deposition of John Twyman, Depositions in the case of *Innes*
v. *Marshall*, 15, Durrett Coll.

possession." [90] Later migrants were unable to establish a title by settling alone, but they continued to invade the lands of absentee investors and to destroy their timber.

Not all of the investors in Kentucky land were absentee speculators. In an era when currency was depreciating wildly, an investment in land was probably the safest repository for money, and many Virginians probably bought land to retain, rather than to increase, their assets. Furthermore, many Virginians bought Kentucky land because they intended to go to Kentucky, and numbers did make the move after their titles were established. Many settlers also came to hold large quantities of land. Those who were in Kentucky between 1776 and 1784, when most of the Virginia warrants were located, were often able to serve as land-jobbers and thus to build up enormous estates. It was, in fact, a rare pioneer who did not leave at least a few hundred acres to his children. Daniel Boone and Simon Kenton, the traditional examples of poverty-stricken pioneers, were perhaps almost the only ones who died poor.

Any pioneer who owned a settlement and preemption right of fourteen hundred acres—and every absentee investor—had more land than he was able to farm. The absentees resented the invasion of settlers, but resident landowners were often glad when migrants came to live on their soil,[91] for life could be lonely and dangerous in a wilderness. One such resident landowner even promised men that they could stay rent-free until the end of the Revolution, if they would settle on his place.[92] As late as 1790 such arrangements existed in parts of Kentucky, for that year one man settled at Mayslick for five rent-free years because he built a cabin and cleared the land.[93] Ordi-

90. John Todd to Wm. Preston, June 22, 1776, Draper Coll., 4 QQ 52.
91. Floyd to Wm. Preston, Nov. 26, 1779, *ibid.*, 17 CC 186–187.
92. "Clinkenbeard Interview," *Filson Club Hist. Qtly.*, II(1927–1928), 103.
93. Drake, *Pioneer Life*, 27–28.

narily owners rented their holdings to landless newcomers. There are a multitude of references in their papers to the renting of land; [94] thus Kentucky was, almost from its very beginning, an area of landlords and tenants as well as of small farms held in fee simple.

The great migration to Kentucky began in the winter of 1778/1779 and came chiefly from Virginia, Pennsylvania, and North Carolina. Some of the migrants were criminals, and some were political outlaws. Others were surveyors, lawyers, and merchants who expected to make a fortune in the West, or gentlemen who hoped to establish great plantations where forests stood. Most, however, were modest, law-abiding citizens, "plain honest peaceable Sober and Industrious People," [95] whose highest aspiration was to own the land on which they lived. Hearing the buzzel of conversation about Kentucky, they built a dream on the promise of free land to settlers or, later, on the strength of treasury warrants.

94. See, for example, James Breckinridge to Lettice Breckinridge, Feb. 26, 1784, Breckinridge Family Papers, I; entry of Sept. 20, 1784, in John C. Fitzpatrick, ed., *The Diaries of George Washington, 1748–1799* (Boston, 1925), II, 294–298; William Christian's will, 1786, in Katharine G. Healy, ed., "Calendar of Early Jefferson County, Kentucky, Wills; Will Book No. 1: April, 1784–June, 1813," *Filson Club Hist. Qtly.*, VI(1932), 5; John Smith to John Preston, May 22, 1786, Preston Papers, #1429, Lib. of Congress; Annie Christian to Elizabeth Christian, Aug. 17, 1787, William Fleming Papers, Washington and Lee College, Lexington, Va.; William Russell to John Breckinridge, June 29, 1790, Breckinridge Family Papers, V; Lucien Beckner, ed., "John D. Shane's Interview with Benjamin Allen, Clark County," *Filson Club Hist. Qtly.*, V(1931), 68; Toulmin, *Western Country*, 80; Lowell Harrison, John Breckinridge: Western Statesman (unpubl. Ph.D. diss., New York University, 1951), 242–243; Otto A. Rothert, ed., "John D. Shane's Interview with Pioneer John Hedge, Bourbon County," *Filson Club Hist. Qtly.*, XIV(1940), 177; Lucien Beckner, ed., "Letter from George Washington to Charles Morgan of Kentucky, 1795," [Jan. 17, 1795], *ibid.*, III(1928–1929), 26–27; R. C. Ballard Thruston, ed., "Letter by Edward Harris, 1797," [to Thomas Christie, Apr. 11, 1797], *ibid.*, II(1927–1928), 164–168.

95. J. M. Nan Harlinger's petition in behalf of the Low Dutch inhabitants of Kentucky, Papers of the Continental Congress, XLI, Fol. 5, no. 95, National Archives.

Often ignorant of legal complexities, these migrants swarmed into the Kentucky forest and settled wherever the prospect seemed good. They cleared away the trees and built their cabins on whatever piece of land was unoccupied, expecting to claim it for their own. They soon learned, however, that unoccupied land was often already claimed and that they were not free to cut trees and build cabins wherever fancy led. Virginia, they found, was no longer giving land to settlers. She would give it to those who came before 1778 and to her men who fought in the Revolution. She would sell it to anyone who could pay the price, and eventually she would offer preemption purchases to settlers who came before 1781. But to the thousands of men who crossed the mountains after 1777 she would give nothing at all, and even to those who came with treasury warrants she would not offer a secure claim.

Virginia's treatment of those migrants who came after 1777 seemed so obviously mistaken that it was hard for settlers to believe. Men who lived in Kentucky bore the heaviest burden of Indian raids; by their very presence on the frontier they protected the interior parts of Virginia, and by their enforced service in the militia they helped secure her title to Kentucky. Yet even repeated petitions did not change Virginia's treatment of settlers.[96] She consistently ignored the men who complained that "almost the whole of the lands . . . are Engrossed into the hands of a few Interested men, the greater part of which live at ease in the internal parts of Virginia." [97] Genuine settlers could not "secure a small quainty of Land any way tolerable to live on." [98] They were "under the disagreeable necessity of going Down the Mississippi, to the Spanish protection, or be-

96. An annotated list of these petitions is given in the Bibliography.
97. Petition to Congress, read 1780, Papers of Continental Congress, Ser. 48, 245, National Archives.
98. Petition to Congress, May 15, 1780 (read Aug. 24, 1780), *ibid.*, 237, also in Theodore Roosevelt, *The Winning of the West* (New York, 1889–1896), II, 398–399.

THE LAND

coming tennants to private gentlemen . . . which is too
rough a medicine ever to be dejested." [99] Many settlers did
go down the river into Spanish territory [100] or into the Ohio
country,[101] decreasing the population of Kentucky and caus-
ing army officers to beg for better laws. Others settled for
second- or third-rate land, and some apparently managed
to digest the medicine.[102]

Even settlers who seemed to hold a valid claim under
Virginia were sometimes unable to establish it. Some,
"through illetrisy, and unable to ascertain the true meaning
of the Law with the Troubles of Indians," had "not Enter'd
their Lands so special and precise as the Law Requires," [103]
while others failed to meet the time limitation. One such
settler was William Lytle. In 1775 he hired a man to make
an improvement on a tract of Kentucky land, assuming this
would entitle him to a settlement right. He himself came
down the Ohio to Kentucky in the spring of 1780. No
sooner had he landed his boat at the Falls of Ohio and led
off his horses than they strayed, and without a horse he
could not make the seventy-five-mile trip to Harrodsburg to
present his claim. Before he could search for the horses he
had to build a cabin for his family; then, "being unac-
quainted with the law and reduced . . . by Sickness and
Misfortunes," he let the time limit expire before he filed
his claim.[104] There was thus no land for William Lytle in
spite of his careful effort to circumvent the old cultivation
law.

99. Petition to Virginia, summer 1779 (read Oct. 14, 1779), Va.
State Lib., also No. 6 in Robertson, ed., Petitions, 46.
100. John Dodge to Thomas Jefferson, Aug. 1, 1780, William P.
Palmer et al., eds., Calendar of Virginia State Papers . . . (1652–
1869) (Richmond, 1875–1893), I, 367–369.
101. Rothert, ed., "Hedge Interview," Filson Club Hist. Qtly.,
XIV(1940), 181.
102. See above, p. 23.
103. Petition to Virginia, spring 1782, Va. State Lib., also No. 15
in Robertson, ed., Petitions, 64.
104. Petition of Lytle, No. 22, ibid., 74–75.

Another settler who lost a claim was Daniel Trabue. He had purchased treasury warrants for two thousand acres and had located his warrants in a choice spot. When the land office opened in Kentucky, he and his brother James went to enter their warrants with the surveyor, but so many people were waiting that they had to cast lots to see who would go first. James was able to make a few of his entries; before they could enter any other locations they had to wait several days. Consequently, they went home again. When the several days had passed, James persuaded Daniel that one of them should stay at home and attend to hoeing the corn. Then James took all their warrants and set off for the land office without Daniel, but on his way he was taken prisoner by Indians. "This was melencholy knews to me," Daniel later recalled, "my land [warrants] gone that had cost me a great Deal   but that Did not Distrys me like the loss of My Brother." James finally returned, but the Indians had taken his pocketbook, and Daniel never did recover his warrants.[105]

Uncertainties about claims were compounded by the tangle of lawsuits that surrounded almost every acre of land. "[We] are like to be overwhelmed in Litigation; which will not only create discords amongst us, but ruin hundreds of poor Families, who being opprest and stript of almost their whole Substance by the Indians, have not the Means of defraying the Expenses of a Land Suit," some settlers complained. "If we prosecute our Claim the last Cow and Horse must be sold to maintain the Suit; or if we decline the Contest, the Land upon which we had Hopes of supporting ourselves and Families in peace during the Remainder of our Lives will be wrested from us."[106] The establishment of a district court in Kentucky[107] eased the

105. Trabue narrative, Draper Coll., 57 J 51–52. See also extracts from the Ashby family letters in *Register*, XLVII(1949), 241.
106. Petition to Virginia, spring 1784 (read June 5, 1784), Va. State Lib., also No. 23 in Robertson, ed., *Petitions*, 76.
107. Hening, ed., *Statutes*, XI, 85–90, 103; see below, p. 53.

expense of land suits but did not decrease their number.
Settlers trying to establish a claim sometimes remained uncertain about it for many years.

Added to the difficulties of claiming land after 1777 was
an Indian war, the frontier version of the American Revolution. Indians were a far more terrible enemy than English
troops. It was their unpredictability, as well as their bar-
barity, that made them frightening. They ranged through
the woods in small parties, striking first here, then there,
almost always without warning. One day they snatched a
baby from its mother's arms and beat out its brains against
a tree; [108] another day they were content to steal a red cloak
that its owner had hung out to dry.[109] Mothers told their
children at night, "Lie still and go to sleep, or the Shawnees
will catch you," and one frontier boy remembered later
that "nearly all my troubled or vivid dreams included either
Indians or snakes—the copper-colored man, and copper-
headed snake, then extremely common." [110] In Jefferson
County during the first nine months of 1781 Indians killed
or took prisoner 131 people,[111] about 13 percent of the total
population.

A favorite technique of Indian warfare, and an effective
one, was to steal the settlers' horses and to kill or scatter
their cattle. Without horses communication was nearly
impossible; without cattle the settlers were likely to suffer
from malnutrition. The Indians may not have realized that
undernourishment breeds discontent, but they surely did
know that people who lacked cows and horses could not

108. Floyd to Thomas Jefferson, Apr. 16, 1781, Palmer, ed., *Cal.
Va. State Papers*, II, 47–49; Lucien Beckner, ed., "Rev. John Dabney Shane's Interview with Mrs. Sarah Graham of Bath County,"
Filson Club Hist. Qtly., IX(1935), 231; Shane's interview with
William McBride, Draper Coll., 11 CC 261.
109. "Clinkenbeard Interview," *Filson Club Hist. Qtly.*, II(1927–
1928), 119.
110. Drake, *Pioneer Life*, 25.
111. Floyd to Jefferson, Apr. 16, 1781, Palmer, ed., *Cal. Va. State
Papers*, II, 47–49; Floyd to William Nelson, Oct. 6, 1781, *ibid.*, 529–
531.

farm a frontier. "We have scarce cattle amongst us to supply, our small Family's," some unfortunate settlers complained, "and many of us that brought good stocks of both Horses and cows, now at this juncture have not left so much as one cow for the support of our familys." [112] Those who lost their cattle were reduced to a diet of corn meal and game, or to game alone. "I thought it was hard times," one settler remembered, "no bred   no salt   no vegitables   no fruit of any kind   no ardent spirrits   indeed nothing but meet . . . [but] hunger is the best of sause." [113]

Settlers living in lonesome cabins scattered through the woods made perfect targets for Indian warfare. A man hardly dared leave his house to cut firewood or hoe his corn, lest he be attacked by Indians lurking in the woods. Even indoors he was not safe; settlers were sometimes massacred in their cabins. It was dangerous to travel in parties of less than half a dozen men. A man who scoffed when warned not to set out in a party of three, who said, "Some time hence their may be Danger but their is none now   I will go and you need not give your self any uneasynys about us," returned within two hours to report that both his companions had been killed and that he had only narrowly escaped death himself.[114] As the war became more fearful many settlers fled into the safer interior regions of Lincoln County.[115] The remainder would have followed their example, a county lieutenant reported, "but are unable to remove by Land having lost most of their Horses already, by the Savages; and the Ohio runs the wrong way." [116]

112. Petition to Virginia, summer 1779, Va. State Lib., also No. 6 in Robertson, ed., *Petitions*, 46.
113. Trabue narrative, Draper Coll., 57 J 13.
114. *Ibid.*, 17–18.
115. Floyd to Nelson, Oct. 6, 1781, Palmer, ed., *Cal. Va. State Papers*, II, 529–531; Floyd to Jefferson, Jan. 15, 1781, *ibid.*, 437–438; John Todd to Jefferson, Apr. 15, 1781, *ibid.*, 44–45.
116. Floyd to Nelson, Oct. 6, 1781, *ibid.*, 529–531.

For self-protection almost all the settlers who stayed in Fayette and Jefferson counties had to spend at least part of the time in forts. There they found a crowded, dirty, and often sickly life. During the days no one dared venture outside the walls without a rifle, and at night even the cattle were brought within. "They was a couragus people but yet I will say they all looked very wild," a fort dweller remembered. "You might frequently see the women a walking around the fort looking and peeping about seeming that they did not know what they was about but [they] would try to incourage one another and hopt for the best." [117] Separated from their crops, men had to brave the dangers of hunting to provide their families with even a monotonous diet. "We might as well die by the sword as famine," [118] one said.

Kentucky settlers thus had two festering wounds inflicted by Virginia. The first was the land situation; the second was the lack of defense. Those who held Virginia titles feared that her failure to defend Kentucky meant she was giving up her claim and that their titles would therefore be worthless. Those who were unable to get Virginia titles resented that, although they had defended Kentucky, the land was taken up by "numbers of monied Gentlemen in the Settlement who live in security and affluence." [119] Men who had received a four-hundred-acre settlement grant thought it was "two small a compensation" for their losses; later settlers thought they should also be given something, having "suffered equally as much as they that first setled, who could only loose their all." [120] Almost all of the settlers disliked the practice of granting land to men who had only built a cabin in Kentucky, without living there. "It had been

117. Trabue narrative, Draper Coll., 57 J 30. See also Beckner, ed., "Graham Interview," Nov. 1780, *Filson Club Hist. Qtly.*, IX(1935), 227.

118. Trabue narrative, Draper Coll., 57 J 49.

119. Petition to Congress, fall 1783 (read Jan. 2, 1784), Papers of Continental Congress, Ser. 41, V, 101–102.

120. Petition to Virginia, summer 1779, Va. State Lib., also No. 6 in Robertson, ed., *Petitions*, 47.

well for us," they said, "if we had all been such cultivators and never come to settle in the country untill there had been a peace." [121]

Shut up in forts, crowded, uncomfortable, and often sick, the settlers became restless. Old women busied themselves making cheese and butter,[122] and young women wove fabric from thread of nettle lint and yarn of buffalo wool,[123] but the men found little to do except hunting and talking. Unable to get to their own land and unwilling to raise crops on another's soil, they did not farm. They seldom had occasion to fight, and when an occasion arose it was not always welcomed. Forts served "as Beds to engender Sedition and Discord in, and as excuses for Indolence, Rags and poverty." The attorney general for the district of Kentucky, disturbed by this situation, concluded that "the active mind of man cannot bear to be unemployed and immediately is casting about to remove the causes of their present confinement." [124]

The land laws of 1779 were undoubtedly one topic of discussion in the forts. "People here exclaim violently against the measure," [125] the surveyor wrote in December 1779. As soon as word of the laws was received that summer a protesting petition circulated at Boonesborough and other Kentucky stations. Among the forty-one petitioners were some of the earliest, if not the most distinguished, Kentucky settlers. They complained both against the small size of settlement grants and against Virginia's failure to grant land to late settlers, and they begged special treatment for them-

121. *Ibid.*
122. Floyd to G. R. Clark, May 22, 1781, James, ed., *Clark Papers*, I, 556–558.
123. "Clinkenbeard Interview," *Filson Club Hist. Qtly.*, II(1927–1928), 114.
124. Walker Daniel to Benjamin Harrison, May 21, 1784, Palmer, ed., *Cal. Va. State Papers*, III, 548–588.
125. Floyd to Wm. Preston, Dec. 19, 1779, Draper Coll., 17 CC 121–124.

selves.[126] Another group of settlers conceived a different remedy for the same problem. In a petition to Congress complaining of unjust Virginia land laws, they begged permission to move across the Ohio River into enemy territory. This move, they said, would have the double virtue of taking the area for the United States and of enabling the petitioners to secure some landholdings.[127]

By the spring of 1780 Kentucky settlers had found Virginia unwilling to change her land laws, and another remedy was offered to heal the wounds of landless and defenseless frontiersmen. This was the idea of remaining loyal to England. The earliest settlers were apparently patriots who supported the cause of American liberty,[128] perhaps because their land titles were granted by the revolutionary government of Virginia and would be valid only if the state's independence were established. At least some of the later settlers were loyalists, however, and their devotion to Virginia and the American cause was surely not increased by Virginia's failure to give them land. A man who came to Kentucky in the winter of 1778/1779 later recalled the crowds of other migrants then. "[We] could hardly get along the road for them; and all grand Tories, pretty nigh. All from Carolina [were] Tories. Had been treated so bad there, they had to run off or do worse." [129] North Carolina had indeed forced her loyalists to leave. They went to England, Nova Scotia, and Canada,

126. Petition to Virginia, summer 1779, Va. State Lib., also No. 6 in Robertson, ed., *Petitions*, 45–47.
127. Petition to Congress, read 1780, Papers of Continental Congress, Ser. 48, 245.
128. In the Draper Coll. (46 J 8) there is a printed copy of the 1774 Continental Congress's nonimportation agreement, signed by 37 Fincastle County residents. Among the signers were Kentuckians-to-be Isaac Shelby, Benjamin Logan, William Russell, James Thompson, and John Adair.
129. "Clinkenbeard Interview," *Filson Club Hist. Qtly.*, II(1927–1928), 98. See also Capt. Nathaniel Hart's comments in Rev. John D. Shane, "The Henderson Company Ledger," *ibid.*, XXI(1947), 46.

to New York and West Florida,[130] and if the recollections
of an old man can be trusted, some went to Kentucky.

After North Carolina loyalists migrated to Kentucky in
1778 and 1779, there were several incidents of loyalism in
Kentucky, but whether the one caused the other we do not
know. There were tories at Strode's Station in 1779; they
left after a year and went to Boone's Station, Boonesborough, and elsewhere.[131] In 1780 a tory from Bryan's
Station, a man named Clark, stole a horse and rode out to
warn invading English troops of an American army's approach.[132] The captain at Boonesborough, a man from
North Carolina named John Holder, was "as grand a Tory
as ever lived," one of his militiamen said.[133] Another militia
commander who was accused of loyalism after a seemingly
precipitate surrender was Daniel Boone himself. Although he
was cleared of the charge by a court-martial, some of his
more ostentatiously patriotic contemporaries were unhappy
about his release.[134]

One pioneer later liked to boast of a fine bargain he
had made with a Kentucky loyalist. The tories at Bryan's
Station, hearing that the British had taken Charleston,
decided to return to North Carolina and fight for the king.
Because the Indians had stolen all their horses, they advertised that they would buy horses in exchange for their
household goods. Josiah Collins of Lexington traded a horse
to one of them named Lambert for a cow, two pots, and
a skillet. Later, visiting at Bryan's Station, he heard the
women telling how the Lexingtonians had cheated Lambert.
It seemed that the horse had grown very ill-natured, had

130. Robert O. DeMond, *The Loyalists in North Carolina during
the Revolution* (Durham, N.C., 1940), 181–201.
131. "Clinkenbeard Interview," *Filson Club Hist. Qtly.*, II(1927–
1928), 98.
132. *Ibid.*, 127; John Bradford, *Historical Notes on Kentucky* (San
Francisco, 1932), 89.
133. "Clinkenbeard Interview," *Filson Club Hist. Qtly.*, II(1927–
1928), 118–119.
134. Trabue narrative, Draper Coll., 57 J 33.

kicked Lambert on the thigh, and had almost crippled him. "I should have minded [the story]," Collins said later, "hadn't they been tories." As it was, the bargain gave him amusement for years to come.[135]

Some of the settlers, apparently loyalists, simply refused to fight for Virginia.[136] One report numbered Kentucky loyalists in the thousands; [137] that was probably propaganda, but it did have some basis in fact. Many settlers, whether motivated by political conviction, by their economic situation, or by sheer cowardice, simply laid down their guns. "Let the great man," they said, "who the land belongs to, come and defend it, for we will not lift a gun in defense of it." [138] A New Yorker in Williamsburg reported in winter 1780 of the Kentuckians in Virginia, "I know they are determined that absentees shall not hold large tracts of land among them without settling and defending them." [139] After Virginia instituted stringent measures against militia delinquents, one man even swallowed a chew of tobacco and became sick enough to escape going on a campaign.[140]

The logic of these settlers was impeccable. If Kentucky

135. John D. Shane's interview with Josiah Collins, *ibid.*, 12 CC 66, 105. For another report of tories from North Carolina at Bryan's Station, see John D. Shane's interview with Joseph Ficklin, *ibid.*, 16 CC 265, 273.

136. Floyd to Wm. Preston, May 31, 1780, *ibid.*, 17 CC 127–129.

137. "The Deposition of Captain John Cox, . . . July 16, 1779," *Virginia Magazine of History and Biography*, XXVI(1918), 372–374. Cox was taken prisoner by some loyalists, and their leader told him that "he had a List of Thousands, who had joined their party, upon the Western Waters." The land on the western waters was Kentucky and Illinois.

138. Letter from "a gentleman of veracity," June 24, 1780, quoted in George Morgan to William Trent, Sept. 12, 1780, Draper Coll., 46 J 59. Abernethy, *Western Lands,* 251, identifies that gentleman of veracity as John Dodge. Not everyone considered Dodge veracious (see George Slaughter to Jefferson, Jan. 14, 1781, James, ed., *Clark Papers,* I, 493–494), but in this case there is another witness to support his testimony, John Floyd, whose word no one doubts.

139. Silas Deane to Robert Morris, Apr. 17, 1780, New-York Historical Society, *Collections,* XXII (New York, 1890), 126.

140. "Clinkenbeard Interview," *Filson Club Hist. Qtly.,* II(1927–1928), 106.

had been undefended, the English would have taken it. English rule might have remedied the wound of inadequate Indian defenses, since the English would surely have restrained their Indian allies from attacks within their own territory. For those who came to Kentucky too late to receive a settlement grant, English government could hardly have been less satisfactory than the rule of Virginia, and it might, after all, be more satisfying. One observer thought this situation was "entirely oewing to a Set of Nabobs in Virginia, taking all the lands there by office-warrants and pre-emption rights." He warned, "Should the English go there and offer them protection from the Indians, the greatest part will join." [141]

141. Letter from "a gentleman of veracity," June 24, 1780, quoted in Morgan to Trent, Sept. 12, 1780, Draper Coll., 46 J 59.

2

POLITICAL DIVISIONS

DURING THE WINTER of 1779 Kentuckians grew accustomed to seeing an unusually tall and handsome young man who wore a scarlet cloak and rode a black horse named Pompey. The man was the surveyor of Kentucky County, John Floyd. The scarlet cloak he had bought in France; the black horse had come from his native state, Virginia. In 1779 John Floyd was only twenty-eight years old, but he had already suffered more adventures than came to most Kentuckians in a lifetime. He had been in Kentucky in 1774, before the first settlement there. During the early years of the Revolution he had commanded a privateer preying on British commerce in the West Indies and had been captured and taken to England. He had escaped from jail there with the aid of the jailer's daughter, had fled to France, and finally had returned to Virginia.[1] With his keen mind and calm disposition, he was one of the most capable men in Kentucky; with his black hair, expressive eyes, and regular features, he was one of the most handsome. His fine manners and lively wit made him also

1. Hambleton Tapp, "Colonel John Floyd, Kentucky Pioneer," *Filson Club Hist. Qtly.*, XV(1941), 1–24.

one of the most charming; men and women alike enjoyed his company.[2]

John Floyd was one of about two dozen men whom Virginia sent west during the frontier years to measure out the land of Kentucky. Healthy and ambitious, the surveyors came from penurious families, but most of them had influential relatives who arranged their appointments. They brought with them the plain but adequate education that was conventional for middle-class Virginians, and some also had a craftsman's training. Yet at heart all the surveyors were planters. Owning little or no land in Virginia, they became surveyors in the hope of gaining title to large Kentucky plantations. Long trips on foot through uncharted forests, foul weather, and Indian threats made their task uncomfortable, but the potential rewards were great.

John Floyd, for example, suffered the same discomforts as any less literate and charming pioneer. He and his wife, Jenny, slept in a tent ten weeks after they arrived; the hard winter of 1779/1780 had struck by the time he got a cabin built. Inside the cabin, which they lined with deerskins to keep out the cold, Floyd's Negro Bob died from frostbite, and the ink in Floyd's pen froze as he tried to write home. Outside the snow piled higher and higher, until it was two feet deep and the ground was frozen fourteen inches down. The bad weather began November 28 and lasted ten weeks; during that time the snow never melted even from the south side of Floyd's cabin. Wild turkeys dropped frozen from their roosts, buffaloes came up to the settlements like domestic animals, and the settlers, too, went hungry. "Money is of no account here," Floyd wrote. Corn was selling for $165 a bushel, and flour was as "dear as gold dust." But

2. For the description of Floyd's disposition, appearance, and manners see Marshall, *Kentucky*, I, 38. For the quality of his mind and his sense of humor see his letters to William Preston in Draper Coll., 17 CC. Floyd was often mentioned affectionately in the Shane and Draper interviews. See, for example, Shane's interview with a woman in Cincinnati, *ibid.*, 13 CC 13. Even the notoriously irascible Humphrey Marshall seems to have liked Floyd: see Marshall, *Kentucky*, I, 38.

Floyd was more fortunate than many others, for Jenny and their son survived, and he lost only one cow during the winter.[3]

The hard winter had barely ended when Floyd and Jenny were forced to move into a garrison; "the Savages are constantly pecking at us," he wrote. Settlers were so crowded in the garrison that Floyd found the very air impure, and his son suffered from flux, a common garrison ailment. Jenny nevertheless managed to make two hundred pounds of cheese for the Virginia troops. They ran short of supplies, and after several polite requests had been ignored, Floyd threatened that they would all be reduced to fig leaves if Jenny were not sent a piece of linen. When the Indian menace finally subsided, he went back to surveying and to farming his fourteen-hundred-acre, settlement and pre-emption grant, Woodstock. In 1782 he was appointed chief justice of the new Kentucky district court, and he presided at the first session of the court in March 1783. He had just returned from the court to his cabin at Woodstock when he was asked to make another trip in a party of five. Jenny, who was expecting a child in two weeks, begged him not to go, but Floyd did not think it too dangerous. He threw his scarlet cloak over his shoulders and left. Within an hour he was struck by an Indian bullet; two days later he died.[4]

3. For descriptions of the hard winter, see "Colonel William Fleming's Journal of Travels in Kentucky, 1779–1780," in Newton D. Mereness, ed., *Travels in the American Colonies* (New York, 1916); Marshall, *Kentucky*, I, 102–103; "Clinkenbeard Interview," *Filson Club Hist. Qtly.*, II(1927–1928), 112; Trabue narrative, Draper Coll., 57 J 45–47; McAfee narrative, Jillson, ed., *Tales*, 47–48. For Floyd himself, see Tapp, "Floyd," *Filson Club Hist. Qtly.*, XV(1941), 1–24. See also the letters from Floyd to Wm. Preston during the winter of 1779/1780 in Draper Coll., 17 CC and 33 S, since Tapp did not use these for his article on Floyd.

4. These details of the Floyds' tribulations are found in Floyd to George Rogers Clark, Aug. 10, 1781, and May 22, 1781, James, ed., *Clark Papers*, I, 529–531, 556–558; Floyd to Wm. Preston, June 1780, Jan. 19, 1780, May 5, 1780, May 31, 1780, Draper Coll., 17 CC 182–183, 120–121, 124–127, 127–129; Shane's interview with a woman in Cincinnati, *ibid.*, 13 CC 13; Tapp, "Floyd," *Filson Club Hist. Qtly.*, XV(1941), 20–22.

Robert Breckinridge, deputy surveyor of Jefferson County, almost married the widowed Jenny Floyd. A shy, compassionate man trained to be a carpenter, he was twenty-eight when he and his brother Alexander went to Kentucky in 1781, both of them just released from British imprisonment and discharged from the Virginia army.[5] By 1784 two of his half brothers were also in Kentucky, living in an isolated cabin on thirty acres of land rented from Jenny Floyd, where, one reported, they had "a fine Corn field and plenty of Milk and Meat." [6] Robert and Alexander Breckinridge probably shared their corn, meat, and milk that winter, for they were both courting Mrs. Floyd. According to legend it was the quiet Robert who won her heart. But he had to make a trip to Virginia before they could be married, and she, fearing as time passed that he would not return, married Alexander just before he arrived.[7] Robert, who eventually became a planter, remained a bachelor all his life.[8]

The oldest and best established of the surveyors was Thomas Marshall, fifty-two when he became surveyor of Fayette County in 1781. A tall, slender, blue-eyed man, more inclined to austerity than to gregariousness, Marshall had served in the Virginia legislature and had distinguished himself as a colonel during the Revolution. He and his son John, a rising young lawyer, were friends of George Washington's; Marshall had once been Washington's neighbor on the east coast, before he began to migrate by steps

5. Harrison, John Breckinridge, 9. For Robert Breckinridge's personality, see the James Taylor diary, Durrett Coll., Univ. of Chicago; Robert Breckinridge to James Breckinridge, July 2, 1788, Breckinridge-Marshall Papers, Filson Club, Louisville, and his letters in the first two volumes of the Breckinridge Family Papers, Lib. of Congress.
6. William Breckinridge to John Breckinridge, Aug. 9, 1784, Breckinridge Family Papers, II.
7. Tapp, "Floyd," Filson Club Hist. Qtly., XV(1941), 22–23.
8. Thomas Marshall Green, The Spanish Conspiracy; A Review of the Early Spanish Movements in the South-West. . . . (Cincinnati, 1891), 144.

across Virginia until he reached Kentucky.[9] When he arrived at Lexington in 1782,[10] he found it a fortress, and his first office was in a log cabin inside the fort.[11] The next year he went back to Virginia and returned to Kentucky down the Ohio River on a flatboat with his wife, several of his fifteen children, and—as another passenger on the boat said—"a parcel of his negroes."[12] Undaunted by an encounter with Indians,[13] they settled on a tract of land in Fayette County that Thomas Marshall called Buck Pond, as fine a plantation as there was in Kentucky.

Marshall appointed his nephew Humphrey Marshall to be deputy surveyor of Fayette County, and that young man

9. Albert Jeremiah Beveridge, *The Life of John Marshall* (New York, 1916–1919), I, 36–37; Maude H. Woodfin in *DAB* s.v. "Marshall, Thomas."

10. The date when Thomas Marshall came to Kentucky is uncertain. Humphrey Marshall, his nephew, said that when he was appointed surveyor in 1781 he was "in the atlantic part of the state, and did not arrive in Kentucky, during the year" (*Kentucky*, I, 121), implying that he did arrive the next year. However, he had not yet arrived in mid-September 1782 (Andrew Steele to Benjamin Harrison, Sept. 12, 1782, Palmer, ed., *Cal. Va. State Papers*, III, 303). The pioneer Josiah Collins said Marshall came "between the Battle of Blue Licks and the campaign," which would put it between July and the end of September 1782 (Draper Coll., 12 CC 105). Cave Johnson, an early settler, also said Marshall opened his Fayette County office in 1782 (autobiography, Durrett Coll.). Another early settler, Andrew Thompson, claimed to have come on the same boat with him in 1783 (Draper Coll., 12 CC 235), and Marshall's son Louis, who was 12 at the time, said his father came in 1784 (*ibid.*, 16 CC 240). Richard H. Collins (*History of Kentucky* . . . [Covington, Ky., 1882], II, 393) gives 1785, clearly a mistake. Louis Marshall also said his father "staid at Lexington a year . . . left it—and settled the first farm north of the Kentucky River." This, together with Josiah Collins's evidence that Lexington was a fort when Marshall opened his first office, suggests that the year 1782 is correct for the arrival and that the year 1783, which the *DAB* gives, is the one in which he moved to Buck Pond. Marshall visited Virginia in the winter of 1784/1785, for his son wrote on Jan. 7, 1785, "My father sets out early in the spring" (John Marshall to George Muter, *Tyler's Historical and Genealogical Magazine*, I[1919–1920], 28). See also A. K. Marshall, *The Western World* (Frankfort, Ky.), Nov. 1, 1806.

11. Shane's interview with Josiah Collins, Draper Coll., 12 CC 105.

12. Shane's interview with Andrew Thompson, *ibid.*, 12 CC 235.

13. Shane's interview with Louis Marshall, *ibid.*, 16 CC 240.

"had his eyes opened to the prospect of resources, never before contemplated"[14] when he first saw Kentucky in 1781. He was then twenty-one, tall and slender, with black hair and piercing black eyes, graceful in manner and correct in dress to the point of eccentricity. Wildly ambitious to claim a share of Kentucky's riches, he seemed capable of any deceit that would increase his wealth. Yet, anxious to make a good impression along with a fortune, he kept his business transactions a secret. He was polite and restrained in company, listening and watching carefully and usually saying little, but in private he resented real and imagined slights.[15] In 1784 he wrote Daniel Boone's romantic autobiography;[16] after that his writing was often a topic of scorn. "For a long time, [he] has been aspiring to distinction as an author," those who distrusted him would say.[17] They never acknowledged that his writing might actually be distinguished, but in fact he had a fine talent for romantic overstatement and could destroy a man's reputation with a stroke of his pen. This ability, added to his precise observation and memory, made his goose-quill pen a dangerous weapon.

Almost all of the surveyors were involved in land speculation. The most conventional arrangement was a partnership with someone, often a member of the Virginia legis-

14. Marshall, *Kentucky* (1812 ed.), 149. Marshall referred to himself in the plural; I have made it singular.

15. A. C. Quisenberry, *The Life and Times of Hon. Humphrey Marshall* (Winchester, Ky., 1892), 17, gives Marshall's physical appearance. As none of his papers have survived, this account of Marshall's character is based on Quisenberry's biography, *ibid.;* on the articles by Jordan Harris [James Wilkinson] in the *Kentucke Gazette* (Lexington), Mar. 29, and Apr. 5, 12, and 26, 1788; on Humphrey Marshall to John Crittenden, published in the *Kentucke Gazette* of Mar. 8, 1788; and on Marshall's general behavior throughout his life. For a similar assessment see E. Merton Coulter in *DAB* s.v. "Marshall, Humphrey." The *Kentucke Gazette* became the *Kentucky Gazette* on Mar. 14, 1789. It is hereafter cited as *Ky. Gaz.*

16. Collins interview, Draper Coll., 12 CC 73.

17. Jordan Harris [James Wilkinson], *Ky. Gaz.* (Lexington), Mar. 29, 1788.

lature, who furnished warrants that the surveyor located. Robert and Alexander Breckinridge had an arrangement of that type with their half brothers, James and John, in Virginia.[18] Alexander Breckinridge carried warrants for 200,000 acres when he went west, and soon the brothers in Kentucky were begging for more warrants.[19] Locating was a good business for surveyors, for they were better equipped than anyone else to find unclaimed acres. Not only did they know the land, recognizing easily the most fertile and potentially most valuable tracts, but they also knew the entries. With a little thought they could tell which tracts had never been entered, which entries were void because they had not been surveyed within the allotted time, and which surveys were forfeited because they were not paid soon enough. Abandoned tracts could be entered in another name, and it was a rare surveyor who did not make such entries.

Like the other surveyors, Humphrey Marshall engaged in several speculative ventures. One was with a Kentuckian named John Clark, who furnished warrants for which Marshall provided entries. They wrote a contract and probably intended to sell the land when prices reached a peak. Land prices were rising constantly throughout the frontier period, however, and it was difficult to determine the optimum time for sale. Finally, Clark appeared one day at the surveyor's cabin in Lexington, announcing that he was ready to sell. Marshall thought it was not yet time. To delay matters he asked to see their contract, and Clark laid it on the table before him. Then he demanded that Clark pay a small debt to Thomas Marshall before they transacted any business. While Clark went to his own cabin, directly across the street, to get the money, Marshall hid the paper. He pretended astonishment at its disap-

18. Harrison, John Breckinridge, 58.
19. Alexander Breckinridge to John Breckinridge, Nov. 8, 1784; James Breckinridge to John Breckinridge, Nov. 18, 1784; and Wm. Breckinridge to John Breckinridge, Dec. 22, 1784, all in Breckinridge Family Papers, II.

pearance, but he refused to sell until it was in hand.[20] Thus outmaneuvered, Clark complained of the transaction to several people, confirming their suspicions of Humphrey Marshall's character.[21] But Marshall, as usual, had accomplished his own end.

Humphrey Marshall also used other techniques for increasing the amount and value of his landholdings. Left in charge of the Fayette surveyor's office while Thomas Marshall was in Virginia preparing to move his family to Kentucky, he earned the hatred of almost everyone in the county by charging—as his enemies later wrote it—"the memorable DOUBLE FEE." [22] He asked that twice the usual fee be paid, in cash, before he would deliver any plats. This action he based on a lawyer's interpretation of a badly written law that had just passed the Virginia legislature. Since his salary was fixed by law he did not profit directly, as he pointed out, and he also paid the double fee himself.[23] But he failed to add what everyone knew, that he might have made an enormous profit indirectly, for plats that lay in the surveyor's office more than twelve months were forfeited by law. If anyone had been unable to pay the double fee and had thus forfeited his survey, Humphrey Marshall would have been the first to know of it and could have entered the land in his own name. He probably intended to do just that. Unfortunately for his plans, Thomas Marshall, who was apparently a person of greater honesty

20. Harris [Wilkinson], *Ky. Gaz.* (Lexington), Apr. 26, 1788. See also the denial of Clark, *ibid.*, May 3, 1788; the six certificates confirming the story told by Harris [Wilkinson], *ibid.*, May 17, 1788; Caleb Wallace to William Fleming, Dec. 27, 1783, Fleming-Christian Correspondence, Hugh Blair Grigsby Papers, Virginia Historical Society, Richmond; A. K. Marshall, *Western World* (Frankfort), Nov. 1, 1806. Neither Marshall nor Wilkinson is very dependable. In this case the weight of evidence seems to be on Wilkinson's side.

21. Certificates published at the request of Jordan Harris [James Wilkinson], *Ky. Gaz.* (Lexington), May 17, 1788.

22. Harris [Wilkinson], *ibid.*, Apr. 5, 1788.

23. Humphrey Marshall, *ibid.*, Apr. 19, 1788.

than his nephew, returned from Virginia in time to disavow the double fee.[24]

Few of the surveyors were as unscrupulous as Humphrey Marshall, but in locating land many used devices that were at best of questionable morality. "This Business has been attended with much villany in other parts," one Kentuckian reported. "Here it is reduced to a System, and to take the advantage of the Ignorance or of the poverty of a neighbour is almost grown into reputation, which must multiply litigation and produce aversions that will not quickly subside." [25] Through these speculative methods almost every one of the early surveyors acquired great quantities of land. Robert Breckinridge patented 20,545 acres, but he seems a virtual pauper by comparison with some others. John Floyd claimed 11,192 acres and a third share in a partnership with two other surveyors involving 390,057 acres; Humphrey Marshall acquired 97,316¼ acres; and Thomas Marshall established title to 127,841 acres. But none of them could compete with the surveyor of Jefferson County. That gentleman, John May, took 831,294 acres of Kentucky.[26]

Humphrey Marshall, Thomas Marshall, Robert Breckinridge, John Floyd, and the other surveyors formed a hard core of Virginia loyalty in Kentucky, an articulate center in a diverse society. It was they who collected and dispensed news, as they went about the country to make their surveys;

24. Wallace to Fleming, Dec. 27, 1783, Fleming-Christian Corres., Grigsby Papers; Harris [Wilkinson], *Ky. Gaz.* (Lexington), Apr. 5, 1788. For a different version of this incident see Christopher Greenup to A. K. Marshall, Oct. 3, 1806, *ibid.*, Oct. 20, 1806.

25. Wallace to James Madison, July 12, 1785, James Madison Papers, V, Lib. of Congress.

26. For Breckinridge's grants, see Willard Rouse Jillson, *The Kentucky Land Grants* . . . , Filson Club Publications, No. 33 (Louisville, 1925), 23, 148. For Floyd's, see *ibid.*, 50–51, 176, and paper dated Mar. 9, 1783, T. J. Clay Papers, 2d Ser., I, Lib. of Congress, also in No. 302, Kentucky Historical Society, Frankfort. For Humphrey Marshall's grants, see Jillson, *Land Grants*, 84, 205–206; for Thomas Marshall's, *ibid.*; and for John May's, *ibid.*, 79–83, 203–205.

it was they who informed Virginia about Kentucky and Kentucky about Virginia. Whether because they owned land under Virginia, because of their official responsibilities, or from sheer love of their native state, they also defended Virginia's claim to Kentucky. They had little interest in politics and certainly never intended to be a political party. If they ever thought about it, they considered themselves the proper leaders of Kentuckians. As the top layer of Kentucky society, they expected to govern Kentuckians in the way the Carters and the Lees had governed Virginians, as an impartial service to society. Anyone who opposed them they thought of as a "faction." Since Virginia had, after all, guaranteed her claim to Kentucky by establishing county governments there, it seemed to the surveyors that there should be no question about the proper authority.

During the frontier years the people of Kentucky were far too diverse to conform to a single authority, as the articulate center of their society expected them to do. In social status the frontiersmen ranged from convict servant to Virginia gentleman; in economic status, from squatter to planter; in politics, from loyalism to patriotism. Even the places of their origin were mixed. Most Kentuckians had migrated to the bluegrass from the mountains, but a substantial number were natives of the coastal and piedmont areas.[27] Half or nearly half of the people of Kentucky had come from states other than Virginia, especially from North

27. Most authorities support the mountain origin of Kentuckians: see Marshall, *Kentucky* (1812 ed.), I, 149–150; Roosevelt, *Winning of the West*, I, 314; John D. Barnhart, *Valley of Democracy: The Frontier versus the Plantation in the Ohio Valley, 1775–1818* (Bloomington, 1953), 32–33. Some settlers from the coast or the piedmont were: William Calk (Kilpatrick, ed., "Journal of Calk," *Miss. Valley Hist. Rev.*, VII[1920–1921], 363); Daniel Trabue (Trabue narrative, Draper Coll., 57 J); and James, William, and Patrick Brown (William Allen Pusey, "Three Kentucky Pioneers: James, Patrick, and William Brown," *Filson Club Hist. Qtly.*, IV[1930], 166).

Carolina and Pennsylvania.[28] An additional 5 percent, perhaps, had come from other nations, chiefly Ireland, Scotland, France, and Germany.[29] "Like the general collection at the last day, they are of all nations, tongues and languages," one visitor to the West reported; "from China, from all parts of Europe, . . . and from every part of America, they are gathered." Or, as another observer wrote, "The people are polite, humane, and hospitable, being a collection from all the civilized parts of the Continent, and from Europe." [30]

Neither the variety of her citizens nor their diverse points of origin distinguished Kentucky from other parts of the nation. In every state there were similar variations in social positions, economic standards, and political beliefs; and in several states—especially Virginia, Pennsylvania, and North Carolina—a large part of the population was not native born. Kentucky was, however, unique in that none of her adult citizens were natives of the area. In 1779 the first

28. This statement, like the one following it, is only an estimate. Little work has been done on the composition of the frontier population. But see Kathryn Harrod Mason, "Harrod's Men—1774," *Filson Club Hist. Qtly.*, XXIV(1950), 230–233; N. F. Cabell, "Some Fragments of an Intended Report on the Post-Revolutionary History of Agriculture in Virginia," *William and Mary Quarterly*, 1st Ser., XXVI(1917–1918), 149*n;* and Marshall, *Kentucky*, I, 441–442.

29. A native of Ireland who settled in Kentucky during the frontier years was Thomas Quirk. Mason, "Harrod's Men," *Filson Club Hist. Qtly.*, XXIV(1950), 232. See also "Clinkenbeard Interview," *ibid.*, II(1927–1928), 114, and Draper Coll., 4 CC 84, 85. Two Scotchmen are mentioned in the Louis Marshall interview, *ibid.*, 16 CC 246. Three Frenchmen in Kentucky were Barthélemi and Pierre Tardiveau and Jean A. Honoré. Howard C. Rice, *Barthélemi Tardiveau, A French Trader in the West* (Baltimore, 1938), 3. The pioneer narratives are full of references to "Dutchmen" who spoke with an accent. See for instance the Trabue narrative, Draper Coll., 57 J, or the Josiah Collins interview, *ibid.*, 12 CC 102. According to Roosevelt, *Winning of the West*, I, 107, these Dutchmen, so called, were actually Germans.

30. Letter from a gentleman in the western country, Dec. 22, 1785, in the *Massachusetts Gazette* (Boston), Mar. 12, 1786, Draper Coll., 32 J 108–110; Alexander Fitzroy, *The Kentuckie Country*, ed. Willard Rouse Jillson (Washington, 1931 [orig. publ. London, 1786]), 11[39].

white child born in Kentucky was only three years old; everyone over the age of three was a citizen by adoption rather than by birth. Those who had come from Virginia were still Virginians in Kentucky, but the land and most of the people were as new to them as to the Pennsylvanians and North Carolinians. The government also was new. Virginians were familiar with its form, but they, like everyone else in Kentucky, witnessed the creation of new counties from the old form. "Citizens generally consisting of such men must make a very different mass from one which is composed of men born and raised on the same spot," one member of the articulate center complained, for "they see none about them to whom or to whose families they have been accustomed to think themselves inferior." [31]

The diversity of Kentuckians and their newness to the area were fertile soil for the growth of opposition to the Virginia-oriented articulate center, and the Virginia legislature planted the seeds of discontent with the land laws of 1779. Most of the non-Virginia immigrants went to Kentucky because the land law of 1777 had implicitly promised them free land. But most of them went after 1777 and were therefore ruled ineligible for a settlement grant by the laws of 1779. They did not receive military-bounty lands from Virginia, and when they purchased treasury warrants, it was difficult to locate the land. Those who came to Kentucky from Pennsylvania and North Carolina consequently felt little loyalty to the Virginia county governments. Although they served in the Virginia militia and voted for delegates to the Virginia General Assembly, they continued to think of themselves as Pennsylvanians and Carolinians and to support their native states against Virginia.[32]

31. George Nicholas to Madison, Sept. 5, 1792, Madison Papers, XV.
32. G. R. Clark to John Clark, Aug. 23, 1780, James, ed., *Clark Papers*, I, 453; Walker Daniel to Fleming, Apr. 14, 1783, Draper Coll., 46 J 78; James Speed to Harrison, May 22, 1784, Palmer, ed., *Cal. Va. State Papers*, III, 588–589.

Land speculators who backed the congressional claim to Kentucky were quick to encourage this discontent. During 1779 one circulated in Kentucky a petition protesting the "instability and inconsistency" of the Virginia legislature,[33] and there soon appeared a sizable party of men who supported the congressional claim against that of Virginia and who wanted to make Kentucky a separate state under Congress. Most of them landless, they expected Congress to annul the Virginia grants and redistribute the land of Kentucky.[34] Few of these men were natives of Virginia; Pennsylvanians and Carolinians predominated.[35] Enough signed their names "yeorge pirtle" or "yoseph dolaen" to suggest that many were foreign born.[36] They were almost all literate, but apparently few were well educated.[37] In that it was a protest against the land laws of 1779, this movement was similar to the toryism of some Kentuckians. It may have replaced loyalism to Great Britain, for it gained strength in 1780 and 1781, just as loyalism was declining.

Arthur Campbell, the most enterprising of the individual speculators, originated the anti-Virginia petition circulated

33. Petition to Virginia, summer 1779, draft in Campbell-Preston-Floyd Papers, Lib. of Congress.

34. John Cowan to Levi Todd, Aug. 21, 1806, Draper Coll., 16 CC 41–42. Of the 52 names signed to one 1782 petition, only 10 are listed in Jillson's *Land Grants* as owning land in 1782. Of these 10, all except 4 held 400 acres or less. Petition to Virginia, spring 1782 (read May 30, 1782), Va. State Lib., also No. 15 in Robertson, ed., *Petitions*, 66. On the petitioners' expectations, see James Ray to Levi Todd, Aug. 26, 1806, Draper Coll., 16 CC 43–44; also see below, p. 65.

35. G. R. Clark to John Clark, Aug. 23, 1780, James, ed., *Clark Papers*, I, 453; Daniel to Fleming, Apr. 14, 1783, Draper Coll., 46 J 78; Speed to Harrison, May 22, 1784, Palmer, ed., *Cal. Va. State Papers*, III, 588–589.

36. Petition to Congress, fall 1783 (read Jan. 2, 1784), Papers of Continental Congress, Ser. 41, V, 101–102, National Archives; petition to Congress, spring or summer 1783 (read Sept. 27, 1783), *ibid.*, 97.

37. This is my impression after examining the names signed on petitions sent to Virginia and to Congress. On the question of literacy two good authorities back me: see Roosevelt, *Winning of the West*, I, 151, and Robertson, ed., *Petitions*, 31.

48   THE PARTISAN SPIRIT

in Kentucky during 1779.[38] A Virginian, he was apparently more interested in making western areas independent than in establishing Congress's control. He sometimes urged the congressional claim and at other times encouraged westerners to separate from Congress as well as from the mother state. He actually created an independent state in western North Carolina and nearly created one in western Virginia.[39] As early as 1780 a Kentuckian wrote to him "to return you thanks on behalf [of] the Kentucky Inhabitants for your attention shown to their distresses." [40] His suggestions later produced a petition to Congress in 1782 and an important new development of the separation movement in 1784.[41] Exactly how Campbell hoped to benefit by these activities is not clear. Motives of personal pique and political ambition have been suggested, as well as his hope of financial profit.[42] One of his contemporaries called him "very able, mean-spirited and jealous"; nonetheless he would eventually win the confidence and respect of several important Kentuckians.[43]

In the early 1780s, however, Arthur Campbell had not yet won the confidence of the articulate center. His most important Kentucky collaborator was Ebenezer Brooks, a small, pompous man of around thirty years who had come from Delaware to Kentucky around 1781, an M.D. and a Presbyterian minister who had been silenced for heresy.[44]

38. This is, at least, strongly suggested by the presence of a draft of the petition in the Campbell-Preston-Floyd Papers, II.
39. Abernethy, *Western Lands, passim*, especially 123–135, 258–273, 288–310.
40. John Todd to Arthur Campbell, July 2, 1780, Arthur Campbell Papers, Filson Club.
41. John Donelson to Campbell, Apr. 20, 1782, Draper Coll., 9 DD 34; see below, p. 76.
42. Abernethy, *Western Lands,* 222.
43. Quoted, *ibid.,* 124; see below, p. 121.
44. See the title page to Ebenezer Brooks's proposed book: A/ Reply to the Age of Reason/in which the/Nature and Necessity of a/Divine Revelation/as the only source of human knowledge/is considered by/Ebenezer Brooks M.D., Timothy Pickering Papers, XXI, No. 309, Massachusetts Historical Society, Boston. I have been

Brooks—"Doctor Brooks," as he was usually called, or "the CRAZY DOCTOR," as his political opponents said [45]—was evidently better educated than most of the surveyors, for he later opened the first Latin school in Kentucky and tutored Thomas Marshall's younger children.[46] Eventually he owned about ten thousand acres of land under Virginia, but by 1784, when he began to acquire it, he was already involved in land transactions with Arthur Campbell.[47] Although once described as "an amiable man," [48] Brooks appeared very silly to most of his contemporaries. He deeded a tract of land to his landlady for no reason except that he had become enamored of her. "The lady not choosing to marry him," as Humphrey Marshall put it, "he did not chuse to marry her" and died a bachelor in 1799, oblivious of the lawsuit that the deed would provoke.[49] Incidents of that kind and his general overeagerness to establish his own importance made Brooks an object of the articulate center's contempt. An anonymous satire on one of them provoked a satire in reply:

unable to find the source of Brooks's M.D. For Brooks as a minister, see *Records of the Presbyterian Church in the United States of America* (Philadelphia, 1904), 462, 472, 476; manuscript minutes of the Leweston [Delaware] Presbytery, 104, 105, 114, Presbyterian Historical Society, Philadelphia. There is no mention of Brooks's silencing in the incomplete Leweston Presbytery minutes; that information comes from the Louis Marshall interview, Draper Coll., 12 CC 242, 244.

45. "A Kentuckean" [Caleb Wallace], *Ky. Gaz.* (Lexington), Nov. 10, 1787.

46. Interview with Nathaniel Hart in Shane, "Henderson Company Ledger," *Filson Club Hist. Qtly.*, XXI(1947), 46; notice of tuition, Mar. 15, 1788, Draper Coll., 18 CC 133; Shane's interview with Louis Marshall, *ibid.*, 12 CC 242, 244; Green, *Spanish Conspiracy*, 203, 211.

47. Jillson, *Land Grants*, 25–26; Ebenezer Brooks to Robert Preston, Oct. 25, 1782, Preston Papers, Va. Hist. Soc.; letter by Brooks, Sept. 1, 1783, Miscellaneous Bound Manuscripts, I, Durrett Coll.; Brooks to Campbell, Nov. 9, 1784, Draper Coll., 11 J 37–38.

48. Campbell to Timothy Pickering, Oct. 7, 1797, Pickering Papers, XXI, Mass. Hist. Soc.

49. "An Observer" [Humphrey Marshall], 55, pamphlet in Wilson Coll., Univ. of Ky.; Campbell to Pickering, July 1, 1799, Pickering Papers, XXV.

You might as well have set your name—
Write as you will, tis all the same;
Your own dull lines their Author tell:
To lie conceal'd you should write well.
By nonsense mark'd, the whole piece looks
To be the work of Doctor Brooks. . . .[50]

The articulate center's opinion of Brooks was much the same as that of the poet.

The Kentucky movement for separation was eventually taken over by some of the eastern land companies who could profit from a destruction of the Virginia claim.[51] Members of the articulate center complained repeatedly about "that Numerous Clan of Partizans or pretended Proprietors residing in Philadelphia." [52] Perhaps the most outstanding agent of the land companies was John Campbell. Not a relative of Arthur Campbell, in spite of his name, he was a native of Ireland who had migrated to America in the mid-1760s.[53] A large, handsome, generous man with somewhat rough manners,[54] Campbell had spent fifteen years as

50. "Verses written extemporarily on the back of an insipid and anonymous satire on Wm. M'Dowell," Thomas Johnson, *The Kentucky Miscellany*, 4th ed. (Lexington, 1821), 14. The fourth edition is the only extant copy of this book.

51. G. R. Clark to Benjamin Harrison, May 2, 1782, James Alton James, ed., *George Rogers Clark Papers, 1781–1784* (Ill. Hist. Soc., Colls., XIX[Springfield, Ill., 1926], Va. Ser., IV), II, 63–65. Hereafter cited as James, ed., *Clark Papers*, II. Clark to Commissioners, Feb. 25, 1783, Palmer, ed., *Cal. Va. State Papers*, III, 448–450; Clark to Harrison, Mar. 8, 1783, James, ed., *Clark Papers*, II, 212–215. There are similar reports in William Christian to Wm. Preston, Feb. 7, 1782, Preston Papers, #1129, Lib. of Congress, and in an article datelined "Richmond Nov 29" in *The Maryland Journal and the Baltimore Advertiser*, Dec. 9, 1783, Draper Coll., 3 JJ 114.

52. G. R. Clark to Harrison, Mar. 8, 1783, James, ed., *Clark Papers*, II, 212–215.

53. William Vincent Byars, ed., *B. and M. Gratz, Merchants in Philadelphia, 1754–1798* . . . (Jefferson City, Mo., 1916); John Campbell's will, July 25, 1786, Misc. Bound MSS, II, Durrett Coll.; Abernethy, *Western Lands*, 35. Arthur Campbell's brother was the John Campbell who supported the separation movement in West Virginia.

54. Collins, *History of Kentucky*, II, 117.

an Indian trader for a Philadelphia mercantile house that
was interested in western lands. He had worked both with
and against Virginia and in the course of a checkered
career had gained a claim to four thousand acres under
Virginia. That claim he located at the most important spot
in Kentucky, the Falls of Ohio, now the site of Louisville.[55]
But he could hope for many times that number of acres if
his land-company claims were established, and so he agitated against Virginia during the frontier period.

Another Kentucky supporter of the congressional claim
who was associated with the land companies was George
Pomeroy. Like John Campbell, Pomeroy came to Kentucky
from Pennsylvania, arriving in Jefferson County between
1778 and 1780—too late to receive a settlement grant.[56]
He seems to have been a man of some means, and he had
wealthy friends, yet the Jefferson County Court in 1781
awarded him four hundred acres of land under an act for
the relief of indigent persons.[57] Presumably they considered
him wanting politically rather than economically; perhaps
they hoped he might be less ardent a partisan if he owned
land under Virginia. But Pomeroy established no title to the
grant and apparently never did own land under Virginia.[58]
Continuing to work for congressional separation, he visited

55. *Ibid.*
56. Marshall, *Kentucky*, I, 162. Pomeroy presumably settled after
1778, because he did not receive a settlement grant, but by 1780,
because his name is signed to two petitions written that year. Petitions to Congress, read 1780, and May 15, 1780, Papers of the Continental Congress, Ser. 48, 245, 237.
57. Pomeroy acted as security for the administrator of an estate
in 1781. Alvin L. Prichard, ed., "Minute Book A, Jefferson County,
Kentucky, March, 1781–September, 1783," 3, *Filson Club Hist. Qtly.*,
III(1928–1929), 61. When the occasion arose he had two friends
who would act as security for him for 500 pounds of tobacco each.
See below, p. 67; "Minute Book No. 1 Jefferson County, Kentucky,
April 6, 1784–December 7, 1785," 37, ibid., VI(1932), 67. For the
400-acre award, see Prichard, ed., "Minute Book A," 15, *ibid.*, III
(1928–1929), 74.
58. At least no grant is listed in Jillson, *Land Grants*. However,
he might have purchased land that had already been patented.

his friends in the East during the winter of 1783/1784, carrying petitions from Kentucky to Congress, and brought back to Kentucky their assurances that Congress would support her claim. He was the most important "separatist" leader in Kentucky.[59]

The supporters of the congressional claim—"partizans," as they were called by the articulate center [60]—were probably more conscious of being a political group than were their opponents, because they were constantly pitting themselves against the established authority of Virginia. Their membership was never very stable, however. Many of the discontented settlers left Kentucky, going down the Mississippi to the Spanish or across the Ohio into British territory,[61] and those who remained probably tended to leave the party as they acquired land under Virginia. Even the landless were irresolute, supporting the movement at one moment and opposing it the next,[62] depending on national developments and on the persuasiveness of their informants.[63] Yet the movement did have at least a few supporters who stayed with it from beginning to end.

"A discontented few," one of the articulate center later called the partisans,[64] thus demonstrating the ex-Virginians' inclination to underestimate their opponents. Actually the party at times amounted to nearly half the population of

59. Walker Daniel to Harrison, Jan. 19, 1784, and May 21, 1784, Palmer, ed., *Cal. Va. State Papers,* III, 555–556, 584–588.

60. G. R. Clark to John Clark, Aug. 23, 1780, James, ed., *Clark Papers,* I, 453; G. R. Clark to Harrison, Mar. 8, 1783, *ibid.,* II, 212–215.

61. See above, p. 25; petition to Congress, read 1780, Papers of Continental Congress, Ser. 48, 245.

62. G. R. Clark to Harrison, May 2, 1782, James, ed., *Clark Papers,* II, 63–65; article datelined "Richmond, June 15" in *Md. Jour.* (Baltimore), June 25, 1782, Draper Coll., 3 JJ 90; S. Clarke to Harrison, Nov. 30, 1782, Palmer, ed., *Cal. Va. State Papers,* III, 384–385.

63. Daniel to G. R. Clark, Sept. 15, 1783, James, ed., *Clark Papers,* II, 246–258; Daniel to William Fleming, Aug. 22, 1783, Draper Coll., 46 J 79.

64. John Cowan to Levi Todd, Aug. 21, 1806, *ibid.,* 16 CC 41–42.

Kentucky.[65] In the spring of 1782 and the winter of 1783/1784 they were numerous enough to frighten the articulate center.[66] "The Ballance stands upon an Equilibrium and one stroke more will cause it to Preponderate to our Irretrievable Wo," [67] a Kentuckian said. "The new invented Ideas of a Separate State," wrote John Floyd, "seems to threaten us on all sides with Anarchy, Confusion, and I may add Destruction." [68]

During 1782 and 1783 the articulate center was strengthened by the judges and attorney general of the recently established district court of Kentucky. These men migrated early enough to be considered later as "ancient settlers," but they were not "pioneers" even though they experienced some of the pioneers' difficulties. Caleb Wallace, for example, had a frightening experience when he brought his family to Kentucky. "Its not worth while to give you a descripshon of our journey," his wife, Rosanna, wrote home, and then added, "The Terror I had on me about the

65. Roosevelt, *Winning of the West*, II, 399, counted 645 names on the statehood petition to Congress of May 15, 1780 (Papers of Continental Congress, Ser. 48, 237), or well over half the adult male population of 1,000. The petitions are so cataloged that it is difficult to tell to which petition the various pages of signatures belong, but it appears that Roosevelt may have counted the 431 names on another petition (read 1780, *ibid.*, 245) with the 240 names that belong to the May 15 document. Even so, the totals for 1780 are impressive. There are 746 names signed to one statehood petition (read Jan. 2, 1784, *ibid.*, Ser. 41, V, 101–102), again about half of the population in the autumn of 1783, when it was circulated. More information about all of these petitions is given in the Bibliography.

66. John Floyd to John May, Apr. 8, 1782, James, ed., *Clark Papers*, II, 54–56; G. R. Clark to Harrison, Mar. 8, 1783, *ibid.*, 212–215; Clark to Edmund Randolph, Oct. 8, 1787, Palmer, ed., *Cal. Va. State Papers*, IV, 346–347; Daniel to Clark, Sept. 15, 1783, James, ed., *Clark Papers*, II, 246–248; article datelined "Richmond Nov 29" in *Md. Jour.* (Baltimore), Dec. 9, 1783, Draper Coll., 3 JJ 114; Daniel to Harrison, Jan. 19, 1784, Palmer, ed., *Cal. Va. State Papers*, III, 555–556; Daniel to Harrison, May 21, 1784, *ibid.*, 584–588; James Speed to Harrison, May 22, 1784, *ibid.*, 588–589.

67. Andrew Steele to Harrison, Aug. 26, 1782, *ibid.*, 269–270.

68. Floyd to May, Apr. 8, 1782, James, ed., *Clark Papers*, II, 54–56.

Indians . . . was past describeing." Nine people had been killed by Indians only fifteen miles from them. The massacre occurred at a place where they had camped the previous night, and they themselves had seen fresh Indian tracks that morning. "It was nothing but the great Mercy of God that preserved us," Mrs. Wallace thought.[69]

The district court was established in Kentucky to discourage the partisans [70] as well as to decide land claims, but it was several years before it accomplished anything toward either end. The salaries were inadequate and, because they were paid from fines collected by the court, uncertain as well.[71] Two men declined appointment to the court, and it was the end of 1785 before a lawyer was found who would accept the position of chief justice.[72] Lacking buildings, records, and law books as well as a chief judge, the court did nothing at its first session in March 1783.[73] Not until June 1785 would any land cases be decided,[74] although that was its most pressing business by far.

The men who did accept appointments in the court were, like the surveyors, planters at heart. Unlike the surveyors, they migrated too late to locate their own plantations. They expected to buy their land and hoped to pay for it with the proceeds from continued judicial preferment. The district attorneys also hoped for an ample law practice on the side.

69. Rosanna Wallace to Anne Fleming, Oct. 23, 1784, Fleming Papers, Washington and Lee.
70. Message of Harrison to General Assembly, Draper Coll., 10 S 78; Daniel to Harrison, May 21, 1784, Palmer, ed., *Cal. Va. State Papers*, III, 584–588.
71. Hening, ed., *Statutes*, XI, 85–90; Caleb Wallace to James Madison, Oct. 8, 1785, Madison Papers, VI.
72. Harry Innes to Harrison, Sept. 9, 1782, Palmer, ed., *Cal. Va. State Papers*, III, 293; *ibid.*, IV, 67.
73. Thomas P. Abernethy, ed., "Journal of the First Kentucky Convention, Dec. 27, 1784–Jan. 5, 1785," *Journal of Southern History*, I(1935), 67–78; Wallace to William Fleming, Dec. 2, 1783, Fleming-Christian Corres., Grigsby Papers; Marshall, *Kentucky*, I, 159.
74. James Hughes, *A Report of the Causes Determined by the Late Supreme Court for the District of Kentucky and by the Court of Appeals, to Which the Titles to Land Were in Dispute* (Lexington, 1803).

"This will be a very excellent Place for your business, as the Attorneys are but few and the business very extensive," one of the Breckinridges wrote his brother John, encouraging him to accept the position of attorney general. "The business is daily agrowing, and the land disputes . . . are almost innumerable. These advantages together with having the satisfaction of living on some of your fine rich soil in this Rich and extensive Country, will add greatly to the happiness of this life." [75] John Breckinridge declined to go to Kentucky at that time, but arguments of this kind did appeal to other young lawyers.

None of the assistant judges had any legal training, but the first two were familiar with intricacies of the land laws. The colorful, capable John Floyd had been surveying in Kentucky for several years when he was appointed to the court in 1783, and his death soon after the first session weakened it considerably. His associate, Samuel McDowell, had been one of the commissioners who ruled on settlement claims in 1780. A blunt, taciturn, self-confident man, tall, erect, and handsome, McDowell had served in the convention that declared Virginia's independence of Britain and in the Virginia legislature. He was forty-seven when he was appointed judge in 1782, sixteen years older than Floyd, but the two men apparently worked together agreeably. Floyd and McDowell selected a surveyor as clerk of the court; then Floyd and Walker Daniel, a young Virginia lawyer who had been appointed attorney general, chose a site for the court. "Danville arose out of the speculation" was Humphrey Marshall's acid comment. In the bluegrass area and near the geographic center of the district, Danville became the leading city of Kentucky and remained so for nearly ten years.[76]

75. William Breckinridge to John Breckinridge, Aug. 9, 1784, Breckinridge Family Papers, II. See also Alexander Breckinridge to John Breckinridge, Aug. 14, 1784, *ibid.*
76. On the appointments to the court and its activities, see Tapp, "Floyd," *Filson Club Hist. Qtly.,* XV(1941), 20–21; Thomas Marshall Green, *Historic Families of Kentucky. With Special Reference*

Caleb Wallace, the third assistant judge of the court, had no more judicial experience than Floyd or McDowell. Like McDowell he had legislative experience, although he was by profession a Presbyterian minister. A plump, jovial man, Wallace had graduated from Princeton College in 1770, at the age of twenty-eight, in the class ahead of the Virginian James Madison. While a member of the Virginia Hanover Presbytery, he had served in the legislature and worked for the separation of church and state. He had married Samuel McDowell's daughter and, after her death, Rosanna Fleming, thus connecting himself with John Floyd and the Breckinridges. In 1780 he became a western land commissioner, along with his father-in-law, Samuel McDowell, and his new brother-in-law, William Fleming. Wallace settled in Kentucky the fall of 1783, while people were still living in garrisons, and as a Presbyterian minister he baptised a baby in one of the forts. Except for the single harrowing trip when he brought his family from Virginia, he remained in Kentucky, attentive to his judicial duties.[77]

George Muter, who accepted the position of chief justice in 1785, was the first judge of the Kentucky district court to have legal training. Ironically, he was also the weakest member of the court. A native of Scotland, at least fifty-five years old, he had been removed from a position as commissioner of the War Office apparently for incompetence, and was perhaps given the appointment for consolation or

to Stocks Immediately Derived from the Valley of Virginia . . . (Cincinnati, 1889), 31–39; Samuel McDowell to Benjamin Harrison, Dec. 22, 1782, Palmer, ed., Cal. Va. State Papers, III, 402; Calvin M. Fackler, "Walker Daniel, the Founder of Danville: One of Kentucky's Almost Forgotten Pioneers," Filson Club Hist. Qtly., XIII(1939), 134–136.

77. Wallace to Harrison, Aug. 14, 1783, Palmer, ed., Cal. Va. State Papers, III, 523; William H. Whitsitt, Life and Times of Judge Caleb Wallace . . . , Filson Club Publications, No. 4 (Louisville, 1888); Shane's interview with James Stevenson, Draper Coll., 11 CC 249; Rosanna Wallace to Anne Fleming, Oct. 23, 1784, Fleming Papers; Wallace to James Madison, Oct. 8, 1784, Madison Papers, VI.

possibly because the governor of Virginia could find no other lawyer to accept it. A short, slight, sallow man who drank too much, he seldom had an opinion of his own and was inclined to follow whomever he was near. He would adopt a crude form of speech whenever it seemed advantageous and even dress in a popular way. More conventional Kentucky lawyers complained of his "tame, complying dependence," but in spite of their contempt, he was an important figure in the Kentucky judiciary.[78]

The first Kentucky attorney general, Walker Daniel, was killed by Indians in 1784 and was replaced by Harry Innes, another Virginia lawyer. Innes had earlier refused the position of judge, the salary being too small to tempt him from the practice of law, but as attorney general he could continue his practice in Kentucky. Like Caleb Wallace a friend of James Madison's, Innes had gone to school with Madison, had studied law with George Wythe, and then had practiced in Virginia for more than ten years. He was thirty-three when he became attorney general of Kentucky in 1785, a balding man of medium height with a long pointed nose, a sufferer from asthma, who stuttered when he was under pressure. Innes had a capacity for justifying whatever he wanted to do to his own satisfaction and that of almost everyone else, mixing indignation and propriety in convincing measures whenever his activities were questioned. He liked comfort and was seldom inclined to work harder than necessary to achieve it; later, when he was a judge, Humphrey Marshall heard him "vow to God, he would never take the responsibility of finding facts in a chancery suit

78. Palmer, ed., *Cal. Va. State Papers*, IV, 67; "The Kentucky Spanish Association," *Western World* (Frankfort), Sept. 6, 1806; Abernethy, *Western Lands*, 301; George Muter to Thomas Jefferson, Mar. 22, 1781, Palmer, ed., *Cal. Va. State Papers*, I, 587–588; the description of Muter in "An Observer" [Humphrey Marshall], 32, pamphlet in Wilson Coll., Univ. of Ky.; see below, p. 172; James Brown to John Brown, Nov. 29, 1790, Jan. 10, 1791, John Mason Brown Collection, Yale University; quoting James Brown to John Brown, Apr. 8, 1795, *ibid.*

upon himself!" Like other members of the district court, he was a planter at heart.[79]

The men attached to the district court in Kentucky— Samuel McDowell, Walker Daniel, Caleb Wallace, George Muter, and Harry Innes—were more interested in politics than the surveyors had been and more fully aware of political problems. Because the court's most important function was the land cases, its members were as aware as the surveyors of the problem of land ownership in Kentucky. They soon took over the work of the articulate center and informed Virginia of Kentucky's progress with more energy and exactness than the surveyors had ever given to that task. Together with the surveyors they thought of themselves as the rightful governors of Kentucky. They never thought of themselves as a party, but they opposed the partisans energetically and so in fact used political tactics. Supported by the men who owned land under Virginia, they were a party of perhaps half the population of Kentucky. Their importance was greater than their numerical strength, however, because their cause was established. The Virginia county governments and district court actually existed in Kentucky, while the hope of separate statehood under Congress was only a dream.

One frontiersman who supported the articulate center was Benjamin Logan. "A large, raw-boned man, fully six feet [tall, who] sometimes fought at fisticuffs," according to another pioneer, Logan weighed nearly two hundred pounds, and his sheer physical strength was reported for

79. On Innes see: Abernethy, *Western Lands*, 301; Innes to Benjamin Harrison, Sept. 9, 1782, Palmer, ed., *Cal. Va. State Papers*, III, 293; Edmund Pendleton to Innes, Aug. 11, 1790, Misc. Bound MSS, II Durrett Coll.; "An Observer" [Humphrey Marshall], 32, pamphlet in Wilson Coll.; "Coriolanus" [Humphrey Marshall], *Ky. Gaz.* (Lexington), Sept. 22, 1792; Innes Papers, Lib. of Congress; and Edward Wiest in *DAB* s.v. "Innes, Harry." For Innes's capacity for self-justification, see for example his letter to Edmund Randolph, July 21, 1787, Palmer, ed., *Cal. Va. State Papers*, IV, 321–323. The Marshall quote is from the "Observer" pamphlet, 47, in Wilson Coll.

hundreds of miles around.[80] He had a hot temper, and was once described as "somewhat arbitrary and overbearing." [81] Logan was one of the earliest settlers; his son William was the first white male born in Kentucky. He came from a former frontier, the Virginia mountains, and he knew the hills, forests, and rivers of Kentucky by heart.[82] Like most of the frontiersmen, he was literate but just barely so; his handwriting to his death was crabbed and difficult to read, and his grammar was his own.[83] The command of the Lincoln County militia was his only responsibility to Virginia. He had neither family nor social ties with the articulate center,[84] and his choleric disposition and lack of education contrasted with their literate, placid assurance. He was not devoted to every detail of their point of view, but he did hold land under Virginia.[85] It was apparently for that reason that he supported them.

Isaac Shelby was another pioneer who supported the articulate center. He, like Logan, came to Kentucky very early from the mountains, but there was hardly any other similarity between the two men. Shelby was a solid man of medium height with sharp strong features and a red face; his education had been plain but adequate for clear composition, correct grammar, and a practiced handwriting. His mind worked slowly, almost sluggishly, but the resulting analysis was usually clear. Except for a rare burst of anger,

80. Quoted in Talbert, *Logan*, 140; Robert S. Cotterill in *DAB* s.v. "Logan, Benjamin."
81. Quoted in Talbert, *Logan*, 140.
82. See *ibid., passim.*
83. See, especially, a letter printed in the *Ky. Gaz.* (Lexington), Nov. 26, 1796. This might be a satire on Logan's composition; however, Talbert, *Logan*, 289, 291n, accepts it as legitimate.
84. Green, *Historic Families*, 120–141.
85. He signed a petition asking revival of the ancient cultivation law. This was not favored by the articulate center, and none of them signed any petition requesting it. Petition to Virginia, spring 1782 (read June 1, 1782) Va. State Lib., also No. 16 in Robertson, ed., *Petitions*, 66–68. More than 5,000 acres had been granted Logan by the end of 1784. Jillson, *Land Grants*, 78–79.

his temper too was slowly aroused and then slowly calmed. By 1784, when he was thirty-four years old, Shelby was capable of mature judgment; yet he remained a sensitive person and all his life was easily hurt. Like Logan, Shelby was not related to the articulate center. He had many important friends through his own family and his marriage into a wealthy North Carolina family, and he and his father were well acquainted with Arthur Campbell; yet he always supported the members of the articulate center. Perhaps this was because he, like Logan, held land under Virginia and because the Virginia claim was always more promising than any other.[86]

Along with Benjamin Logan and Isaac Shelby, thousands of Kentuckians supported the articulate center, men like Thomas Bell, Samuel Kelly, Robert Sanders, David Vance, all of whom held land under Virginia.[87] Their biographies can seldom be traced beyond that fact. They would probably have denied belonging to a party; perhaps they were even unaware of it. Years later, when they wrote their memoirs or recalled ancient events, they seldom mentioned matters political. They talked about the beauty of the country, the hardships of the trip, land disputes, and Indian troubles, but they seldom spoke of politics. Yet, even though it became unimportant to them, even if they were unconscious of it, these men grouped themselves in a way that we now call "political," and so we can refer to them—for lack of a better term—as a "party."[88]

* * *

86. On Shelby see: Samuel M. Wilson in *DAB* s.v. "Shelby, Isaac"; Shelby Papers at Lib. at Congress, Filson Club, Ky. Hist. Soc., Univ. of Chicago, and Univ. of Ky.; Campbell-Preston-Floyd Papers, Lib. of Congress; and Campbell Papers, Draper Coll., 8–10 DD. Shelby held nearly 6,000 acres by the end of 1784. Jillson, *Land Grants*, 18.

87. These are among the names signed to a petition to Virginia, spring 1782, Va. State Lib., also No. 24 in Robertson, ed., *Petitions*, 78–79. All are listed in Jillson, *Land Grants*, as holding land under Virginia.

88. For a discussion of the use of the word "party," see the Bibliography, pp. 260–264.

The separation movement began in obscurity in 1779.[89] Apparently directed from Virginia by Arthur Campbell, it was encouraged by his friends who lived in Kentucky or who went there on business.[90] Someone recalled twenty-five years later that "the persons who came forward in the business were old Mr. [John] Kincade"—whom Campbell had befriended in 1779 [91]—"some of his sons and a schoolmaster named Eades," [92] perhaps Ebenezer Brooks. None of these were men of importance. The partisans evidently did not have an adequate leader until 1782, when agents of the land companies began to support and encourage them.[93] George Pomeroy was probably one of these agents. He had been in Kentucky before 1782 and had supported the separation movement from the beginning, but he did not appear as a leader until 1783.[94]

In the spring of 1782, and perhaps earlier, agents of the land companies circulated copies of Thomas Paine's *Public Good,* which argued the invalidity of Virginia's claim to Kentucky.[95] "An Inflamatary Pamphlet," according to some settlers it "produced Considerable Desentions amongst

89. See above, p. 47; G. R. Clark to John Clark, Aug. 23, 1780, James, ed., *Clark Papers,* I, 453.

90. John Donelson to Arthur Campbell, Apr. 20, 1782, Draper Coll., 9 DD 34.

91. John Kinkead to Campbell, July 8, 1779, Campbell Papers, Filson Club.

92. James Ray to Levi Todd, Aug. 26, 1806, Draper Coll., 16 CC 43–44.

93. See above, p. 50.

94. See above, p. 51; Pomeroy's name appears on two 1780 petitions to Congress. Petition, read 1780, and petition, May 15, 1780, Papers of Continental Congress, Ser. 49, 245, 237. He is first mentioned in Daniel to Harrison, Jan. 19, 1784, Palmer, ed., *Cal. Va. State Papers,* III, 555–556.

95. Petitions to Virginia, spring 1782 (one read May 30, 1782), Va. State Lib., also Nos. 15 and 24 in Robertson, ed., *Petitions,* 62–66, 78–79; Marshall, *Kentucky,* I, 161–162; Thomas Paine, *Public Good, Being an Examination into the Claim of Virginia to the Vacant Western Territory, and of the Right of the United States to the Same. To Which Is Added, Proposals for Laying off a New State, To Be Applied as a Fund for Carrying on the War, or Redeeming the National Debt* (Philadelphia, 1780).

them." [96] During 1783 the agents spread reports that Congress had actually declared the Virginia claim invalid; [97] this device was especially effective because it stirred the fears of those who held land under Virginia as well as the hopes of those who had none. To give weight to such reports they circulated anonymous letters reputedly written by members of Congress, attributing congressional delay to an unwillingness to cause confusion during the war and promising that when peace came Kentucky would be made a separate state. [98] "These Letters," one of the articulate center noted, "are circulated with great Industry and read with as much avidity and a firm persuasion of the Truth of their contents." [99]

Both the friends of Arthur Campbell and the land-company agents found that their most useful device was the petition. Aided by letters from Campbell and from congressmen recommending that the people "remonstrate frequently in order to bring about the matter more easily," they sent, between 1780 and 1784, at least four petitions to Congress and five to Virginia complaining of the land laws and the district court and asking that Kentucky be made a separate state. [100] Usually composed by partisan supporters

96. Petition to Virginia, spring 1782 (read May 30, 1782), Va. State Lib., also No. 15 in Robertson, ed., *Petitions*, 62–66.

97. Walker Daniel to William Fleming, Apr. 14, 1783, Draper Coll., 46 J 78; Daniel to Fleming, Aug. 22, 1783, *ibid.*, 79; Daniel to G. R. Clark, Sept. 15, 1783, James, ed., *Clark Papers*, II, 246–248; petition to Congress, spring or summer 1783 (read Sept. 27, 1783), Papers of Continental Congress, Ser. 41, V, 97; article date-lined "Richmond Nov 29" in *Md. Jour.* (Baltimore), Dec. 9, 1783, Draper Coll., 3 JJ 114; petition to Virginia, spring 1782, Va. State Lib., also No. 27 in Robertson, ed., *Petitions*, 78–79.

98. Daniel to Fleming, Apr. 14, 1783, Draper Coll., 46 J 78; Daniel to Harrison, May 21, 1784, Palmer, ed., *Cal. Va. State Papers*, III, 584–588.

99. Daniel to Fleming, Apr. 14, 1783, Draper Coll., 46 J 78.

100. Donelson to Campbell, Apr. 20, 1782, *ibid.*, 9 DD 34; Daniel to Fleming, Apr. 14, 1783, *ibid.*, 46 J 78. The petitions to Congress were those of May 15, 1780, Papers of Continental Congress, Ser. 48, 237; fall 1781, mentioned in three letters to Levi Todd, Aug.–Sept. 1806, in Draper Coll., 16 CC 39–44; spring 1782 (read

rather than by the leaders,[101] these petitions were introduced
at a meeting in the settlements or garrisons [102] and then
copied laboriously by men more accustomed to a plow than
a pen. After the copies were carried from cabin to cabin to
be signed, they were finally taken to Congress by someone
traveling that way or by partisans commissioned for the
task.[103]

The articulate center tended to ignore Arthur Campbell's
activities, perhaps because he was a Virginian like themselves and related by marriage to John Floyd, the
Breckinridges, and Caleb Wallace, or possibly because his
friends were ineffectual at their worst and at their best
were willing to support the district court.[104] Pomeroy and
other agents of the land companies could not be over-

Aug. 27, 1782), mentioned in N.-Y. Hist. Soc., *Colls.*, XI (New
York, 1878), 145–150; and fall 1783 (read Jan. 2, 1784), Papers
of Continental Congress, Ser. 41, V, 101–102. The petitions to Virginia were those of summer 1779, Campbell-Preston-Floyd Papers,
Lib. of Congress; Dec. 1781, mentioned in No. 24, Robertson, ed.,
Petitions, 78–79; spring 1782 (read May 30, 1782), Va. State Lib.,
also No. 15, *ibid.,* 62–66; fall 1782, mentioned in No. 17, *ibid.,*
68–69; and fall 1783, *Md. Jour.* (Baltimore), Dec. 19, 1783. See the
Bibliography for an annotated list of petitions.

101. Two petitions of spring 1782 were certainly not composed by
John Donelson, who called the meeting to introduce them, for the
style is entirely unlike his. Petition to Congress, spring 1782, mentioned in N.-Y. Hist. Soc., *Colls.*, XI, 145–150; petition to Virginia,
spring 1782 (read May 30, 1782), Va. State Lib., also No. 15 in
Robertson, ed., *Petitions,* 62–66. All of the petitions except that of
fall 1783 to Virginia, *Md. Jour.* (Baltimore), Dec. 19, 1783, were
evidently written by people unused to composition and copied by
unpracticed hands.

102. Donelson to Campbell, Apr. 20, 1782, Draper Coll., 9 DD
34; S. Clarke to Benjamin Harrison, Nov. 30, 1782, Palmer, ed.,
Cal. Va. State Papers, III, 384–385; three letters to Levi Todd, Aug.–
Sept. 1806, Draper Coll., 16 CC 39–44.

103. Many of the names were obviously signed in family groups
and therefore presumably not at a community meeting. On the trans-
mission of the petitions, see Donelson to Campbell, Apr. 20, 1782,
Draper Coll., 9 DD 34; John Cowan to Todd, Aug. 21, 1806, *ibid.,*
16 CC 41–42; Daniel to Harrison, Jan. 19, May 21, 1784, Palmer,
ed., *Cal. Va. State Papers,* III, 555–556, 584–588.

104. Ebenezer Brooks signed a petition supporting the district
court. Petition to Virginia, spring 1782, Va. State Lib., also No. 24
in Robertson, ed., *Petitions,* 78–79.

looked, however. Although the members of the articulate center recognized the economic motivation,[105] they usually thought of the movement as a plot to destroy their personal reputations and authority.[106] Convinced of the justness of their own ideals, they referred to partisan leaders as "false malitious persons," "a small party of blackguards," or "designing and perverse members of Society," and suggested that they were actually attempting to gain power or prestige.[107] "You are sensible how fond some perticular classes of people are, of spreading reports prejudicial to others," one member of the articulate center complained, perhaps referring to Ebenezer Brooks. "A low character, in the Eastern part of the State, he fits himself out, comes to the fronteers, supposes on his rout, that although of an Inferior Class in his own neighborhood [he] will be at least Equal to the First in the Country he is going to. [He] push[es] himself into Company and perhaps Gets kicked out, and Emediately makes a point of Exclaiming, not only for sake of revenge, but is in hopes that strangers will view him as a man of consequence." [108]

By 1782, with the invasion of land-company agents into Kentucky, the articulate center was forced to defend its position. To counter the partisans' letters from congressmen,

105. Daniel to Fleming, Apr. 14, 1783, Draper Coll., 46 J 78; G. R. Clark to Commissioners, Feb. 25, 1783, Palmer, ed., *Cal. Va. State Papers*, III, 448–450.

106. John Floyd to John May, Apr. 8, 1782, James, ed., *Clark Papers*, II, 54–56; S. Clarke to Harrison, Nov. 30, 1782, Palmer, ed., *Cal. Va. State Papers*, III, 384–385; G. R. Clark to Commissioners, Dec. 15, 1782, *ibid.*, 396–397; John Montgomery to Commissioners, Feb. 22, 1783, *ibid.*, 441–444; Clark to Harrison, Mar. 8, 1783, James, ed., *Clark Papers*, II, 212–215.

107. Montgomery to Commissioners, Feb. 22, 1783, Palmer, ed., *Cal. Va. State Papers*, III, 441–444; G. R. Clark to Harrison, May 2, 1782, James, ed., *Clark Papers*, II, 63–65; Daniel to Clark, Sept. 15, 1783, *ibid.*, 246–248; S. Clarke to Harrison, Nov. 30, 1782, Palmer, ed., *Cal. Va. State Papers*, III, 384–385; Clark to Commissioners, Dec. 15, 1782, *ibid.*, 396–397.

108. Montgomery to Commissioners, Feb. 22, 1783, *ibid.*, 441–444.

they circulated their letters from Virginia; to offset the petitions, they begged Virginia to defend her interests.[109] Supporters of the articulate center sometimes called meetings, especially when they knew their opponents were meeting, and on two occasions a riot broke up partisan gatherings.[110] At elections to the Virginia General Assembly they made fun of partisan candidates. Of one they told a story that his wife came to the door and called, "Andrew come to your mush. The pegs have been in it, and will be in it again." [111] "Mush" was the mountaineers' name for what easterners called "hominy," and "pegs" was distinctly a mountain pronunciation for "pigs"; this was a way of saying that the candidate, having not lived in eastern Virginia, was too inexperienced in political matters to be trusted with a legislative post.

Kentuckians reached a peak of separatist enthusiasm during the winter of 1783/1784. Filled with the rumors spread by partisan leaders and excited by the prospect of annulment of Virginia land claims that they supposed would follow statehood, landless settlers began to choose the sites they would take when the land was redistributed. Many even moved onto the land they had taken, marked the trees to show it was theirs, built cabins, and began to plant crops.[112] They thought the land would be given away by "head-rights," in settlement grants,[113] so they probably expected their possession of the land would give them a prior claim. Since the land they were choosing and settling was already

109. Daniel to Fleming, Aug. 22, 1783, Draper Coll., 46 J 78; petitions to Virginia, spring 1782, spring 1783 (read May 21, 1783), Va. State Lib., also Nos. 24, 17 in Robertson, ed., *Petitions*, 78–79, 68–69.
110. Donelson to Campbell, Apr. 20, 1782, Draper Coll., 9 DD 34; three letters to Levi Todd, Aug.–Sept. 1806, *ibid.*, 16 CC 39–44.
111. Shane interview, *ibid.*, 16 CC 269–270.
112. Article datelined "Richmond Nov 29" in *Md. Jour.* (Baltimore), Dec. 9, 1783, Draper Coll., 3 JJ 114; Marshall, *Kentucky*, I, 162; Wallace to Madison, Nov. 12, 1787, Madison Papers, VIII.
113. John Cowan to Todd, Aug. 21, 1806, Draper Coll., 16 CC 41–42.

claimed under Virginia, members of the articulate center found this development thoroughly frightening.[114] One of them even predicted bloodshed.[115]

When partisans began to occupy land already claimed under Virginia titles, the articulate center was finally provoked into strong legal action. Both George Pomeroy and his fellow partisan, a man named Galloway, were indicted by the attorney general, Walker Daniel, and brought to trial.[116] Galloway had circulated petitions privately in Fayette County and then had declared openly that the Virginia title was "no better than an oak leaf"; Pomeroy, whom the attorney general considered "the first mover, at least the ostensible cause of the Disturbance," had circulated several petitions and then carried them to Congress. Having made the indictment against Pomeroy, Daniel was, as he reported, "for a considerable time almost at a loss to know under what Law he should be punished. To prosecute him for high crimes and misdemeanors, was unprecedented not only in this new country, but in the State: it would have been difficult to have fixed the matter, and to have brought him under the description: his crime did not amount to Treason, tho' the consequences were nearly as serious and alarming." He "therefore had recourse to our old Law, almost absolute, for the punishment of Divulgers of false news." [117]

The cases of Galloway and Pomeroy demonstrated both the enthusiasm of partisans and the strength of the Virginia government in Kentucky. Galloway's trial, in the log cabin that served as Fayette's courthouse, was attended by a great crowd of people, among them many Jefferson County partisans, who were noisy and rude until they realized the local

114. Daniel to Harrison, Jan. 19, 1784, Palmer, ed., *Cal. Va. State Papers*, III, 555–556.
115. Article datelined "Richmond Nov 29" in *Md. Jour.* (Baltimore), Dec. 9, 1783, Draper Coll., 3 JJ 114.
116. This may have been the George Galloway whose daughter Pomeroy married. Will of George Galloway, Healy, ed., "Jefferson County Will Book No. 1," *Filson Club Hist. Qtly.*, VI(1932), 18.
117. Daniel to Harrison, Jan. 19, May 21, 1784, Palmer, ed., *Cal. Va. State Papers*, III, 555–556, 584–588; Marshall, *Kentucky*, I, 162.

citizens were taking the trial seriously.[118] A large crowd also attended Pomeroy's trial by the Jefferson County Court four months later, in May 1784, but there the separatists behaved, Walker Daniel thought, with "the most perfect Decorum." [119] Galloway was given only a moderate fine; [120] Pomeroy, however, was fined two thousand pounds of tobacco and bound to good behavior with two sureties.[121] Daniel was surprised by the eagerness of Pomeroy's friends to act as security. "Instead of Indignation and Resentment, at being brought into contempt and ridicule by his false-hoods and misrepresentations," he noted, "they seemed to mourn at his conviction." [122]

Pomeroy and Galloway ceased to agitate after their trials, and no further efforts were made toward a con-gressional separation. Congress had effectually ruled out that possibility when it accepted Virginia's cession of the Northwest Territory in March 1784, for in doing so it had also implicitly accepted Virginia's authority over Kentucky and her consequent right to grant land there. The petition for which Pomeroy had so laboriously collected signatures, which he had carried to Philadelphia himself, was ignored in Congress.[123] When word of the cession reached Kentucky —probably in May, around the time of Pomeroy's trial— partisans must have realized that they could no longer hope for Congress to appropriate the land of Kentucky and annul the Virginia titles. Yet the reasons for the separation move-

118. Daniel to Harrison, Jan. 19, 1784, Palmer, ed., *Cal. Va. State Papers*, III, 555–556; Marshall, *Kentucky*, I, 162.
119. Daniel to Harrison, May 21, 1784, Palmer, ed., *Cal. Va. State Papers*, III, 584–588.
120. Daniel to Harrison, Jan. 19, 1784, *ibid.*, 555–556. The offi-cial record of this trial was lost when the Fayette Courthouse burned in 1803.
121. "Minute Book No. 1, Jefferson County," 37, in *Filson Club Hist. Qtly.*, VI(1932), 67.
122. Daniel to Harrison, May 21, 1784, Palmer, ed., *Cal. Va. State Papers*, III, 584–588.
123. Delegates to the governor of Virginia, Feb. 20, 1784, Ed-mund C. Burnett, ed., *Letters of Members of the Continental Con-gress* (Washington, 1921–1936), VII, 446.

ment still existed. The land laws were still unjust, Indians continued to menace, and some settlers were still cooped up in forts where sedition could brew.[124] Moreover, there were still some men in Kentucky who wanted to enhance their own importance by challenging the leadership of the articulate center.

Limited now to the leadership of Arthur Campbell's friends and a few discontented speculators, yet unwilling to abandon hope for a redistribution, partisans continued to work for a separation. They might accomplish it with the consent of Virginia, as was provided for in the Virginia Constitution of 1779, or they might declare "unconditional" independence of the mother state, as Campbell's state of Franklin (now Tennessee) would soon do. In either case they would probably apply for admission into the Union after the separation, thinking Congress might be sympathetic toward their goals even though it would not actively intervene in Kentucky now. In either case the partisans would have to win control of the new Kentucky government before they could redistribute the land. That did not seem an impossible task in the spring of 1784. "I am persauded [sic] that no two thinking men in the District, of honest disinterested Intentions, at present, wish a separation from the Eastern part of the State," Walker Daniel wrote after the trial of Pomeroy, "[but] I am at a loss to say how long they will continue in their present Sentiments."[125] The next day another Kentuckian wrote, even more pessimistically, "I fear the Faction will increase, and ere long we shall revolt from [Virginia] Government in order to try if we can govern ourselves, which in my opinion, will be jumping out of the frying Pan into the Fire."[126]

*   *   *

124. Daniel to Harrison, May 21, 1784, Palmer, ed., *Cal. Va. State Papers*, III, 584–588.
125. *Ibid.*, 588.
126. James Speed to Harrison, May 22, 1784, *ibid.*, 588–589.

"I begin to think that the time for a separation is fast approaching, and has perhaps actually arrived," Thomas Marshall's son John wrote to George Muter less than eight months later, answering a letter in which Muter described "the situation of affairs in the western country." [127] In the half year between Pomeroy's trial and the end of 1784, members of the articulate center had reconsidered the whole question of separation, and some of them, including Muter, had come to favor it. Neither the "Congressional separation" for which George Pomeroy had worked nor the "unconditional separation" now advocated by Arthur Campbell satisfied them, however. What they wanted was a "constitutional separation," begun in an orderly way, preceded by a contract guaranteeing the land grants that Virginia had made to Kentuckians.

Between May and December 1784 it had become obvious that Kentucky was no longer a frontier; [128] this was probably the most important factor in the articulate center's change of mind. The end of the Revolution had promised an end to the Indian war, allowing Kentuckians to move out of the forts and begin serious farming. "Plenty abounded," Humphrey Marshall later recalled; "cattle, and hogs, were seen to increase, and thrive to an astonishing degree; and the fields were burthened with Indian corn." [129] The first market crops were harvested in Kentucky in the fall of 1784 and sent on flatboats down the Mississippi soon after.

As Kentuckians settled on their farms and planted crops, they also began to build permanent residences. Until 1783

127. John Marshall to George Muter, Jan. 7, 1785, *Tyler's Qtly. Hist Gen. Mag.*, I(1919–1920), 28.
128. Marshall, *Kentucky*, I, 161, puts the end of the frontier at 1783, noting the establishment then of horse races, schools, stores, and distilleries, the coming of preachers, and the increase in trading. Roosevelt, *Winning of the West*, II, 213, probably drawing on Marshall, also points to the year 1783 and notes many of the same things; he then (III, 16) points to the year 1785, with the building of houses and gristmills and the growth of villages.
129. Marshall, *Kentucky*, I, 161.

every house in Kentucky had been a log cabin, but that year Thomas Marshall built a two-story log house, and in 1784 similar buildings began to appear all over the district.[130] In 1785 someone in Lexington hewed the logs for his house, to make them square and smooth; about the same time someone in Louisville put glass windows in a building, and a frontier boy ran home crying "O ma! there is a house down here with specs on!"[131] Several people built stone houses in 1783 and 1784,[132] Isaac Shelby built one in 1786, and in 1783 Benjamin Logan built a frame house, the first in Kentucky.[133]

The end of the war also meant that all the would-be Kentuckians who had postponed their move on account of Indian troubles and all those who had been serving in the armies could go to Kentucky. In three years the population of Kentucky jumped from about five thousand to about forty thousand, and the amount of money in circulation increased proportionately. The presence of the new settlers and their money changed the whole life of Kentucky. Lexington and Louisville became flourishing towns, and several smaller villages appeared; in 1785 Louisville had a population of three hundred, living in one hundred buildings in three parallel streets, and Lexington supported

130. Marshall's home was Buck Pond, now in Woodford County. William E. Railey, *History of Woodford County* (Frankfort, Ky., 1938), 306–307. Similar houses were, for example, the home of John Clark, Mulberry Hill (1784), near Louisville and the Adam Rankin house (1784), 215 West High St., Lexington. Mulberry Hill is discussed in Rexford Newcomb, *Architecture in Old Kentucky* (Urbana, Ill., 1953), 32. For the Rankin house see Clay Lancaster, *Ante Bellum Houses of the Bluegrass* (Lexington, 1961), 6.

131. Lucien Beckner, ed., "John D. Shane's Notes on an Interview with Jeptha Kemper of Montgomery County," *Filson Club Hist. Qtly.*, XII(1938), 156; Collins, *History of Kentucky*, II, 373.

132. For example, the William Crow house (1783) in Boyle County (Newcomb, *Architecture*, 38); the Robert Boggs house (1784) about eight miles southeast of Lexington (Lancaster, *Ante Bellum Houses*, 16–17); the Jel Du Puy house (1784) in Woodford County (Newcomb, *Architecture*, 38).

133. Newcomb, *Architecture*, 38; Talbert, *Logan*, 189.

two silversmiths.[134] Ebenezer Brooks started his Latin school in 1784, and the Transylvania Seminary opened in 1785, along with several other schools.[135] Ministers began to migrate to Kentucky in 1783,[136] and Lexington built its first log church in 1784.[137] Merchandising became a profitable employment, and suddenly almost a dozen stores appeared —six at Lexington, two at Danville, and at least two at Louisville.[138] Kentuckians who had previously ordered supplies from Virginia and depended on travelers to transport them could now purchase in Kentucky corduroy, chintz, and dimity, queensware and delft, lemons and crosscut saws.[139] Merchants urged the people to raise tobacco to exchange for goods and guaranteed a good price for it.[140]

134. Roosevelt, *Winning of the West*, III, 16; letter from a gentleman in the western country, Dec. 22, 1785, in *Mass. Gaz.* (Boston), Mar. 12, 1786, Draper Coll., 32 J 108–110; Noble W. and Lucy F. Hiatt, *The Silversmiths of Kentucky, 1785–1850* (Louisville, 1954), xv.

135. Interview with Nathaniel Hart in Shane, "Henderson Company Ledger," *Filson Club Hist. Qtly.*, XXI(1947), 46; Collins, *History of Kentucky*, II, 183–184.

136. Marshall, *Kentucky*, I, 161; Vernon P. Martin, "Father Rice, the Preacher Who Followed the Frontier," *Filson Club Hist. Qtly.*, XXIX(1955), 324–330. But see the Josiah Collins interview, Draper Coll., 12 CC 73.

137. Charles R. Staples, *History of Pioneer Lexington, 1779–1806* (Lexington, 1939).

138. Lexington stores were started by: Peter January (n.d.), James Wilkinson (1784), Alexander and James Parker (1784), George Gordon and John Coburn (1784), and Robert Barr (1784). Staples, *Pioneer Lexington*, 27–30. Also William Butler (1784?), Butler interview, Draper Coll., 15 CC 46. The Danville storekeepers were Walker Daniel (1782) and Hugh Shiell (1784). Calvin M. Fackler, *Early Days in Danville* (Louisville, 1941), 24–25; "Letters of General James Wilkinson," *Register*, XXIV(1926), 259. Those in Louisville were Daniel Broadhead (1783) and Tardiveau and Honoré (1782?). Collins, *History of Kentucky*, II, 372; Rice, *Tardiveau*, 3.

139. James Wilkinson to Hugh Shiell, undated (probably 1784), "Letters of Wilkinson," *Register*, XXIV(1926), 260–262; Wilkinson to Shiell, July 4, 1784, *ibid.*, 259–260; Ann Wilkinson to John Biddle, spring 1788, "Letters of Mrs. Ann Biddle Wilkinson from Kentucky, 1788–1789," *Pennsylvania Magazine of History and Biography*, LVI(1932), 42–43.

140. Nicholas Meriwether to William Meriwether, Aug. 1784, No. 662, Ky. Hist. Soc.

By 1784, or 1785 at the latest, most of the good land in Kentucky had been taken;[141] the land that remained unclaimed was undesirable either because of its quality or its location. Like the inevitable piling up of lawsuits,[142] this furnished another sign of the end of the frontier. The lawsuits began at this time both because uncontested locations were no longer available and because the district court began its sessions in 1783. A host of lawyers to argue them started their westward migrations at the end of the Revolution. The first professional, full-time attorney arrived in the summer or fall of 1783[143] and was soon followed by about half a dozen practicing attorneys, so that by 1785 the Kentucky bar included a number of men. They were an important addition to the articulate center.

Almost everyone in Kentucky, even the most loyal Virginians, had expected all along that the district would eventually be a separate state. Divided by the Allegheny Mountains, Kentucky and Virginia were distinct geographic areas with distinctly separate lives. Virginia stretched along the Atlantic coast, her rivers ran southeast, and she faced London. Kentucky, however, was inland. The Ohio River, flowing west, offered easy transportation from the east to Kentucky, but there was no easy passage from Kentucky back to Virginia. The western waters ran northwest into the Ohio and then south down the Mississippi, so Kentucky faced New Orleans. The planters of Virginia had found it most profitable to spread along the river banks and to live by trading with the rest of the world, but the planters of Kentucky found it best to live in the interior. Even if Indian

141. William Christian to Gilbert Christian, Aug. 13, 1784, Draper Coll., 5 QQ 124; letter from a gentleman in the western country, Dec. 22, 1785, in *Mass. Gaz.* (Boston), Mar. 12, 1786, *ibid.*, 32 J 108–110.

142. Floyd to Preston, Mar. 27, 1783, *ibid.*, 33 S 320; Alexander Breckinridge to John Breckinridge, Aug. 8, 1784, Nov. 8, 1784, Breckinridge Family Papers, II; Wm. Breckinridge to John Breckinridge, Aug. 9, 1784, *ibid.*

143. See below, p. 79.

attacks had not forced them inland, they would have found that the best land did not always lie on navigable rivers. Living in the forest, limited by the mountains and the current of the rivers, they had to be self-sufficient.

Even if Kentucky and Virginia had been geographically a unit, the sheer distance involved would have made a connection difficult. From Danville to Richmond it was about 750 miles, an exhausting journey and a time-consuming one. The distance meant that Indian expeditions could not be authorized quickly, and it made appeals to the Supreme Court in Richmond costly. It meant that qualified men were unwilling to sit in the Virginia General Assembly unless they had other business in the East to justify so long an absence, and it meant that Kentuckians remained in ignorance of the laws long after they were passed. The distance prohibited any organized postal service and left the mail to depend on private travelers; thus the *Virginia Gazette* did not circulate regularly in Kentucky, and Kentuckians' information was almost as often rumor as it was fact. "The papers of any date . . . would be new in this Part of Country," one of the Breckinridges complained in the summer of 1784, "and the Acts of Assembly are not to [be] had in this part of this Country." [144]

The distance between Virginia and Kentucky made the administration of Kentucky difficult and led to the passage of many unfortunate or unnecessary laws. The condition of the district court was a particularly sore spot with the articulate center. They were distressed, first, because the court was accomplishing nothing and, second, because the payment of judges' salaries from fines—as provided by the legislature of Virginia—opened a door for corruption. [145]

144. Wm. Breckinridge to John Breckinridge, Aug. 9, 1784, Breckinridge Family Papers, II. See also Wm. Breckinridge to John Breckinridge, Feb. 7, 1785, *ibid.*
145. Resolution at the Dec. 1784 convention, Abernethy, ed., "Journal of First Convention," *Jour. So. Hist.*, I(1935), 67–78; see above, p. 54.

Third, they thought Kentuckians had to pay for their court twice, since they paid the usual taxes from which other Virginia courts were supported and still had to support their own from fines.[146] Finally, they were afraid that inadequate salaries would force the judges to resign and the court to close, and they feared the consequences if it did. "Anarchy and confusion must follow, because faction and error will bring the County Court into Contempt: their authority will immediately be trampled on and disregard[ed]," one wrote. "If we have no superintending Court, which we cannot have without Funds to support it, a Revolution in this Country will ensue, and then no man can say that he is sure of his property an hour." [147]

The land laws were, if possible, an area even more sensitive than the district court. Kentuckians found most objectionable a tax of five shillings per hundred acres imposed by Virginia on patents in 1782.[148] Curiously, however, it did not evoke any protest until after the October session of 1784, when a revision made it more lenient; [149] perhaps it was not enforced until after the revision.[150] The tax applied only to lands patented under treasury warrants and even then only to the amount of land exceeding fourteen hundred acres—if the land was in a single plot (even if it was in several surveys) or if it was granted under a single patent. Thus it did not touch many Kentuckians directly, but it was expected to reduce the value of all Kentucky lands.[151] It weighed most heavily, of course, on men who dealt in very large quantities of land, the surveyors and other speculators,

146. *Ibid.*
147. Daniel to Harrison, May 21, 1784, Palmer, ed., *Cal. Va. State Papers,* III, 584–588.
148. Hening, ed., *Statutes,* XI, 121.
149. *Ibid.,* 445. The only references I have found to it before the revision are both calm: Floyd to Preston, Mar. 28, 1783, Draper Coll., 17 CC 144–149; Abraham Hite to Richard C. Anderson, Mar. 8, 1784, Anderson Papers, Box 1, Va. State Lib.
150. Charles Yancey to Daniel Boone, Jan. 14, 1785, Draper Coll., 25 C 1.
151. *Ibid.*

and brought an angry protest from at least one surveyor. "The people here," he said, "are a good deal enraged at the Government of Virginia which I expect will force us to a Separation sooner than we are prepared for it." [152]

A third factor in the articulate center's discontent with the government of Virginia was the matter of Indian warfare. The Indian menace had eased with the end of the war, and by 1784 the interior parts of Kentucky were solidly settled and seldom saw an Indian. But it would be many years before Kentuckians ceased to have an Indian problem. As late as 1789 twenty-two people would be killed and twelve wounded and over a hundred horses taken in frontier attacks during a bad three-month period.[153] These raids had the effect of pushing the frontier back toward the interior settlements and sometimes of forcing the people into garrisons again.[154] The situation was never as serious after 1784 as it had been during the war, but it was still distressing. Moreover, it was frustrating, because Virginia law permitted only defensive fighting. By the time the militia could gather after a raid on a lonely frontier cabin, the Indians had long since left the area; thus the Kentuckians were in fact unable to defend themselves. "We complain much," one settler wrote, "that the Legislative Body have

152. Christopher Greenup to Charles Simms, July 19, 1785, Charles Simms Papers, I, Lib. of Congress. See also William Nelson to William Short, Oct. 16, 1785, William Short Papers, I, Lib. of Congress. Both of these letters I found through Abernethy's reference to them, *Western Lands,* 303. He attributes the beginning of the movement for constitutional separation to this law, but he mistakenly dates the law in May 1784, although he refers to Hening, ed., *Statutes,* XI, 445, which was the Oct. session. No similar land tax was passed at the May session. In fact, news of the revised land tax had probably not yet reached Kentucky when the November 1784 meeting took place.

153. Unidentified newspaper account in Samuel McDowell to Beverley Randolph, July 26, 1789, Palmer, ed., *Cal. Va. State Papers,* V, 8.

154. Levi Todd and James Garrard to Edmund Randolph, Mar. 29, 1788, *ibid.,* IV, 419–420; Alexander S. Bullitt to Randolph, May 16, 1787, *ibid.,* 284–285.

tied the Hands of the Kentucky people in such a manner as to prevent our lifting Arms against those who daily invade us." [155]

It was the Indian problem that brought the next partisan move, in November 1784, and prompted the articulate center to decide on the question of separation. The occasion was the quarterly session of the district court, when the men of Kentucky gathered in Danville to transact their business and exchange news, standing in the muddy street, and to talk politics over drinks of rum at the tavern. Benjamin Logan had just returned from a trip to the Southeast with news that the Cherokee and Chickamauga Indians were planning to invade Kentucky; he was convinced that an offensive expedition was the only means of thwarting their plan. Probably acting as militia lieutenant of Danville's county, he called together the most important of the men in town to discuss the situation.[156] (Earlier, in April 1782, acting "as a private person," he had called a similar meeting in Lincoln County to discuss "matters of public choncern.") [157] Aware that no one in Kentucky had authority to authorize an expedition, Logan feared there was not time enough to get permission from Richmond. The situation, he thought, was critical and called for immediate action.

The partisan move came after the articulate center, including McDowell, Wallace, and Muter, had stood firm against an expedition, arguing that it would be altogether illegal. They were, after all, responsible for enforcing the

155. Todd to Randolph, Apr. 30, 1787, *ibid.*, 277. See also Todd to Patrick Henry, Sept. 16, 1785, *ibid.*, 53.

156. The basic sources for the Nov. 1784 meeting are Ebenezer Brooks to Arthur Campbell, Dec. 9, 1784, Draper Coll., 11 J 37–38, published in Temple Bodley, *History of Kentucky* (Chicago, 1928), I, 354–356; Caleb Wallace to Madison, Sept. 25, 1785, Madison Papers, VI; "A Farmer" [Harry Innes], *Ky. Gaz.* (Lexington), Oct. 18, 1788; William Littell, *Political Transactions in and concerning Kentucky, from the First Settlement Thereof, Until It Became an Independent State, in June, 1792* (Frankfort, Ky., 1806), 12; Marshall, *Kentucky*, I, 190–193.

157. Notice of Benjamin Logan, Draper Coll., 32 J 66.

laws of Virginia. Then "an obscure little man" (as Ebenezer Brooks described the event to Arthur Campbell), "your humble servant, arose and discussed the point, both with respect to law and order." He apparently persuaded the articulate center that the expedition could be justified, for a motion favoring it carried unanimously. Enjoying his "fair victory over a Doctor, a lawyer, and a quandam priest"—Wallace's brother-in-law William Fleming, George Muter, and Caleb Wallace himself—he was dismayed when the meeting received word that the Southern Indians had become peaceful, for it meant that the expedition would not be held and the authority of Virginia not challenged. After someone suggested that the meeting petition Virginia for more independence in Indian affairs, Brooks, relying on the discontent of such supporters of the articulate center as Benjamin Logan and Isaac Shelby, moved that it was a proper time to demand a separation from Virginia.[158]

Once again the articulate center was able to use the tools of law and order against a partisan. They simply ignored Brooks's motion. No one seconded it, and it died a natural death.[159] But they did decide to call a more formal convention to consider the military situation, even after word came that the Indians were no longer threatening attack. This convention, to consist of one representative elected by each militia company, was to meet in Danville on December 27, 1784, only seven weeks away.[160] It would be unofficial, because it was not called by any legally constituted authority,

158. Brooks to Campbell, Nov. 9, 1784, *ibid.*, 11 J 37–38, published in Bodley, *Kentucky*, I, 354–356.

159. This becomes apparent from a reading of the sources. Brooks does not say that the meeting voted to adopt his motion, as he surely would if that had been the case; yet neither Littell nor Marshall says that the motion was voted down. (Littell's information came in part from Caleb Wallace, who was at this meeting.)

160. See the standard sources for the Nov. 1784 meeting cited in n. 156 above. All these writers agree that the convention of Dec. 1784 was called to consider the military situation rather than the question of statehood.

but it would not be illegal. Because the matter to be discussed was military, it would represent the entire Kentucky militia; yet, since most men served in the militia, in a sense it would represent the whole population of Kentucky.[161]

The December convention, Brooks wrote to Arthur Campbell, "may be an introduction to important events." [162] The decision to call a convention he saw as a victory for himself. Previously the articulate center had supported the Virginia government and opposed separation, distrusting everything Brooks had tried to do. In calling a convention to discuss the military situation, they now showed discontent with the Virginia government and, perhaps, indicated a willingness to work with Brooks. They had not declared themselves in favor of separation, but it looked as though they might soon take that step. In November 1784 matters looked very hopeful for the partisans.

161. Talbert, *Logan*, 196, suggests that the convention of Dec. 1784 represented the entire population even though it was elected through the militia. It is true that free males between the ages of 18 and 50, with certain exceptions, were required to serve in the militia (Hening, ed., *Statutes*, XI, 476–477, XII, 10), so the first convention did represent most of the voting population. However, this seems to have been coincidental; those who called the convention were concerned with the military situation and therefore presumably with the militia, not the civil population.
162. Brooks to Campbell, Nov. 9, 1784, Draper Coll., 11 J 37–38, published in Bodley, *Kentucky*, I, 354–356.

3

THE STRUGGLE FOR
STATEHOOD

On his way to Kentucky in the summer of 1783,[1] John
Brown was riding in twilight through the wilderness when
he sighted the fires of an Indian party ahead. Hoping to
pass around the Indians without being seen, he and his three
companions pressed ahead, but their horses stumbled on
some rocks. Brown thought he had never heard such a noise
as they made. Through the mountain stillness that magnified
every sound, the Indians heard it too and began pursuit.
Brown and his companions rode hard all night and all the
next day, stopping only once to give the horses some grass.
That night they crawled into the bushes off the trail to get
some sleep, then raced on. They had barely reached the
gates of the fort at Crab Orchard, the closest settlement in
Kentucky, before the Indian party appeared on top of the

---

1. The date of John Brown's arrival in Kentucky is usually given
as 1782. Collins, *History of Kentucky,* II, 252; E. Merton Coulter in
DAB s.v. "Brown, John." It can be fixed after Mar. 1783 by a letter
from John Floyd to William Preston, Draper Coll., 33 S 320, Wis.
Hist. Soc., and before Oct. 1783 by a letter addressed to John Brown
in Danville, Ky., Preston Papers, #1242, Lib. of Congress.

hill behind them. They later learned that the Indians actually had been planning an attack.[2]

John Brown, thus saved by a few feet and a few minutes, was one of the lawyers whose arrival announced the end of the frontier in Kentucky. In 1783 he was twenty-six years old, a man of medium height with pleasant, youthful features, rosy cheeks, and a figure already growing stout.[3] "He looked able to take on himself a share of the defence of the country, a circumstance not unnoticed," [4] according to Humphrey Marshall. His cultured speech marked him a gentleman; he had attended Princeton College, had graduated, like Caleb Wallace, from William and Mary, and had studied law under Thomas Jefferson. The son of a well-known Presbyterian minister in Rockbridge County, Virginia, and related to John Floyd, Caleb Wallace, and the Breckinridges, he knew many of the important men in Virginia and had already established his reputation as a lawyer.[5] "I have heard a great character of Mr. John Brown," Floyd had written. "Mr. Wallace gives him the greatest praise of all the young men of his acquaintance, and others have told me they thought he would be eminent in his profession." [6]

With his clear, analytical mind John Brown was able to break any abstract problem into its various parts and then arrange the parts in an intelligible way.[7] This made him a fine lawyer, and Kentuckians soon developed great confidence in his legal abilities.[8] During 1785 his legal fees

2. Shane's interview with David Humphrey, Draper Coll., 16 CC 292.

3. Marshall, *Kentucky*, I, 279; Trumbull portrait of John Brown in the Yale Art Gallery.

4. Marshall, *Kentucky*, I, 279.

5. Coulter in *DAB* s.v. "Brown, John."

6. Floyd to Wm. Preston, Mar. 27, 1783, Draper Coll., 33 S 320.

7. See, for example, a paper signed "J. B.," *ca.* Jan. 1820, in Henry Clay Papers, Wilson Coll., Univ. of Ky., abstracted in James F. Hopkins, ed., *The Papers of Henry Clay*, II(Lexington, 1961), 748–749.

8. John Brown to John Breckinridge, Sept. 20, 1784, Breckinridge Family Papers, I, Lib. of Congress; Barthélemi Tardiveau to Crè-

amounted to several hundred pounds, and he was actually paid £218,[9] more than the established salaries of the assistant judges and probably more than the chief judge actually received. In dealing with immediate personal problems Brown was less clear than he was with abstract legal ones. Shy and severely restrained, sensitive to rebuffs, he was characterized by his most perceptive friend as "a young man of respectable talents, but timid, without political experience, and with very little knowledge of the world."[10] Troubled by an occasional piety that assailed him in times of crisis and a consistent moral uncertainty, he always tried to do the right thing, but it was difficult for him to discover just what was right. During his college years he had leaned on an uncle; now he would depend on his friends.[11]

The articulate center quickly adopted John Brown. In the next few years many lawyers and planters would migrate from Virginia to Kentucky, but he happened to be the first who came after the war ended. It was probably for that reason that he became as important in Kentucky as he did. "His friends want him to take up a political career, in which they are of the opinion that he will cut a distinguished figure," a visitor to Kentucky reported. "Competent people tell me that in Virginia he is inferior only to Mr. Madison."[12] Estimating his ability thus, Kentuckians elected him to the Virginia Senate in 1784, and he continued to represent them for the next twenty years. Under other circumstances his personality might have forbidden the backslap-

---

vecoeur, May 25, 1789, Rice, *Tardiveau*, 30–31; Marshall, *Kentucky*, I, 280.

9. John Brown's account book, at Liberty Hall in Frankfort, Ky.

10. James Wilkinson to Esteban Miro, Feb. 14, 1789, in Charles E. A. Gayarré, *History of Louisiana* (New Orleans, 1854–1867), III, 240–247.

11. John Mason Brown Papers, Yale Univ.; John Brown Papers, Ky. Hist. Soc.; Orlando Brown Papers, Filson Club; Preston Papers, Draper Coll.; Innes Papers, Lib. of Congress.

12. Tardiveau to Crèvecoeur, May 25, 1789, Rice, *Tardiveau*, 30–31.

ping and backbiting of politics, but in 1784 John Brown was clearly the most capable man in the district.

Another lawyer who arrived in Kentucky at the end of the frontier period was Benjamin Sebastian, Jr.,[13] a Virginian of around forty years, formerly an Anglican clergyman.[14] Sebastian came in 1784 with the highest of recommendations, described as "one possest of every Amiable quality you Could wish to find in a Human Creature," who "will prove a Valuable Acquisition to Any Society he may chance to Settle Among." [15] A handsome, able man who carried himself with dignity, he soon became indolent and inactive,[16] and as the years passed he developed a conviction that the world owed him more comfort than it had given. "He is too fickle and whimsical a man to be depended on," one acquaintance wrote; "this is the character he has borne through Life hitherto, and which he will carry to his Grave." [17] Sebastian never seemed to have quite enough money; eventually he would turn away from the law for financial profit [18] and finally would bother his friends with whining letters about his difficulties.[19] But in the 1780s he must have been a pleasant companion.

Perhaps the most outstanding of the Virginia planters who went west at the end of the frontier period was John Fowler, who hoped like many to recoup his finances in Kentucky. The son of a planter, Fowler had enjoyed con-

13. "Kentucky Spanish Association," *Ky. Gaz.* (Lexington), Sept. 11, 1806. The copy of this article in *Western World* (Frankfort) is no longer extant.

14. Isaac J. Cox in *DAB* s.v. "Sebastian, Benjamin."

15. Letter of Thomas Hart, Sept. 30, 1784, Thomas Hart Papers, Wilson Coll.

16. James Brown to John Brown, Nov. 29, 1790, Jan. 10, 1791, Apr. 8, 1795, J. M. Brown Papers, Yale Univ.

17. George Mason to Thomas Marshall, Oct. 16, 1789, T. J. Clay Papers, 1st Ser., II, Lib. of Congress.

18. Benjamin Sebastian to Wilkinson, Jan. 5, 1790, Gayarré, *Louisiana*, III, 275–276.

19. See for example his letter to James Brown, Oct. 16, 1806, Benjamin Sebastian Papers (photostats), Western Kentucky State College, Bowling Green.

siderable luxury since his marriage. His Virginia home was furnished with a harpsichord and a chamber organ, wedding presents from his father-in-law, in addition to a dozen tablecloths, several dozen pieces of queensware and glassware, and other implements of elegant living.[20] But his expenses had too consistently exceeded his income; in 1783, at the age of twenty-seven, he signed over his belongings to creditors,[21] and the next year he and his wife moved to Kentucky. Choosing a fertile tract of land in Fayette near Thomas Marshall's Buck Pond, the Fowlers lived with the Marshalls while their house was being built.[22] Life in the West must have seemed primitive, although the Fowlers continued to maintain a high standard even there.[23] "The first teacups and saucers I ever saw were there [at the Fowler house]," [24] one native later recalled. Even before his move to Kentucky, Fowler had begun speculating in Kentucky lands; [25] eventually he would patent more than 100,000 acres and buy and sell an additional 100,000.[26] By the end of 1784 he already had some 44,000 acres,[27] and his mind naturally turned to politics.

Fowler, Sebastian, and Brown soon became close friends with Harry Innes, Caleb Wallace, Samuel McDowell, and George Muter. People would soon call them "the court party," because the group included the judges of the district court, the attorney general, and the most important lawyers, and because they did become a political party.[28] But these

20. Ila Earle Fowler, *Captain John Fowler of Virginia and Kentucky; Patriot, Soldier, Pioneer, Statesman, Land Baron and Civic Leader* (Cynthiana, Ky., 1942), 12.
21. *Ibid.*, 11.
22. *Ibid.*, 26.
23. See the note by M. K. J. on "John Fowler to Constituents," Feb. 28, 1803, No. 308, Ky. Hist. Soc.
24. James Stevenson interview, Draper Coll., 11 CC 250.
25. John Fowler to Henry Lee, Aug. 15, 1784, *ibid.*, 31 CC 5.
26. Fowler, *John Fowler*, 24.
27. Jillson, *Land Grants*, 50.
28. Marshall, *Kentucky*, I, 322. Although the term "court party" was a generic one in the 18th century, meaning the party that sup-

men were friends before they were a party,[29] and they shared more than merely the business of the court and the politics of the district. Similar backgrounds and aspirations drew them together. Brown, Innes, Wallace, and McDowell could, through a web of intermarriages, consider themselves relatives—one way or another they were all members of the numerous and far-flung Preston family of western Virginia[30]—and Brown for a time courted McDowell's daughter.[31] All of them except McDowell were unusually well educated, and all except Sebastian were Presbyterians. All knew and corresponded with important Virginians, especially James Madison. Their wives, too, were compatible, visiting each other for long periods and sending each other greetings in their husbands' letters.[32] All planters at heart, the members of the court party built fine houses and furnished them well as soon as conditions permitted a stable life. John Fowler awed his neighbors with teacups and saucers, John Brown erected a handsome brick house with a ballroom, and Harry Innes ordered china from Baltimore[33] while most Kentuckians still ate with their knives and fingers from homemade wooden trenchers.[34]

---

ported the incumbent administration, Humphrey Marshall specifically says that on this occasion it was used "on account of the leaders, with the exception of Wilkinson, being members either of the bench or bar of the supreme court for the district." (I have edited the punctuation of this quotation.) Interestingly enough, members of the county courts were not automatically drawn into the court party. Although the county courts in Kentucky functioned much like their prototypes in Virginia, the membership seems to have represented not so much wealth and social status as the political makeup of the particular county. I am indebted to Joan W. Coward for a list of county court members during the prestatehood period.

29. See the depositions of Caleb Wallace and Samuel McDowell, *Innes* v. *Marshall*, 25–28, 65, Durrett Coll., Univ. of Chicago.

30. Orlando Brown, *Memoranda of the Preston Family* (Frankfort, Ky., 1842); Green, *Historic Families*, 192–195.

31. Marshall, *Kentucky*, I, 181. But see a news item in *Western World* (Frankfort), Aug. 16, 1806.

32. Fowler, *John Fowler*, 31–33.

33. Innes Papers, XVIII, Nos. 35, 37–38.

34. Marshall, *Kentucky*, I, 123; Stevenson interview, Draper Coll., 11 CC 250.

Perhaps even more important than similar backgrounds and aspirations in holding the court party together was their mutual respect for James Wilkinson, who came from Philadelphia in December 1783 to open a store in Lexington. "General Wilkinson [is] a particular friend of mine," John Brown said,[35] and the other court party members would have concurred. Wilkinson's round face was open, mild, and intelligent, and his manners were polite yet democratic. A short, plump person—Humphrey Marshall, from his vantage point of six feet two, acidly described Wilkinson's figure as "not quite tall enough to be perfectly elegant" but "compensated by its symmetry"—the twenty-six-year-old general had a manly walk and appeared healthy and active.[36] With his flair for the dramatic, Wilkinson even made a memorable event of mounting a horse. Ignoring the stirrup, he put his hand on the saddle and sprang onto the horse's back.[37] When he was short of money, he never whined as Sebastian did; instead he laughed and made a little arrangement to keep him until next week.[38] When there was something to be written, he composed it in a florid style that delighted his friends.[39] When someone misused him, he replied with a fine invective.[40] It was he who imported brandies for Harry Innes to drink and silks for Mrs. Innes to wear;[41] it was he who built the first house in Lexington with glass window panes[42] and owned the first

35. John Brown to Thomas B. Craighead, Dec. 22, 1786, in David Meade Massie, *Nathaniel Massie, A Pioneer of Ohio* (Cincinnati, 1896), 113–114.
36. Marshall, *Kentucky*, I, 165; Humphrey interview, Draper Coll., 16 CC 292.
37. *Ibid.*
38. See especially his letters to Hugh Shiell, No. 1058, Ky. Hist. Soc., published in "Letters of Wilkinson," *Register*, XXIV(1926), 259–267.
39. Marshall, *Kentucky*, I, 213; Littell, *Political Transactions*, 31. But see Caleb Wallace to James Madison, Sept. 25, 1785, Madison Papers, VI, Lib. of Congress.
40. See below, pp. 153–154.
41. Harry Innes in account with James Wilkinson, Apr. 3 to Dec. 6, 1789, Innes Papers, XXIII, Pt. i.
42. Collins, *History of Kentucky*, II, 181.

coach-and-four in Kentucky, with two riders mounted on black horses.[43] For dramatic promise and for actual accomplishment no man in the West could equal James Wilkinson.[44]

In 1784 Wilkinson's friends knew him as a spirited, adventuresome man who had attained a far higher rank than they in the Revolution. His luxurious style of living, frequent parties, and free-flowing spirits suggested that he was wealthy;[45] his casual references to important eastern acquaintances made him seem important;[46] and the obvious devotion of his beautiful, accomplished wife, Ann Biddle, offered an answer to any questions about his worth.[47] Wil-

43. Stevenson interview, Draper Coll., 11 CC 250; see below, pp. 145–146.

44. Wilkinson was a constant letter writer and a paper saver of the first order. "He kept copies of all the letters he ever wrote," an acquaintance said. "I went to the house near Philadelphia—he was in the midst of his papers, knee deep, all around him on the floor." Humphrey interview, Draper Coll., 16 CC 292. In the course of many moves most of his own papers were destroyed or lost, but many of them are published in his three-volume *Memoirs of My Own Time* (Philadelphia, 1816), and great quantities of letters from him have survived. To students of Kentucky history the most interesting are those in Cuban and Spanish archives, of which there are some copies in English at the Filson Club (the Pontalba Papers, collected by Thomas Bodley, and Some Letters of James Wilkinson, copied and trans. by D. C. and R. D. Corbitt) and in Spanish at the Lib. of Congress (Archivo General de Indias, Papeles Procedentes de Cuba) and the Univ. of Chicago (six bound volumes copied for John Mason Brown, now in Durrett Coll.). Many of these are published in Gayarré, *Louisiana,* III; William R. Shepherd, "Wilkinson and the Beginnings of the Spanish Conspiracy," *Am. Hist. Rev.,* IX (1903–1904), 490–506; *ibid.,* 533–537, 748–766; and in many books and articles on Wilkinson. In the Innes Papers one entire volume consists of the business papers that Wilkinson left with Innes when he left Kentucky in 1791, plus some of his letters to Innes. There are some 40 letters to John Brown in the J. M. Brown Papers, Yale Univ., and in many other collections scattered over this continent and Europe. There are many references to Wilkinson in the Draper and Shane interviews, and other source materials appear in every early work on Kentucky history. A few are cited above, immediately below, and throughout this study.

45. Marshall, *Kentucky,* I, 245.

46. For an example of this kind of reference see Wilkinson to Miro, May 15, 1788, Draper Coll., 33 J 133.

47. "Letters of Ann Biddle Wilkinson," *Pa. Mag. Hist. Biog.,* LVI(1932), 33–35.

kinson's friends were boundless in their admiration and delighted to be associated with him.[48] Partly, perhaps, to encourage their devotion and partly because he needed their help, Wilkinson allowed them to do him favors. He let Innes handle his business and legal affairs without charge;[49] he made Fowler godfather to one of his children[50] and, at another time, moved in with him for a year or two;[51] he entrusted his political business to John Brown.[52] For a period of several years he scrawled regular letters to John Brown, three to ten pages of venom and charm. "You must feel happy in corresponding with a man of his abilities,"[53] Brown's brother wrote.

In 1784 no one in Kentucky realized just how complex Wilkinson's character really was. His friends knew, of course, that he had the best of intentions, that he wanted to please everyone, even at great inconvenience.[54] Within a few years, seeing the invective with which he replied to criticism, they probably realized that he was instinctively defensive when he failed to please. They might also have guessed this from the care with which he saved papers.[55] Perhaps Wilkinson's comrades realized that he wanted to be admired, but they probably did not understand the depth of that longing, so great that he enjoyed wealth and physical comfort less for their own sake than because he thought they brought admiration.[56] Certainly they were unaware of

48. Marshall, *Kentucky*, I, 282; James Ripley Jacobs, *Tarnished Warrior, Major-General James Wilkinson* (New York, 1938), 42.
49. See the volume of Wilkinson papers in the Innes Papers.
50. Fowler, *John Fowler*, 31.
51. Stevenson interview, Draper Coll., 11 CC 250.
52. Letters from Wilkinson to John Brown, J. M. Brown Papers, Yale Univ.
53. James Brown to John Brown, Oct. 20, 1790, *ibid*.
54. For an example see John Fowler to Henry Lee, summer 1786, Draper Coll., 6 BB 45, quoted in Fowler, *John Fowler*, 26–27.
55. See n. 44, above.
56. For the clearest illustration of Wilkinson's desire for admiration see "Letters of General James Wilkinson addressed to Dr. James Hutchinson, of Philadelphia," *Pa. Mag. Hist. Biog.*, XII (1888), 55–64.

the complexity of his entangled financial affairs and the way that he had overextended himself to achieve an appearance of wealth.[57] Neither did Wilkinson's friends realize how often he failed to distinguish clearly between the truth as it was and the truth as he wished it to be. What he said was always related to fact,[58] and he said it so convincingly that people believed him and—this is what confused the issue—he believed himself.[59] If anyone doubted him, he was deeply hurt and told another lie to assuage the doubt.[60] In the end he was caught in an inextricable tangle of his own distortions, but in 1784 that was many years away.

From the beginning Wilkinson, like other members of the court group, had nothing to do with the partisans. "As a native of Maryland and living sometime in Philadelphia the party was very communicative to him," one of the articulate center reported. "The decided unequivocal manner

57. See below, pp. 106, 202.

58. The problem with Wilkinson is how far he can be believed. Most Kentucky authors have considered his Spanish letters as fabrications out of whole cloth; see for instance Temple Bodley, "Introduction," *Reprints of Littell's Political Transactions in and concerning Kentucky, and Letter of George Nicholas to his Friend in Virginia, also General Wilkinson's Memorial,* Filson Club Publications, No. 31 (Louisville, 1926), and Elizabeth Warren, "Senator John Brown's Role in the Kentucky Spanish Conspiracy," *Filson Club Hist. Qtly.,* XXXVI(1962), 158–176. Most other authors have taken what they liked of the Spanish letters and discounted the rest; see Arthur P. Whitaker, *Spanish American Frontier, 1783–1795: The Westward Movement and the Spanish Retreat in the Mississippi Valley* (Boston, 1927), and Abernethy, *Western Lands.* Actually there is no evidence that contradicts Wilkinson's testimony in any of his contemporary letters, and there is occasionally some support for what he says. For example, John Brown in his three letters to Gardoqui (Gardoqui Papers, I, 379–386, IV, 402–405, V, 66–69, Durrett Coll.) gives the same account of affairs in Kentucky that Wilkinson does in his letters to Miro (Gayarré, *Louisiana,* III, 223–240, 240–247). Consequently it seems reasonable to credit Wilkinson's contemporary accounts of events. His *Memoirs* are not, however, so reliable.

59. See, for example, his letters to Hugh Shiell, No. 1058, Ky. Hist. Soc., published in "Letters of Wilkinson," *Register,* XXIV (1926), 259–267. His belief in himself shows most clearly in his *Memoirs.*

60. See Wilkinson to John Brown, undated [ca. 1792], No. 1058, Ky. Hist. Soc., almost certainly an example of his use of a second lie to cover an initial distortion.

in which he delivered to them his Sentiments on this Subject
had very considerable effect. He took pains to set them
right." [61] Wilkinson had a finger in almost every Kentucky
pie, including shipping, wholesale purchasing, retailing, a
monopoly on salt, lead, and silver mining, banking, manufacturing, ferrying, and of course planting.[62] Several different kinds of land speculation were among his enterprises,
and within the next five years he patented some 35,000
acres under Virginia.[63] That alone is sufficient to explain
his antagonism toward the partisans. In addition he must
have realized that the articulate center included virtually
everyone worth impressing and that they would be the
dominant force in Kentucky politics for many years to
come.

Toward the end of 1784 members of this court party began to favor a separation for Kentucky.[64] In this stand they

61. Walker Daniel to Benjamin Harrison, May 21, 1784, Palmer,
ed., *Cal. Va. State Papers*, III, 584–588.
62. Agreement between Wilkinson and Daniel Brodhead, May 4,
1784, Misc. Bound MSS, I, Durrett Coll.; Innes and Horatio Turpin,
Ky. Gaz. (Lexington), Dec. 15, 1787; Wilkinson and Peyton Short
to Isaac Shelby, Dec. 19, 1789, enclosing Wilkinson and Short, To
the Planters of Kentucky, Misc. Bound MSS, II, Durrett Coll.;
Short, *Ky. Gaz.* (Lexington), Jan. 23, 1790; Wilkinson's letters to
Shiell, No. 1058, Ky. Hist. Soc., published in "Letters of Wilkinson,"
Register, XXIV(1926), 259–267; Thomas D. Clark, "Salt, A Factor
in the Settlement of Kentucky," *Filson Club Hist. Qtly.*, XII(1938),
44; Josiah Collins interview, Draper Coll., 12 CC 72, 108; Fowler
to Henry Lee, summer 1786, *ibid.*, 6 BB 45; Thomas Speed, *The
Political Club, Danville, Kentucky, 1786–1790*, Filson Club Publi-
cations, No. 9 (Louisville, 1894), 159–160; Collins, *History of Kentucky*, II, 514; Wilkinson, *Ky. Gaz.* (Lexington), Jan. 16, 1790.
63. Agreement between John Lewis and Wilkinson, July 3, 1784,
Lewis Papers, Box 1, Durrett Coll.; Wilkinson to James Hutchinson,
June 20, 1785, *Pa. Mag. Hist. Biog.*, XII(1888), 56–61; Wilkinson,
Ky. Gaz. (Lexington), June 27, 1789, Aug. 8, 1789, Jan. 9, 1790;
Wilkinson to Innes, Feb. 29, 1792, Innes Papers, XXIII, Pt. i; Jillson,
First Landowners of Frankfort, passim; Jillson, *Land Grants*, 136–
137.
64. John Marshall to George Muter, Jan. 7, 1785, *Tyler's Qtly.
Hist. Gen. Mag.*, I(1919–1920), 28; Innes to William Fleming, June
20, 1785, Fleming Papers, Washington and Lee; Wilkinson to
Hutchinson, June 20, 1785, *Pa. Mag. Hist. Biog.*, XII(1888), 56–61;

joined the partisans, who had worked more than five years for independence, leaving behind their surveyor brethren who still wanted to protect their land by maintaining the Virginia connection.[65] The court party continued to think of itself as a separate political group, however, and thus continued to distinguish itself from partisans. This was in part because the friendship between members of the party was rooted in common interests and long acquaintance and so was far stronger than any alliance provoked by a mere coincidence of political views. Also, the court party and the partisans were working for different ends, even though they happened to be using the same means. Partisans preferred a separation through Congress—or since that was now impossible, an "unconditional" separation without the consent of Virginia—that would put them in control of the district and enable them to redistribute the land granted by Virginia. The court party, on the other hand, wanted a "constitutional" separation through Virginia that would leave them in power to prevent a partisan redistribution of land.

"We conceive the People of this District do not at present enjoy a greater portion of Liberty than an American Colony might have done a few years ago had she been allowed a Representation in the British Parliament." [66] Explanations like this one, pregnant with suggestion, soon became standard rhetoric for members of the court party when they wrote home to justify their interest in separation. Virginia is a tyrant, they implied, citing a host of Virginia laws

---

Wallace to Madison, July 12, 1785, Madison Papers, V; Samuel McDowell to Fleming, Nov. 11, 1785, Draper Coll., 2 U 137; Thomas Marshall to George Nicholas, Apr. 26, 1789, Innes Papers, XXII.

65. Material on the surveyors' position at the time is scanty, but for the Marshalls see Jordan Harris [Wilkinson], Ky. Gaz. (Lexington), Apr. 26, 1788; for James Thompson, another surveyor, see Arthur Campbell to John Edmundson, Aug. 26, 1785, Palmer, ed., Cal. Va. State Papers, IV, 100–101; for Joseph Crockett see his letter to A. K. Marshall, Oct. 3, 1806, Western World (Frankfort), Nov. 1, 1806.

66. Wallace to Madison, July 12, 1785, Madison Papers, V.

utterly inappropriate to the needs of Kentucky.[67] Members of the Virginia legislature, probably puzzled by the sudden concern over ancient laws that had never been enforced in Kentucky, immediately made new regulations for horse-breeding, speyed mares, and the advertising of stray horses in Kentucky.[68] The legislature's answer to any request from Kentucky, both before and after the court party's conversion to separation, was always so prompt that the charge of unresponsiveness seems more than a little contrived.[69]

Virginia's taxation of Kentuckians was particularly aggravating to the court party. Inveighing both against "partial taxes," as they called them, and against double taxation, they agreed that "laws which from their nature impose Taxes on the Inhabitants of the Western Waters only, whether expressly, or from their operation are greevous and against the fundamental rights of the People." [70] They found the law "imposing a duty on merchandise brought into the district" an example of double taxation, for merchandise was also taxed "on first importation"; the district judges, they thought, should not be supported out of local fines, because the people of Kentucky also paid their proportion to support the eastern judges. As for "partial taxes," the most striking example was the tax of five shillings laid on every hundred acres of large patents.[71] This tax the court party supported initially, even though it was "partial," but later, when it had been repealed, they cited it as an example of Virginia's tyranny. Apparently they favored it in 1784

67. Abernethy, ed., "Journal of First Convention," *Jour. So. Hist.*, I(1935), 72–73. For evidence that this list of grievances was drawn up by the court party, see "A Virginian" [Ebenezer Brooks], *Ky. Gaz.* (Lexington), Sept. 1, 1787.

68. Hening, ed., *Statutes*, XII, 373.

69. So thought "A Virginian" [Brooks], *Ky. Gaz.* (Lexington), Aug. 25, 1787; "Cornplanter" [Brooks], *ibid.*, Sept. 13, 1788; and "An Early Inhabitant," *ibid.*, July 26, 1806.

70. Abernethy, ed., "Journal of First Convention," *Jour. So. Hist.*, I(1935), 75.

71. *Ibid.*

because it touched few of them personally and might have had an effect they greatly desired, of forcing the sale of large holdings and thus making more land available to new purchasers; but when it had been repealed they did not scruple to talk as though they had opposed it all along.[72]

In justifying their decision to support a separation, the court party stressed that "the remote situation of this District from the seat of Government is burthensome to its Inhabitants and subjects them to many greevances which can not be redressed whilst it remains a part of Virginia." [73] As examples they pointed to the expense of lawsuits at Richmond, surely a small consideration since there was now a district court in Kentucky, the absence of any power in Kentucky to pardon those sentenced to death, a humanitarian concern but again negligible in importance since there had been no executions in Kentucky, and the legal ignorance of Kentuckians, who could not know the laws until long after they were passed and sometimes not until after they were expired. The last complaint was all too true, but it could easily have been remedied at the slight expense of hiring a messenger to carry copies of the laws to Kentucky.

Members of the court party most frequently stressed the difficulty of defending Kentucky against Indian attacks as a reason for separation, and this would remain their most useful argument for several years to come.[74] The Virginia legislature allowed Kentuckians to fight the Indians only defensively, requiring the governor's authorization for an

72. "A Kentuckean" [Caleb Wallace], Ky. Gaz. (Lexington), Sept. 15, 1787.
73. Abernethy, ed., "Journal of First Convention," Jour. So. Hist., I(1935), 77. See also "An Early Inhabitant," Ky. Gaz. (Lexington), July 26, 1806.
74. See, for instance, Wallace to Madison, Sept. 30, 1786, Madison Papers, VI; Innes to Edmund Randolph, July 19, 1787, Palmer, ed., Cal. Va. State Papers, IV, 321–323; Innes to John Brown, Dec. 7, 1787, No. 473, Ky. Hist. Soc.; Innes to Henry Knox, July 7, 1790, quoted in Bradford, "Notes on Kentucky," Ky. Gaz. (Lexington), May 4, 1827; "An Early Inhabitant," ibid., July 26, 1806. See also Marshall, Kentucky, I, 256–257.

offensive expedition. Against that law the court party argued that offensive strikes were often necessary to prevent Indian attacks and that immediate action was frequently called for. The eight or so weeks required for the round trip to Richmond was too long to be practical when an offensive expedition was needed; thus, they said, Kentucky should have an executive authority on her side of the mountains. With the Indian situation as their major argument for a separation, members of the court party habitually exaggerated the Indian problem when they wrote East.[75] Harry Innes, as attorney general, was particularly assiduous about stressing the many deaths from Indian attacks and the great numbers of prisoners and horses taken by the Indians. His totals were impressive, but considered in relation to the total population they become almost insignificant.

Another argument used by members of the court party for several years to come stressed the danger that partisans might seize Virginia-granted lands. "Repeated attempts had been made to introduce anarchy into the district, which proved abortive more through want of talents in the promoters than opportunity," Caleb Wallace later described his decision to support a separation. "Much of our most valuable Lands have been marked since my acquaintance with the District by those who avowed their expectation that a more equal distribution would shortly take place. . . . Supposing that a constitutional Separation would be the best preservative against the confusion that threatened us, I espoused the measure." [76] This reasoning was especially calculated to appeal to the pocketbooks of the Virginia legislators, many of whom owned land in Kentucky.

Actually, the danger from partisans was slight at the end of 1784 and soon became nonexistent. The number of partisans actually working for a redistribution of Kentucky land had diminished as more people acquired land under

75. Marshall, *Kentucky*, I, 216.
76. Wallace to Madison, Nov. 12, 1787, Madison Papers, VIII.

Virginia; now only in Jefferson County and in outlying parts of Fayette were there substantial numbers of people who wanted an "unconditional" separation. By 1785 almost everyone in Kentucky expected that a separation would eventually take place, but most thought the district was not yet ready for independent government.[77] Even the court party, in the midst of arguments for separation, occasionally acknowledged the unreadiness of the district.[78] Many Kentuckians, content under the government of Virginia, were the more willing to postpone separation because a new government would certainly mean high taxation, whereas under Virginia they had never yet been required to pay the tax for general revenue.[79] (Kentuckians paid the tax on patents and the duty on imports, but not the tax for general revenue.)

Thus the arguments offered by the court party for separation from Virginia—the tyranny of Virginia, partial and double taxation, inconveniences from the remoteness of Kentucky, the difficulty of defending Kentucky, and the danger from partisans—were all apparently weak excuses contrived by the court party to persuade their Virginia brethren. That the court party began to favor a separation in the winter of 1784/1785 is clear; why they favored it is not clear. In part, perhaps, they were persuaded by the obvious advance of Kentucky from a frontier to a more nearly self-sufficient community. But this material advance alone is an utterly inadequate explanation for the passionate support the court party soon gave to the cause of separation.

Some Virginians, fearful about their own claims in Ken-

77. "A Real Friend to the People" [Samuel Taylor], Ky. Gaz. (Lexington), Apr. 25, 1789; Marshall, Kentucky, I, 217.
78. See, for instance, a letter from a man in Danville, May 31, 1785, in Md. Gaz. (Baltimore), July 1, 1785, Draper Coll., 3 JJ 138–139; Wallace to Madison, July 12, 1785, Madison Papers, V; Christopher Greenup to Charles Simms, July 19, 1785, Simms Papers, I, Lib. of Congress.
79. Muter to Madison, Sept. 23, 1786, and Wallace to Madison, Sept. 30, 1786, both in Madison Papers, VI; Marshall, Kentucky, I, 217.

tucky, thought the separatists actually wanted to take control of all the vacant land, including the land granted to nonresidents of the district.[80] This idea was plausible. Members of the court party had come to Kentucky to claim and speculate in land, but they arrived after most of the good land was taken. If they looked enviously at the 97,000 acres of Humphrey Marshall, the 128,000 acres of Thomas Marshall, or the 831,000 acres of John May,[81] they hardly dared to challenge those holdings, for the Marshalls and the Mays were at hand to complain. But there remained the 254,484 acres of Christopher McConnico, the 344,783 acres of Thomas Shore, the 211,417 acres of David Ross, the 241,451 acres of Kennon Jones, and the 232,047 acres of John Banister.[82] Not one of these men was in Kentucky to notice whether the court party took some quiet action that might lead to the control over their land.[83]

Another factor that distinguished the court party may have influenced their decision to work for separation. Unlike either the partisan leaders or their surveyor friends, the party was intrigued with the possibility of developing Kentucky as a commercial center, and they would soon add to this interest the hope that Kentucky might be a center of manufacturing. "Never before have I heard so much talk of agricultural and commercial projects; never before have I seen the spirit and taste for enterprise developed in so many different shapes," one traveler wrote after a visit in 1784 to Danville, where most of the court party lived. "No one speaks, no one dreams of anything here save the sites of cities, of ferries, of bridges, of mills, of roads, of new communications, of clearings, of efforts in agriculture, of the construction of houses."[84]

80. William Nelson to William Short, July 17, 1785, Oct. 16, 1785, Wm. Short Papers, I, Lib. of Congress.

81. See above, p. 43.

82. Jillson, *Land Grants*, 95–96, 121–122, 111–112, 69–70, 18.

83. At least none of them signed any of the petitions in Robertson, ed., *Petitions*.

84. Crèvecoeur, "Sketch of the River Ohio," Durrett Coll.

Envisioning the time when Kentucky would ship out everything needed by the whole Southwest, when raw materials would be sent to Kentucky for conversion into valuable manufactured products, when Kentuckians would import for their own use only exotic luxuries, the court party must have realized that the district could advance faster toward that goal if it became a separate state. With so enterprising an entrepreneur as James Wilkinson in their midst, they must surely have noted that statehood would give them control over the Ohio River, which formed their northern boundary and served in addition as a commercial artery across almost half of the nation. As a state, Kentucky could tax every item carried down the Ohio, for every item must land at Louisville to be carried around the falls there. That tax could serve to prevent other areas from exporting to the Southwest, or it could be used to raise revenue; in either case it would raise the price of imports into Kentucky, discourage Kentuckians from buying imported merchandise, and thus encourage local manufactures.

If the court party supported a separation because of the vacant lands and nascent industries of Kentucky, they did not mention either to their friends in the East. Virginians, they knew, would not look kindly on a plan to confiscate nonresident lands; in fact, talk about confiscation might lead Virginia to refuse a separation in Kentucky, and the district might be thrown into a condition chaotic enough for partisans to seize control. Similarly, if the Philadelphia land companies heard there was a new plan for separation, they might send new agents to support the partisans in Kentucky and thus accomplish an "unconditional" rather than a "constitutional" separation. Moreover, those land companies were financed in several cases by the mercantile and manufacturing houses of Philadelphia, another reason why they might take some action if they heard rumors that the court party planned to control the Ohio trade and encourage Kentuckians to make their own necessities. Considerations such as these may have led the court party as early as 1784 to develop a habit of explaining themselves with less than the whole truth.

In fact, the court party's decision to support a separation was so sudden and so contrary to the popular sentiment that some people thought it could not be explained by the Indian situation, the condition of the district court, the obvious advancement of civilization in Kentucky, or even by all of those factors together. To these critics it seemed plain that the court party wanted, above all else, to rule in Kentucky and that when they found their leadership threatened they had taken measures to insure continued control.[85] The desire to rule, it seemed, explained the haste with which the December 1784 convention met, only seven weeks after the November meeting, and the lack of publicity before the elections to it. Because the articulate center's leadership was generally accepted, these critics thought, members of the court party knew they would be elected unless an issue was made of their position. Consequently they held the elections so quietly that in several only two or three votes were cast.[86]

Yet the court party did not have a majority of delegates when the convention of militia representatives met on December 27, 1784, the first of a bewildering series of Kentucky conventions. The Jefferson County delegation of ten, led by John Campbell, was almost entirely partisan, apparently correctly representing that county's political sentiment. As the point where most settlers from Pennsylvania landed, and as the county most troubled by Indian raids,

85. Daniel Boone to Patrick Henry, Aug. 16, 1785, Draper Coll., 12 S 51–54; Wallace to Madison, Sept. 30, 1786, Madison Papers, VI; "A Virginian" [Ebenezer Brooks], *Ky. Gaz.* (Lexington), Sept. 1, 1787; "A Real Friend to the People" [Samuel Taylor], Apr. 25, 1789, *ibid.;* Marshall, *Kentucky,* I, 216.

86. "A Real Friend" [Taylor], *Ky. Gaz.* (Lexington), Apr. 25, 1789.

Jefferson had a high percentage of malcontents. At least three or four of the seven Fayette delegates were partisans, for Fayette's situation was similar to Jefferson's, although less serious. Even Lincoln County—the home of the district court, the county most solidly settled and least troubled by Indians, and the residence of most well-established Kentuckians—had elected about half a dozen partisans, including Ebenezer Brooks, among its twenty members. Two of the thirty-seven delegates to the convention were surveyors and about eighteen were partisans, leaving at most only about seventeen court party supporters.[87]

When Ebenezer Brooks arose in the convention and proposed an immediate separation, supporting the motion by reading letters from people like Arthur Campbell and a long essay of his own composition,[88] he was opposed, another partisan noted, by "several very pacific souls, together with something like the influence of that baneful aristocratic Spirit that is so much complained of in all the southern states." [89] The court party had not yet announced its change of mind on the question of separation; seeking a constitutional separation rather than a partisan independence and thus unwilling to cooperate with Brooks, it insisted that "decent moderate language is the best." "Angry words are only the ebullitions of a disorderly multitude," one said; "wiser men will always be sparing of hard words, but

87. Roll of members, in Abernethy, ed., "Journal of First Convention," Jour. of So. Hist., I(1935), 67–78. Basic sources for the first convention are this journal; Wallace to Madison, Sept. 25, 1785, Madison Papers, VI; "A Virginian" [Brooks], Ky. Gaz. (Lexington), Sept. 1, 1787; "A Kentuckean" [Wallace], ibid., Sept. 15, 1787; "A Farmer" [Harry Innes], ibid., Oct. 18, 1788; "A Real Friend" [Taylor], ibid., Apr. 25, 1789; Littell, Political Transactions, 12–13; Marshall, Kentucky, I, 196–206.

88. Muter to Madison, Feb. 20, 1787, Madison Papers, VII; "A Native of Virginia" [William Ward], Ky. Gaz. (Lexington), Sept. 22, 1787; "A Farmer" [Innes], ibid., Oct. 18, 1788.

89. Letter from a gentleman in Kentucky, Jan. 16, 1785, in Pennsylvania Packet (Philadelphia), Mar. 23, 1785, Draper Coll., 2 JJ 370–372.

prepare for *hard blows,* if necessary." [90] By arguing that the convention had authority only to discuss military problems, they managed to postpone any action at all on separation.

Instead of declaring an immediate independence from Virginia, as Brooks proposed, the members called another convention for May 1785, specifically to consider the question of statehood. The delegates were to represent the actual population, rather than the militia companies, as in this convention, or the counties, as in the Virginia legislature, and no property restriction was placed on suffrage. The last provision passed almost unnoticed, for the twenty-five-pound fee for voting imposed by Virginia law had never been enforced in Kentucky.[91] Representation on the basis of population, however, became a controversial matter. Partisans later charged that the court party had engineered the change to gain control of the next convention.[92] By reducing the Jefferson delegation from ten to eight they might eliminate two partisans; by increasing the Fayette delegation from seven to eight they might add a member of the court party; and by cutting the Lincoln delegates from twenty to twelve they might squeeze out Ebenezer Brooks and the several other partisans from that county. Confronted with such charges, the court party defended proportionate representation as a true republican measure.[93]

To create popular support for a constitutional separation, the convention adopted a list of Kentucky's grievances against Virginia. This was a court party measure, members of that group having prepared the long list ahead of time.[94] Brooks thought they gathered grievances "with as much earnestness as if they were searching for hidden trea-

90. *Ibid.*
91. Marshall, *Kentucky,* I, 197–198.
92. Innes to Fleming, May 1, 1785, Fleming Papers; "A Real Friend" [Taylor], *Ky. Gaz.* (Lexington), Apr. 25, 1789; see p. 101 below.
93. Innes to Fleming, June 20, 1785, Fleming Papers; Marshall, *Kentucky,* I, 197.
94. "A Virginian" [Brooks], *Ky. Gaz.* (Lexington), Sept. 1, 1787.

sure," [95] but some of their complaints—those on the Indian situation, the district court, and the land laws [96]—were really significant. Perhaps the most important was a resolution against the holdings of nonresidents, [97] which stated that "to grant any Person a larger quantity of Land than he designs Bona Fide to seat himself or his Family on, is a greevance." [98] Only one resolution, a motion to condemn the five-shillings land tax, seems to have aroused controversy. [99] The surveyors and some of the speculating partisan leaders opposed that tax; the court party opposed their motion, and Samuel McDowell demanded a roll-call vote. The resolution passed, however, twelve to nine, with the court party—McDowell, Caleb Wallace, Isaac Shelby, Benjamin Logan, and Logan's brother John—solidly in opposition, with partisans and the two surveyors supporting it, and with most of the convention abstaining. [100]

During the first convention the court party had led partisans to believe they would support a separation if it were accomplished in a constitutional manner rather than as a declaration of independence from Virginia, but they had never stated that position clearly. After the convention they continued to speak against separation as they had in previous years, perhaps because there was so little popular interest in the measure. [101] When John Campbell, leader of the

95. *Ibid.*

96. See above, pp. 91–93.

97. This explanation, given by one Virginian (Nelson to Wm. Short, July 17, 1785, Short Papers), seems to be the most plausible. For other explanations see Abernethy, *Western Lands*, 305–306, and Barnhart, *Valley of Democracy*, 69–70.

98. Abernethy, ed., "Journal of First Convention," *Jour. So. Hist.*, I(1935), 75–76.

99. See above, p. 74.

100. Abernethy, ed., "Journal of First Convention," *Jour. So. Hist.*, I(1935), 75.

101. "A Real Friend" [Taylor], *Ky. Gaz.* (Lexington), Apr. 25, 1789. George Muter wrote, "Those for a Separation, have perhaps not been altogether so candid in their informations to the people as could have been wished" (to Madison, Sept. 23, 1786, Madison Papers, VI), perhaps referring to this situation; there is also an oblique reference in Wallace to Madison, Sept. 30, 1786, *ibid.*

Jefferson County partisans, heard that the court party still opposed a separation, he began to doubt the results of the convention scheduled for May 1785, which other partisans expected to resolve in favor of separation. Suggesting that the change in the basis of representation was a scheme of Lincoln and Fayette to control the coming conventions, he persuaded the voters of Jefferson to elect twelve representatives, the same number given to Lincoln, instead of the eight they were allowed. In addition he arranged the election of twelve partisans from Nelson County, which the Virginia legislature had just cut off from Jefferson, an area where large numbers of Maryland Catholics were just settling and attempting to acquire land.[102] Thus the old Jefferson County elected twenty-four delegates, four more than the combined total of Lincoln and Fayette and enough to control the convention. "We shall have no Convention this month," Harry Innes complained; "Col. Campbell has marred the whole plan." [103]

The second convention did meet as scheduled, but on the opening day, May 23, 1785, only the Fayette and Lincoln County delegations had appeared.[104] They were clearly dominated by the court party—Harry Innes, Caleb Wallace, George Muter, Samuel McDowell, and Benjamin Logan—even though James Wilkinson was too sick to attend [105] and Ebenezer Brooks once again represented the

102. Benedict J. Webb, *The Centenary of Catholicity in Kentucky* (Louisville, 1884), 26.
103. Innes to Fleming, May 1, 1785, Fleming Papers.
104. Basic sources for the second convention are two extracts from the minutes, May 27 and 28, 1785, in Fleming Papers; list of members in Collins, *Kentucky*, I, 354; Innes to Fleming, June 20, 1785, Fleming Papers; Wallace to Madison, Sept. 25, 1785, Madison Papers, VI; "A Virginian" [Brooks], *Ky. Gaz.* (Lexington), Sept. 1, 1787; "A Farmer" [Innes], *ibid.*, Oct. 18, 1788; "A Real Friend" [Taylor], *ibid.*, Apr. 25, 1789; Littell, *Political Transactions*, 13–14, 61–66; Marshall, *Kentucky*, I, 196–206.
105. Wilkinson to Richard C. Anderson, May 26, 1785, Anderson Papers, Box 1, Va. State Lib., Wilkinson to Hutchinson, June 20, 1785, *Pa. Mag. Hist. Biog.*, XII(1888), 56–61.

Lincoln County partisans. Without waiting for the Jefferson and Nelson County delegations, the convention elected as president the oldest, most distinguished, and most judicious member of the court party attending, Samuel McDowell, and then proceeded to consider a constitutional separation. Four days later fourteen of the twenty-four delegates from Jefferson and Nelson appeared, demanding, with John Campbell as spokesman, that the convention be reorganized and the minutes of the previous four days erased from the journal. The delegates reached a compromise in conversations "out of doors." Each member expressed his opinion; when it became apparent that the court party favored a separation in spite of their public statements to the contrary, the Jefferson and Nelson delegates agreed that the journal entries for the first four days could stand.[106] In exchange, the Lincoln and Fayette members consented to admit the Jefferson and Nelson delegates without examining their doubtful certificates of election.[107] Only John Campbell disapproved of this proceeding. Realizing, apparently, that partisans were about to lose control of the separation movement, he refused to consent to the compromise and went home.[108]

This second convention actually accomplished nothing, even though it adopted both a petition to Virginia asking a separation and a declaration of independence from Virginia. The declaration, evidently prepared in advance by James Wilkinson, was circulated as an address to the people; Humphrey Marshall, still opposed to a separation, thought it "calculated to arouse their feelings—awaken their fears—and infuse into their minds, disaffection towards the existing state of things." [109] The petition was not sent to Virginia; in-

106. Innes to Fleming, June 20, 1785, Fleming Papers.
107. *Ibid.*; extract from the minutes of the second convention, May 27 and 28, 1785, *ibid.*
108. Innes to Fleming, June 20, 1785, *ibid.* Campbell's name consequently did not appear on the list of delegates. Collins, *History of Kentucky,* I, 354.
109. Marshall, *Kentucky,* I, 206.

stead it was referred, together with the whole question of separation, to a third convention in August 1785. Clearly unwilling to act on separation without stronger popular support,[110] the court party apparently also wanted to strengthen its position relative to the partisans. Since they had been gaining strength with each convention, they probably hoped that a third election would give them a majority. Certainly they expected that another election would give James Wilkinson an opportunity to speak for separation. As their most persuasive orator, he could do more than anyone else to gain support for a constitutional separation; for him, primarily, the third convention was called.[111]

When the convention met, on August 8, 1785,[112] the members finally accomplished their predestined business of petitioning Virginia for a separation. Among the delegates were Samuel McDowell, who was again elected president, George Muter, Caleb Wallace, Harry Innes, Benjamin Sebastian, Benjamin Logan, and Wilkinson. One commentator observed there were "some more important personages [present], than were in the last [convention]." [113] The assemblage was clearly dominated by the court party; none of the surveyors was a member, nor were partisan leaders John Campbell and Ebenezer Brooks elected. The placid petition to Virginia that had been referred from the last convention was discarded, and Wilkinson—who, as Humphrey Marshall said, "held a glowing pen"—composed a more florid document.[114] In spite of his ending assertion that "we have discarded the complimentary style of adula-

110. *Ibid.*, 205.
111. Wilkinson to Hutchinson, June 20, 1785, *Pa. Mag. Hist. Biog.*, XII(1888), 56–61; Marshall, *Kentucky*, I, 213.
112. Basic sources for the third convention are the list of members in Collins, *History of Kentucky*, I, 354; Wallace to Madison, Sept. 25, 1785, Madison Papers, VI; "A Virginian" [Brooks], *Ky. Gaz.* (Lexington), Sept. 1, 1787; "A Farmer" [Innes], *ibid.*, Oct. 18, 1788; "A Real Friend" [Taylor], *ibid.*, Apr. 25, 1789; Littell, *Political Transactions*, 14, 66–72; Marshall, *Kentucky*, I, 207–220.
113. A note in back of a letter from Kentucky, Aug. 19, 1785, Draper Coll., 3 JJ 208.
114. Marshall, *Kentucky*, I, 206, 212.

tion and insincerity," employing "the plain, manly, and unadorned language of independence," [115] Wilkinson's expressions were wordy and diffuse. Caleb Wallace later confessed, "I am not pleased with the Splendid Dress in which they are clothed." [116] But most of the convention was pleased, and the petition was sent to the Virginia legislature.

When the third meeting ended, the court party had gained leadership of the separation movement, had offered their own arguments for separation as reasons endorsed by all Kentuckians, and—they thought—had arranged that Kentucky would soon be a state. In explaining their position, they had told less than the whole truth to their Virginia friends, and they had been less than honest with their constituents while campaigning for seats in the conventions. All of this they had done for the good of Kentucky. Raised in a tradition where educated men were expected to use their knowledge for the public benefit, they had taken control as those best trained in law and hence in the science of government. Inexperienced, idealistic, ambitious young men, they believed that their plans for the disposition of lands and for the encouragement of manufactures were the best of all possible plans for Kentucky. And they never for a moment doubted that they would be chosen to govern the new state and put those plans into effect.

Confident that a separation would soon be accomplished,[117] the court party spent the summer and fall of 1785 making plans for the new government of Kentucky. Caleb Wallace and George Muter asked James Madison's advice on a constitution for the new state,[118] and James Wilkinson requested a friend in Pennsylvania "to give me your own, and to promise for me from the most able of your Ac-

115. The petition is No. 25 in Robertson, ed., *Petitions*, 79–82.
116. Wallace to Madison, Sept. 25, 1785, Madison Papers, VI.
117. Marshall, *Kentucky*, I, 199.
118. Muter to Madison, Jan. 6, 1785, and Wallace to Madison, July 12, 1785, in Madison Papers, V.

quaintances, your and their Ideas of that System of Government, which is best suited to the genius of our Country and the Times." [119] Wallace also considered means of preventing "a dangerous interval of Anarchy" during the change in government. He thought the third convention, controlled by the court party, might be "recognized and empowered to direct the Choice of another for the purpose of adopting a Form of Government and organizing it: and in the mean Time it may be provided that all Officers civil and Military shall continue to enforce the Laws of the present Government with such exceptions as the Case may require." [120]

While the court party was contemplating forms of government, Kentuckians heard a piece of news that shocked them all. The Spanish, who owned New Orleans, had closed the Mississippi River to American trade. Kentuckians had been concerned about the river for a long time, but only two years previously the treaty of peace ending the Revolution had guaranteed them, they thought, the former British right of navigation. They had raised their first large crop the next summer, 1784, and had shipped it on flatboats down the river the spring of 1785. Now the boatmen returned to say that everything had been confiscated.[121] Not only was the labor of a year lost; since the river was their only route to a market, the news meant that there was no longer any outlet for Kentucky produce. Kentuckians who had hoped their tobacco and lard would bring in a few dollars a year and those who had expected to make the district an important commercial center were alike distressed by the news.

"The Want of an Export Trade will render us incapable of defraying the Expences of a Separate Government," Caleb Wallace thought, although "a Legislature of our own

119. Wilkinson to Hutchinson, June 20, 1785, *Pa. Mag. Hist. Biog.*, XII(1888), 56–61.
120. Wallace to Madison, Oct. 8, 1785, Madison Papers, VI.
121. "A Real Friend" [Taylor], *Ky. Gaz.* (Lexington), Apr. 25, 1789.

might do much to regulate Trade or supply the Deficiency." [122] Members of the court party were deeply troubled, and their passion for a separation was intensified. "A Free Trade out of the Mississippi and we are a blessed People indeed," James Wilkinson exclaimed; "it would push Kentucky most rapidly to Individual opulence and Public wealth. . . . But without trade . . . Kentucky will be subject to domestic discord, Individual Poverty and public wretchedness." He added, " 'Tis an inestimable prize and we are all unanimously ready to wade to it through Blood." [123] Wilkinson's feelings were even more extreme than most. He was already involved in the river trade [124] and, deeply in debt, was probably counting heavily on next year's shipments.

The new year, 1786, began with discussions of the impending separation, but the court party's optimism quickly turned to dismay when they received copies of the enabling act passed by Virginia.[125] The act provided that in the event of a separation Kentucky must pay its just part of Virginia's public debt; recognize all Virginia land grants as valid, making no new grants that would interfere with those already made by Virginia; and neither tax the lands of nonresidents higher than those of residents nor interfere in the free navigation of the Ohio. The act called for yet another convention to be held, in September 1786, elected on the basis of representation by counties; if that meeting accepted Virginia's terms and if Congress consented before June 1787 to the creation of a fourteenth state, the authority of Virginia could cease at any time "posterior to September 1, 1787." [126]

122. Wallace to Madison, Oct. 8, 1785, Madison Papers, VI.
123. Wilkinson to Hutchinson, June 20, 1785, *Pa. Mag. Hist. Biog.*, XII(1888), 56–61.
124. Agreement between Wilkinson and Daniel Brodhead, May 4, 1784, Misc. Bound MSS, I, Durrett Coll.
125. Marshall, *Kentucky*, I, 226.
126. Hening, ed., *Statutes*, XII, 37–40.

"The Kentucky Bill passed under some restrictions which I do not think consistant with the policy of that District," Harry Innes complained, "but there was only one Party to the Contract, therefore the other has the Election [only] to recede or accept." [127] In copying the act he underlined the guarantee of Virginia titles and the provision against imposing higher taxes on nonresidents, thus perhaps indicating one reason for the court party's discontent with the law. Caleb Wallace suggested another ground of discontent when he wrote James Madison to complain that Kentucky should have control of the Ohio trade.[128] Probably members of the court party were most dissatisfied with the delay that the law imposed. They had expected Kentucky to become a separate state immediately after Virginia consented, but now they found themselves so entangled in red tape that it would take two more years to establish independence. To their impatience that was a hard blow.[129]

In Virginia, James Madison noted "the apparent coolness of the Representatives of Kentucky as to a separation since these terms have been defined" and thought it "indicated that they had some views which will not be favored by them. They disliked much to be hung up on the will of Congress." [130] The court party apparently did have some such views, and about this time they evidently began to consider the possibility of declaring an immediate independence from Virginia. This was exactly what Ebenezer Brooks had proposed in the first convention. Then they had opposed the plan, perhaps to prevent partisans from gaining control in the district; now they favored it, possibly because they

127. Innes to Fleming, Feb. 11, 1786, Fleming Papers.
128. Wallace to Madison, Sept. 30, 1786, Madison Papers, VI.
129. Marshall, *Kentucky*, I, 226.
130. Madison to George Washington, Dec. 9, 1785, in Gaillard Hunt, ed., *The Writings of James Madison* . . . (New York, 1900–1910), II, 196–200; see also Madison to James Monroe, Dec. 9, 1785, *ibid.*, 201–202, and Madison to Thomas Jefferson, May 12, 1786, in Julian P. Boyd, ed., *The Papers of Thomas Jefferson* (Princeton, 1950—), IX, 519.

had established political control themselves. An "absolute separation"—a "violent separation," as it came to be called —would leave Kentuckians free to handle their lands and the Ohio trade as they chose, enable them to deal with the Mississippi question, eliminate all the delay of going through Virginia and Congress. Freed from Virginia, they could then negotiate with Congress for an admission on their own terms.

Meanwhile the surveyors had also begun to favor separation from Virginia.[131] "The country party," as they would soon be called,[132] became the staunchest supporters in Kentucky of the enabling act that Virginia had passed. Their support of separation really represented no change of position. They had opposed it before Virginia consented, but now that the mother state had given permission they favored it; in both cases they were obeying the laws of Virginia. Through the enabling act they had gained a security missing before, the knowledge that their immense landholdings were considered inviolable. As long as Kentuckians moved toward an orderly "legal" or "constitutional" separation, the country party needed not worry; they were threatened only by the prospect of an "immediate" separation.

Now the position of the surveyors and that of members of the court party differed widely, even though they were all part of the old articulate center and shared a common Virginia background. The court party lived in town—most of them in Danville, the judicial center of the district, or in Lexington—and were chiefly involved in the practice of law. The surveyors, involved in the problems of land ownership, lived on their plantations. Whereas the court

131. Marshall, *Kentucky*, I, 216. Marshall makes his support of separation even more plain in the 1812 ed., 354, and in "An Observer," 10, pamphlet in Wilson Coll. See also Joseph Crockett to A. K. Marshall, Oct. 13, 1806, *Western World* (Frankfort), Nov. 1, 1806, and the letter of A. K. Marshall to the editor of the *Ky. Gaz.* (Lexington), Oct. 20, 1806.
132. Marshall, *Kentucky*, I, 322.

party disliked the enabling act, the surveyors approved it wholeheartedly; when the court party began to talk of an immediate independence, the surveyors favored only a legal separation. The court party thought of the western settlements as an area distinct from the East; the surveyors were more conscious of the unity of the American nation. Their reactions to the closing of the Mississippi were thus equally unlike. The court party, hoping to make Kentucky a center of manufacturing and commerce, angrily determined to open the river; the surveyors, less concerned about the growth of Kentucky industries, apparently hoped that the closing of the river would force the development of East-West trade routes and thus tie Kentucky to the eastern states.[133]

While the articulate center debated whether the separation should be legal or immediate, one by one the partisan leaders, disturbed that the court party had seized leadership of the separation movement and conscious of the strength of Congress and Virginia, began to turn against separation and argue that Kentucky needed the support of Virginia to get the river opened. During the summer of 1785 one obscure Lincoln County partisan, Samuel Taylor, had risen to importance by working against separation. Taylor, a former deputy surveyor from Virginia,[134] had previously advocated unconditional independence.[135] After the members of the third convention were elected, when it became apparent that the court party would be in control, Taylor began to stir the people of Lincoln County against their

133. See the statement of Thomas Marshall's friend George Washington in Fitzpatrick, ed., *Diaries of Washington*, II, 326, and the letter of John Marshall—son of Thomas and first cousin of Humphrey—to George Muter, Jan. 7, 1785, *Tyler's Qtly. Hist. Gen. Mag.*, I(1919–1920), 28.

134. Samuel Taylor, a paper read before the Harrodsburg Historical Society, Apr. 7, 1932, by Neva L. L. Williams, now in the possession of George M. Chinn, Ky. Hist. Soc.

135. Muter to Madison, Feb. 20, 1787, Madison Papers, VII; "A Real Friend" [Taylor], *Ky. Gaz.* (Lexington), Apr. 25, 1789.

representatives. Taking advantage of popular apathy toward the question of separation, he circulated a petition instructing the convention to postpone any action. The election had aroused so little interest that he was able to get more people to sign his petition than had voted for delegates. It was ignored by the convention, however, and the convention journal was later altered to remove all references to it.[136]

The position of partisans had been difficult all along, but it had become doubly complex as the court party began to support a separation. Many of the landless settlers who had supported the partisan program now probably gave their support to the court party plan of separation. But the partisans desired separation only as a means to another end, the redistribution of Kentucky land. Their more perceptive leaders realized that the court party would not use separation to accomplish a redistribution and that they must therefore oppose that group. Consequently John Campbell refused to join in the compromise of the second convention, and Samuel Taylor began to oppose separation. The partisan plan had been conceived and developed by speculators who hoped for personal gain from redistribution. Because they already owned large quantities of land, under Virginia as well as from land companies, these partisan leaders often aligned themselves with the surveyors, as at the first convention when partisans and surveyors had combined to condemn the five-shillings tax. Now partisans and surveyors continued to find a common interest in their attachment to the eastern states and their opposition to the court party.

Thus by the middle of 1786 there were three distinct positions on the question of separation, and all three were reversals of positions previously held. The partisans, who had favored a separation through Congress that would annul the Virginia land titles, were now against any separation.

136. "A Real Friend" [Taylor], *Ky. Gaz.* (Lexington), Apr. 25, 1789; Samuel Taylor, *ibid.,* July 26, 1806.

The articulate center, who had previously opposed a separation, was now split. One group, centering around Thomas and Humphrey Marshall, favored a legal separation through Virginia that would guarantee their land titles; the other, centering around James Wilkinson, was disgusted with Congress and Virginia and wanted to declare the independence of Kentucky immediately. "Congress by not asserting the right of the Union to the navigation of the Mississippi, a right derived from Nature and founded on Treaty, betray the trust reposed in them," Wilkinson wrote. "The people here from ignorance of the subject, and from that blind obeyance which used to Characterize the Colonies, are divided in sentiment—but they shall be informed or I will wear out all the Stirrups at every Station." [137]

These three parties would continue to exist through seven more conventions in the next four years. To men raised in a tradition where political service was considered service to the community, unused to political machinations, unaccustomed to thinking of themselves as politicians at all, the three-party politics of Kentucky must have been confusing. But they soon learned the basic rule—that it took two parties to make a majority—and combined as the situation allowed. Partisans and the country party had in common both their reliance on the eastern states and (at least among the leaders) their large landholdings; partisans and court party shared a desire to open the Mississippi; court and country parties had a common Virginia background and thus common standards for a government. Any combination was possible, and all combinations would appear in the four years to come.

A poll of citizens would probably have shown that a majority opposed separation from 1786 until 1790. [138] Even

137. Wilkinson to Hutchinson, May 4, 1786, *Pa. Mag. Hist. Biog.*, XII(1888), 62.
138. John Brown to John Breckinridge, May 20, 1786, Breckinridge Family Papers, III; Wallace to Fleming, July 13, 1786, Fleming-Christian Corres., Grigsby Papers; Levi Todd to Patrick Henry, June

the court party frequently mourned the "lack of unanimity" among the people and often, when running for office, talked as though they opposed separation.[139] They seldom claimed that separation was the will of the majority,[140] but argued only that the "leading characters" favored statehood and that it would be in the best interest of the district. Partisan leaders consistently insisted that a majority opposed separation and urged the people to vote.[141] "Our petitioning for a New State," one partisan wrote as early as 1785, "is entirely against the Voice of the people at large." [142]

But the voice of the people was silent. All the available evidence indicates that most Kentuckians, whatever position they would have taken in a poll, regarded the question of separation with a general lack of interest. Never once throughout the period of statehood conventions was there a public response even remotely like that in the earlier period, when almost half the population had signed petitions for a congressional (partisan) separation.[143] During the July 1785 election to the third convention, the number of people who voted was so few that Samuel Taylor could get more than that number of signatures for his petition, apparently in a single Sunday's work; [144] at the decisive elec-

---

22, 1786, Palmer, ed., *Cal. Va. State Papers,* IV, 151; Muter to Madison, Sept. 23, 1786, Madison Papers, VI; Wallace to Madison, Sept. 30, 1786, *ibid.* Most people thought the agitation against separation ceased about 1790. Nicholas to Madison, May 3, 1790, *ibid.,* XIII; Nicholas to John Brown, Dec. 31, 1790, No. 715, Ky. Hist. Soc. The weight of evidence sustains this view. For some continued opposition to separation, however, see Samuel Terrill to Garritt Minor, July 7, 1790, Terrill-Carr Papers, Univ. of Virginia. This letter was discovered by Joan W. Coward.

139. See the items cited in *ibid.;* "A Real Friend" [Taylor], *Ky. Gaz.* (Lexington), Apr. 25, 1789.

140. An exception is Samuel McDowell to William Fleming, Sept. 23, 1787, Fleming Papers.

141. "A Real Friend" [Taylor], *Ky. Gaz.* (Lexington), Aug. 25, 1789; "H. S. B. M.," *ibid.,* Dec. 24, 1791; "Valerius," *ibid.,* May 2, 1789.

142. Daniel Boone to Patrick Henry, Aug. 16, 1785, Draper Coll., 12 S 51–54.

143. See above, pp. 52–53.

144. See above, pp. 109–110.

tion of October 1788 only five hundred people voted in Fayette, out of thirty-five hundred eligible to vote.[145] "The people think of nothing else than cultivating their lands and increasing their plantations," James Wilkinson complained at a particularly low point.[146] No doubt the increasingly wide ownership of lands and the comparatively peaceful condition of Kentucky during most of this period were largely responsible for public complacency.

If the people of Kentucky had been interested in the question of separation, they might have influenced the attitudes and actions of their leaders. As it happened, the leaders operated without any restraints except those imposed by their own disagreements; later, when the court party urged Kentuckians to be unanimous, what they sought was unanimity of the politicians, for by then they knew that the will of the people was no barrier to any action. Because the people took so little interest in separation, it is impossible to follow the turns of their thought, nor is their thought an important part of the story. It is only possible to follow the leaders, who determined the outcome. Here "party" means, as it generally did in the eighteenth century, a small group of men associated to gain a particular end.

The newly changed political opinions of all the three parties became apparent during the August 1786 elections for the fourth convention. In Fayette County, James Wilkinson was running against several opponents, among them Humphrey Marshall. Wilkinson's friends announced that he would speak on the first day of the five-day election in favor of an immediate separation; a large crowd gathered, and he spoke for three hours and a half. Basing his arguments for immediate independence on the need to avoid further delay, he probably pointed to the year that had already

145. "Valerius," *Ky. Gaz.* (Lexington), Nov. 15, 1788.
146. Wilkinson to Esteban Miro, Jan. 26, 1790, Gayarré, *Louisiana,* III, 280.

been lost because of the Virginia enabling act and emphasized the need for immediate action to open the Mississippi. For the benefit of Humphrey Marshall, who objected that an immediate separation would be an illegal and dangerous course, Wilkinson explained that the phrase "posterior to September 1, 1787," in the enabling act meant before and not after that date. Then Marshall, with his fine legal mind and his gift for sarcasm, reduced Wilkinson to a nice dilemma. "Either he does not know the meaning of the word, 'posterior'; or he means to impose on his audience," Marshall announced. "In the one case, he is unfit to guide—in the other, unsafe to follow." [147]

Wilkinson, however, won the election. "I pleased myself, and, what was more consequential, every Body else, except my dead opponents," he reported. "These I with great facility turned into subjects of ridicule and derision." But according to Humphrey Marshall, Wilkinson won only by a trick. Marshall charged that the sheriff, a Wilkinson supporter, sensed a general feeling against Wilkinson and delayed opening the polls until late in the day, after Wilkinson's opponents had returned to their homes in the country, announcing that they would not vote until the last day of the election. Then, according to Marshall, on the last day the militia officers, who were also supporting Wilkinson, called a muster in outlying parts of the county and prevented the anti-Wilkinson bloc from voting at all. Whichever way it happened, Humphrey Marshall did not hold a seat in the fourth convention, and Wilkinson did. "I find myself now," he wrote, "more easy, prompt, and eloquent in a public debate, than I ever was in private conversation, under the greatest flow of spirits." [148]

During the elections of August 1786 Ebenezer Brooks

147. Wilkinson to Hutchinson, Aug. 18, 1786, *Pa. Mag. Hist. Biog.*, XII(1888), 63–64; Marshall, *Kentucky*, I, 242–243. Marshall, writing later, quoted himself in the past tense; I have changed it to the present.
148. Wilkinson to Hutchinson, Aug. 18, 1786, *Pa. Mag. Hist. Biog.*, XII(1888), 63–64; Marshall, *Kentucky*, I, 244.

joined Samuel Taylor in opposing a separation. A year earlier he had run for the third convention on a proseparation
platform; now the court party, habitually contemptuous of
partisans, accused him of changing his mind only because
he had been defeated.[149] Brooks retaliated by calling his opponents "the aristocrats" and by charging that only aristocrats wanted a separation. He used the term to refer to the
court and country parties combined, and with some justice,
for the old articulate center included most of the large land-
holders in the district (except for a few partisans), all of
the educated men (with the single exception of Brooks himself), and virtually all of the officeholders. There was also
much justice in his charge that only aristocrats wanted a
separation, for it does seem that the only strong supporters
of separation, either immediate or legal, were the members
of the court and country parties. Brooks read at militia
musters and posted at the tavern a parody he had written [150] in which his opponents from the articulate center,
wondering whether "to serve or not to serve," asked

> . . . Who would bend to earth
> And groan and sweat to gain the approbation
> Of ev'ry fool that hath a vote to give!
> Who with an air of friendship would conceal
> The high contempt that evil men deserve?

and finally confessed that

> . . . the dread of being too obscure[,]
> That awful state from whence so few can rise
> To claim the notice due to human beings[,]
> Puzzles the will and makes us still push on.
> Thus vanity makes cowards of us all.[151]

At this election partisans also developed a second line of
argument that was to serve them for several years, the argu-

149. "A Native of Virginia" [William Ward], *Ky. Gaz.* (Lexington), Sept. 22, 1787.
150. *Ibid.*
151. "A Paraphrase" [Ebenezer Brooks], *ibid.*, Aug. 25, 1787.

ment against taxation. Brooks later declared that many Kentuckians had gone west especially to avoid taxes, and another Kentuckian wrote, "The object with a number of people for removing to this retired corner, was, to avoid Taxation, but so soon as the Separation shall take place, the Taxes must also take place." [152] Whether or not that was so, it does appear that many Kentuckians were content with the government of Virginia precisely because it did not tax them. As an argument for separation the court party had said, in their address to the people adopted at the second convention, that Virginia was about to begin enforcing the tax for general revenue in Kentucky. Now, as an argument against separation, partisans distributed a handbill written by "A Planter," who revealed that the leading men planned to keep their property clear of taxes and to place the burden of support for the new government on the poor by instituting a poll tax as soon as a separation took place.[153] They argued that Virginia would continue to collect no taxes in Kentucky while Kentuckians lacked an outlet for their produce; and, above all, they contended that a few people intended to rule Kentucky for their own personal profit and satisfaction.[154] Ebenezer Brooks edited a petition opposing separation that had been written by Samuel Taylor, at best no scholar. Taylor read it aloud in church one Sunday, collected some seventy signatures of people whom the court party thought "obscure," and set off with it for Richmond.[155]

152. "Cornplanter" [Brooks], ibid., Sept. 13, 1788; Samuel Terrill to Garritt Minor, July 7, 1790, Terrill-Carr Papers. See also Caleb Wallace to William Fleming, July 13, 1786, Fleming-Christian Corres., Grigsby Papers.

153. George Muter to Madison, Sept. 30, 1786, Madison Papers, VI.

154. Ibid.; Caleb Wallace to James Madison, Sept. 30, 1786, ibid.

155. Muter to Madison, Feb. 20, 1787, Madison Papers, VII; "A Real Friend" [Taylor], Ky. Gaz. (Lexington), Apr. 25, 1789; "Kentucky Spanish Association," ibid., July 22, 1806.

A few members of the fourth convention, called by Virginia to ratify the terms of separation, gathered in Danville on September 26, 1786,[156] in an atmosphere of confusion. Ebenezer Brooks was there, and it now appeared that he had aided the petition Samuel Taylor was taking to Richmond. Among the court party members he was joking about his new opposition to a separation, perhaps because he fancied himself their intellectual equal and was embarrassed by the difference of opinion.[157] The court party found his jokes less than amusing; they were seriously afraid that the convention might fail to ratify the terms offered by Virginia.[158] With many of the delegates away fighting Indians, the convention failed to reach a quorum. A few members met from day to day to keep the convention alive, among them Thomas Marshall, Caleb Wallace, George Muter, Harry Innes, James Wilkinson, and John Brown,[159] who although a member of the Virginia legislature had chosen to remain in Kentucky for the convention.[160]

Continuing to meet from day to day—since most of them were obliged to stay in Danville anyway for the district court—these few members petitioned Virginia to extend the

156. Materials on the fourth convention are scant indeed. The journal was apparently already lost by the time Humphrey Marshall wrote his *History of Kentucky,* first published in 1812, and there is no extant list of members. See Wallace to Fleming, Sept. 27, 1786, Fleming-Christian Corres., Grigsby Papers; Muter to Madison, Feb. 20, 1787, Madison Papers, VII; "A Farmer" [Harry Innes], *Ky. Gaz.* (Lexington), Oct. 18, 1788; "A Real Friend" [Taylor], *ibid.,* Apr. 25, 1789; Littell, *Political Transactions,* 15–17; Marshall, *Kentucky,* I, 253–256.

157. James Speed to Fleming, Sept. 27, 1786, Fleming Papers.

158. Wallace to Fleming, July 13, 1786, Fleming-Christian Corres., Grigsby Papers; Muter to Madison, Sept. 23, 1786, Wallace to Madison, Sept. 30, 1786, both in Madison Papers, VI.

159. These are among the names signed to a letter to the governor of Virginia, Dec. 22, 1786, printed in Green, *Spanish Conspiracy,* 76–77. The letter came from Danville and evidently from the fourth convention.

160. Green, *Spanish Conspiracy,* 116, points out John Brown's presence in Danville despite his other obligations, a suggestion confirmed by Mary Howard to John Brown, Jan. 15, 1787, Preston Papers, #1479, Lib. of Congress.

time allowed for Congress's consent,[161] for it seemed unlikely that the fourth convention would reach a quorum before spring, and by then it would be too late to gain congressional assent before the June 1787 date required by the enabling act. As they waited through the rest of September and then October, November, and December, these members talked about separation and forms of government. Their conversations grew into a "Political Club" in December 1786, with formal debates at a Danville member's home every Saturday night, sometimes lasting until the small hours of the morning.[162] They resolved on January 6, 1787, with Harry Innes and John Brown introducing the question, "that an immediate separation of this District from the State of Virginia will tend to its benefit" and on January 13 that a separation would be beneficial "upon the terms prescribed in the act." [163]

Meanwhile the few delegates attending the fourth convention received important news that made them even more eager for a separation. Sometime in January, Thomas Marshall learned from his son John in Richmond that Congress proposed to surrender the Mississippi River to Spain for twenty-five years.[164] Congress's secretary of foreign affairs, John Jay, was negotiating with the Spanish minister, Diego de Gardoqui, and Congress had entered the vote in its secret journal, but it was hardly secret. Soon George Muter received a letter from James Madison asking, "Would Kentucky purchase a free use of the Mississippi at the price of its exclusion for any term, however short?" [165] Muter hastily

161. Muter to Madison, Sept. 23, 1786, Madison Papers, VI.
162. The history of the club, as far as it is known, is recorded in Speed, *Political Club*. Speed noted that "the roll of members shows that nearly all were members of the conventions" (5), but like other Kentucky historians he failed to notice the chronological moment of founding and the consequent likelihood that the club grew out of the fourth convention's impatience for a quorum.
163. *Ibid.*, 107, 111, 112.
164. Littell, *Political Transactions*, 79. Green, *Spanish Conspiracy*, 107–108, established that the letter was received in January.
165. Madison to Muter, Jan. 7, 1787, *Tyler's Qtly. Hist. Gen. Mag.*, I(1919–1920), 29–30.

replied, "I have not mett with one man, who would be willing to give the navigation up, for ever so short a time, on any terms whatever." [166] Everyone in Kentucky—court party, country party, and partisan alike—was deeply disturbed by the news. "The late commercial treaty with Spain," another Kentuckian wrote, "has given the western Country an universal shock, and struck its Inhabitants with an amazement." [167]

Eventually, late in January 1787, a quorum of the fourth convention gathered in Danville. Although the members were considerably less unanimous than those of the second and third conventions, they did vote by a majority of more than three to one to accept Virginia's terms of separation.[168] But the vote had no sooner been taken than Samuel Taylor arrived from Virginia bringing a second enabling act just passed by the legislature.[169] Instead of extending the time allowed for Kentucky to petition Congress, as the court party had requested, the legislature had called yet another convention—which would be the fifth—to be held that summer of 1787 and had moved the dates for Congress's assent and the actual separation another year into the future.[170] Enraged at this development, members of the court party charged that Taylor's partisan petition had persuaded the legislature that Kentuckians did not want a separation and insisted that Taylor was personally to blame.[171] To their further annoyance Taylor claimed, "I had no hand in the matter, but merely to be bearer of the petition, at the particular request of my constituents." [172]

166. Muter to Madison, Feb. 20, 1787, Madison Papers, VII.
167. Letter from a man at the Falls of Ohio, Dec. 4, 1786, in Arthur Campbell to Edmund Randolph, Feb. 16, 1787, Palmer, ed., *Cal. Va. State Papers,* IV, 242–243.
168. "A Farmer" [Innes], *Ky. Gaz.* (Lexington), Oct. 18, 1788.
169. *Ibid.*
170. Hening, ed., *Statutes,* XII, 240–243.
171. Muter to Madison, Feb. 20, 1787, Madison Papers, VII.
172. "A Farmer" [Innes], *Ky. Gaz.* (Lexington), Oct. 18, 1788. According to the 18th-century convention, Taylor is quoted as referring to himself in the third person; I have changed the reference to first person.

Puzzled now by the legal status of the fourth convention, the members debated whether it had been dissolved by this second enabling act. Finally, deciding that it had been, they disbanded. George Muter protested that decision, and his protest was soon confirmed by a letter from James Madison.[173] This letter Muter handed around among his court-party friends; now they knew that the legislature had intended the fourth convention to continue and that they could therefore have taken some action on separation. But now it was too late, for they could see no means of calling the convention together again.[174] The fault, they thought, was Samuel Taylor's, for he had failed to make the legislature's intention plain. Muter lamented, "Those of the people that were against a Separation, exault exceedingly; they think they have gained a victory and plume themselves upon it, highly indeed." [175]

About this time some Kentuckians began to consider the possibility that the district might separate from the Union as well as from Virginia and apply for aid to the British, who still held the Northwestern posts, or to the Spanish, who held New Orleans and thus controlled the Mississippi trade, as they had just demonstrated.[176] It was evidently the court party who adopted this extreme point of view, the expectation of foreign aid becoming an integral part of their idea that Kentucky might make a "violent separation" from Virginia. Apparently James Wilkinson spoke for all his political

173. Madison to Muter, Jan. 7, 1787, *Tyler's Qtly. Hist. Gen. Mag.*, I(1919–1920), 29–30.
174. Muter to Madison, Feb. 20, 1787, Madison Papers, VII.
175. *Ibid.*
176. Journal of General Richard Butler, Oct. 5, 1785, Jan. 2, 1786, 30, 216–219, Durrett Coll.; Thomas Jefferson to Archibald Stuart, Jan. 25, 1786, Boyd, ed., *Jefferson Papers*, IX, 217–219; William S. Smith to Jefferson, May 21, 1786, *ibid.*, 554–557; petition of delegates from the western waters and of sundry officers, Nov. 17, 1786, misc. legislative petitions, Box G, #1579, Va. State Lib.; John Campbell to Madison, Feb. 21, 1787, Madison Papers, VII; Madison to Jefferson, Mar. 19, 1787, Boyd, ed., *Jefferson Papers*, XI, 219–223.

friends when he said, "I can but lament the acrimonious spirit which seems to be kept up by the People of the United States, and Britain—Surely 'tis hard policy and must tend to the Injury of both." As Wilkinson explained it, "the People of Kentucky alone, could dislodge every Garrison the Spaniards have on or in the neighborhood of the Mississippi before this day twelve months, with ease and certainty."[177] Then they would rely on the British navy to open the Gulf of Mexico for their vessels. All this was not just talk and bluff, for Wilkinson had already been approached by a British agent.[178]

Members of the court party had followed with interest the developments just to their south, where settlers in western North Carolina had established a state called Franklin, written a constitution, declared their independence, and begun independent operation while applying to Congress for admission to the Union. This was the process which the court party had expected Kentucky to follow. In Franklin it had been accomplished under the leadership of Arthur Campbell, the erstwhile opponent of the court party. Now Harry Innes and Benjamin Logan began to communicate with Campbell; soon John Brown and Samuel McDowell were also among his regular visitors and correspondents,[179] which strongly suggests that they looked to him for support in planning an absolute or violent separation for Kentucky.

"I have been reflecting on the Hint you hold out of a general coalessence of the Western Country," Harry Innes

177. Wilkinson to Hutchinson, June 20, 1785, *Pa. Mag. Hist. Biog.*, XII(1888), 56–61.

178. John Campbell to Madison, Feb. 21, 1787, Madison Papers, VII; Wilkinson's first memorial, Sept. 5, 1787, in Bodley's "Introduction" to *Reprints of Littell's Political Transactions, cxxiv–cxxv.*

179. Benjamin Logan to A. Campbell, May 18, 1787, Palmer, ed., *Cal. Va. State Papers*, IV, 287; A. Campbell to Randolph, June 18, 1787, *ibid.*, 297–298; Harry Innes to A. Campbell, Sept. 19, 1788, Draper Coll., 9 DD 51; A. Campbell to John Brown, Dec. 29, 1787, Campbell Papers, Filson Club; Samuel McDowell to A. Campbell, Sept. 23, 1787, Draper Coll., 9 DD 46; deposition of McDowell, *Innes* v. *Marshall,* 64, Durrett Coll.

later wrote Arthur Campbell; "it is a subject of serious consideration." [180] Thinking, as they did, of the western settlements as an area geographically and economically separate
from the eastern states, it was natural that they should
consider the possibility of a political unity among them. And
from that thought it was a short step to a comparison between the current position of the western settlements and
that of the colonies at the time of the American Revolution. The court party had, in fact, been making that comparison for more than two years already. They had worked
hard in the first convention of December 1784 to stir up a
sense of grievance among the people, and in the second
convention of May 1785 they had actually patterned their
address to the people after the Declaration of Independence.[181]

Now the party received a communication from a committee of correspondence at Pittsburgh that was well
adapted to their frame of mind.[182] Frustrated because it was
taking so long to accomplish the separation, they were also
grieved by the Mississippi situation. They were already
aware that all the American settlements along the Ohio and
Mississippi were distressed by Congress's apparent willingness to barter away their right of navigation, but they had
taken no decisive action. Now, on March 29, 1787, apparently prompted by the Pittsburgh communication, four
members of the court party—George Muter, Harry Innes,
John Brown, and Benjamin Sebastian—addressed a circular letter to the people of Kentucky asking that they elect
representatives to meet in Danville the first Monday of
May 1787, "to take up this project of Congress; to prepare a spirited but decent remonstrance against the cession;
to appoint a committee of correspondence . . . ; to appoint delegates to meet representatives from the several

180. Innes to A. Campbell, Sept. 19, 1788, Draper Coll., 9 DD 51.
181. See p. 99–100 and p. 102 above.
182. Littell, *Political Transactions,* 17.

districts on the western waters, in convention, should a convention be deemed necessary; and to adopt such other measures as shall be most conducive to our happiness." [183] This was distinctly a revolutionary approach.

The convention of May 1787,[184] which met midway between the fourth and fifth conventions, was unofficial like the first three conventions and unlike the fourth and fifth which were called by the Virginia legislature. Its program, however, was the most ambitious yet conceived. The meeting was not only to send a memorial to Congress but also to select a committee of correspondence and elect delegates to a meeting of all the western settlements. Moreover, it was asked to "adopt such other measures as may be most conducive to our happiness": it was, in short, given a blanket power. But the convention actually did nothing more than choose a committee of correspondence.[185] The court party worked hard to get up a remonstrance, but "it seemed"— as Humphrey Marshall put it—"so much like impelling a cannon ball with drop shot, that it was however declined by a large majority." [186] The convention adjourned after several days, ostensibly because the legislature of Virginia had passed several resolutions strongly opposing the cession of the Mississippi. In fact, however, these resolutions had

183. This letter is published in almost every work dealing with these events, for example, *ibid.*, 78–79; Marshall, *Kentucky*, I, 259–260; John M. Brown, *Political Beginnings*, 243–244; Green, *Spanish Conspiracy*, 109–110. There are several copies in the Draper Coll., but as far as I know none that can be called an "original."

184. The sources for this convention of May 1787 are very scanty. Except for the letter cited in n. 183 there is no contemporary source except Wallace's fleeting reference to committees of correspondence in his letter to Madison, Nov. 12, 1787, Madison Papers, VIII. There are three later discussions by contemporaries: Littell, *Political Transactions*, 18; Marshall, *Kentucky*, I, 267–268; and John Bradford, "Notes on Kentucky," *Ky. Gaz.* (Lexington), Feb. 9, 1827. Bradford's account is based on Littell. The court party was more than willing for the people of Kentucky to forget this convention, which is no doubt the reason it was never given a number.

185. Wallace to Madison. Nov. 12, 1787, Madison Papers, VIII.

186. Marshall, *Kentucky*, I, 268. I have edited the punctuation of this quotation.

been passed some six months before, on November 29, 1786, and the court party had known of them when they called this convention.[187] The convention failed, not because its work had been done by the Virginia legislature, but because it could not muster support in Kentucky for an immediate, illegal, separation.

Humphrey Marshall, recalling twenty years later the court party's insistence on a separation, attributed it to the influence of James Wilkinson. Apparently Wilkinson did first publicize their determination, in August 1786,[188] but his friends soon carried on without him. During the convention of May 1787, which probably suffered from his absence, he was en route to New Orleans, having devised a bold scheme that promised not only to retrieve his sinking finances but also to win the admiration of everyone in Kentucky. He personally would open the Mississippi to the Kentucky trade! Persuading his Kentucky friends to make a serious trial of the trade situation, he collected from them —evidently without any investment at all—a shipment of hams, butter, and tobacco which he sent on flatboats toward New Orleans early in the spring of 1787.[189] Then, "loudly exclaiming," as Humphrey Marshall put it, "against restraints on the rights of navigation and free trade," he himself followed in April, "leaving his countrymen enraptured with his spirit of free enterprise and liberality, no less than with his unbounded patriotism." [190] Since his departure had been imminent since the middle of March, and probably before then,[191] he did not sign the court party's

187. This is established by Green, *Spanish Conspiracy*, 107–108; he draws on Marshall, *Kentucky*, I, 261–267.

188. See above, pp. 113–114.

189. Arthur P. Whitaker, "James Wilkinson's First Descent to New Orleans in 1787," *Hispanic American Historical Review*, VIII (1928), 85; "A Kentuckian" [James Wilkinson], *A Plain Tale* (New York, 1807).

190. Marshall, *Kentucky*, I, 271. I have edited the punctuation of these two passages.

191. Henry Carbury to Richard C. Anderson, Mar. 20, 1787, Anderson Papers, Box 1.

circular letter of March 29, 1787, and he was absent during the convention that it called.

In New Orleans Wilkinson claimed that his trip had been sponsored by the "leading characters of Kentucky," [192] meaning both the court and country parties. Whether or not this was true may never be known. But it is known that the court group had reached a peak of disgust with the American nation just before Wilkinson's departure, and it seems plausible to believe that they, at least, were interested in the trip. It may well be, as Wilkinson claimed, that they wanted to investigate the possibility of Spanish aid to Kentucky, in the event of a violent separation, as well as to test the trade situation.

* * *

My customers will excuse this, my first publication, as I am much hurried to get an impression by the time appointed. A great part of the types fell into pi in the carriage of them from Limestone to this office, and my partner, which is the only assistant I have, through an indisposition of the body has been incapable of rendering the smallest assistance for ten days past.[193]

Thus inauspiciously began the publication on August 11, 1787, of the district's first newspaper, the second newspaper west of the mountains, the Lexington *Kentucke Gazette*. Ever since the first convention of December 1784 citizens of Kentucky had been conscious of the need for a newspaper in the district; [194] they had invited printers from both Philadelphia and Richmond to settle in Kentucky, but without avail. Finally a Kentuckian had volunteered for

192. Wilkinson's first memorial, Sept. 5, 1787, published in William R. Shepherd, "Wilkinson and the Beginnings of the Spanish Conspiracy," *Am. Hist. Rev.*, IX(1903–1904), 501.

193. Quoted in George W. Ranck, *History of Lexington, Kentucky* (Cincinnati, 1827), 125. There is no longer an extant copy of this first issue of the *Ky. Gaz.*

194. Abernethy, ed., "Journal of First Convention," *Jour. So. Hist.*, I(1935), 67–68.

the task; the fourth convention of September 1786–January 1787 promising its support, he had sent to Pittsburgh for a press and other materials.[195] John Bradford, the editor, was "no printer, or self taught," but with an assistant who was a printer he managed to make the newspaper a success.[196]

Beginning publication less than two weeks before the elections for the fifth convention and hardly more than a month before the convention itself, the *Kentucke Gazette* immediately became a vehicle for political controversy. During these first few months the printer seems to have accepted everything that was offered for publication. Except for enforcing his eccentric spelling "Kentucke," he printed all contributions without any noticeable editing of grammar, punctuation, or spelling, and sometimes even without benefit of proofreading. All political pieces were printed over an obviously assumed name, such as "Hezekiah Stubblefield" or "Philip Phillips," or more often over some such signature as "A Native of Virginia" or "A Kentuckean," for it was considered indelicate in the eighteenth century to mention either one's own name or the name of anyone else in a political article. But there was seldom any secret about the authorship of these articles, and persons being calumniated were always clearly identified. The argument over separation, conducted now in public, soon became bold and bitter.

The newspaper controversy was initiated by Ebenezer Brooks, who published his parody of Hamlet in the second

195. [John Bradford], "The Printer of the Kentucke Gazette to the Public," *Ky. Gaz.* (Lexington), Aug. 18, 1787; John Bradford, "Notes on Kentucky," *ibid.*, Mar. 2, 1787; Dwight Mikkelson, The *Kentucky Gazette:* The Herald of a Noisy World (unpubl. Ph.D. diss., University of Kentucky, 1963).

196. Marshall, Kentucky, I, 271; Samuel M. Wilson, "John Bradford, Not Thomas Parvin, First Printer in Kentucky: An Open Letter," *Filson Club Hist. Qtly.*, XI(1937), 145–151; Willard Rouse Jillson, "The Role of Thomas Parvin—An Open Letter, in reply," *ibid.*, 238–240; Samuel M. Wilson, "John Bradford, Kentucky's First Printer: A Wide Open Letter," *ibid.*, 260–269.

issue, August 18, 1787, and then in the third issue began a series of articles against separation over the signature "A Virginian." Brooks offered the arguments that had already become conventional for partisans, who were now as firmly opposed to separation as the court party was determined to accomplish it. "This controversy," he wrote, "has changed its appearance very much since the time of its commencement." In the beginning the district of Kentucky had valid grievances against Virginia, both "in the administration of government, and in a great inattention in the assembly to the interests of this country," but the grievances had since been remedied. "As the present government ceases to be charged with evil designs; as we are sensible of the advantages we have, but cannot tell the advantages we have not; as the present debate turns upon theory and speculation; as the great [men] alone can be gainers and the people may suffer by a revolution; it should be delayed to a further period." In his second article, on September 1, Brooks wrote the first history of the statehood movement to show how the court party had pursued the elusive goal of separation through four conventions with increasing fervor as their reasons for separating diminished.

Brooks's "Virginian" series prompted immediate answers from the court party. Long ago they had begun to make fun of partisans; now they continued in the same vein. On September 15 one court party supporter complained that the Virginian's style seemed "calculated to insinuate itself into the Passions, and by that means, bias the judgment and excite ridicule rather than convince the understanding, and moralize the heart." [197] A week later, reminding readers of the partisans' change of position while ignoring his own party's reversal, he charged that the Virginian called himself "a Pennsylvanian" when he was "so piping hot for a sapa-

197. "Noviciatus" [William Ward], *Ky. Gaz.* (Lexington), Sept. 15, 1787. William Ward is established as a supporter of the court party by "An Observer" [H. Marshall], 25, pamphlet in Wilson Coll.

ration," recalled Brook's defeat for the third convention and his subsequent change of position, and paraphrased Brooks's parody to describe the consequence:

> . . . Ay, there's the rub!
> To be out voted or to be out wited,
> To cease to claim success by confidence
> Must give you pause and stop your resolution;
> This is the intolerable sad reflection
> Which drags you on with so much fruitless toil
> And makes a calamity of our Convention! [198]

An article by Caleb Wallace also complained of Brooks's change of position, suggested that he "could not brook the total defeat he met" in the first convention when he proposed an immediate separation, and concluded that this defeat was responsible for his "inveterate malice" toward those who favored separation. Once again Wallace enumerated the reasons for a separation, concentrating on the necessity of an adequate defense and the need to regulate the navigation of the Mississippi, but adding, "This is so much an Inland Country, that our main resource must ever be in our Manufactures." [199]

Before this newspaper quarrel could continue, the fifth convention met on September 17, 1787.[200] The court party poet had commented on the election:

> From low and abject themes, my grov'ling muse
> Now upward soars, and loftier subjects chuse:

198. "A Native of Virginia" [Ward], *Ky. Gaz.* (Lexington), Sept. 22, 1787.

199. "A Kentuckean" [Caleb Wallace], *ibid.*, Sept. 15, 1787.

200. Basic sources for the fifth convention are the list of members in Collins, *History of Kentucky,* I, 354; the proceedings of the fifth convention, Draper Coll., 3 JJ 364; extracts from the journal, *Ky. Gaz.* (Lexington), Nov. 17, 1787, Mar. 1, 8, 1788; Samuel McDowell to A. Campbell, Sept. 23, 1787, Draper Coll., 9 DD 46; McDowell to Fleming, Sept. 23, 1787, Fleming Papers; Wallace to Madison, Nov. 12, 1787, Madison Papers, VIII; Innes to John Brown, Dec. 17, 1787, No. 473, Ky. Hist. Soc.; "A Farmer" [Innes], *Ky. Gaz.* (Lexington), Oct. 18, 1788; Littell, *Political Transactions,* 24–25, 84–88; Marshall, *Kentucky,* I, 275–278.

Mercer's grand election here display,
And sing the glories of that pompous day.
M'Dowell, Jouett, Taylor, take their place,
With panting breast each anxious for the race.
Soon Jouett mounts his Pegasus on high,
And Taylor's ragged ruffians rush him nigh:
In sullen gloom, M'Dowell moves along,
Nor hopes for suffrage from the blackguard throng.
All vote for Taylor, Taylor every soul;
And Mercer pours her filth on Taylor's poll.[201]

Of the thirty-four delegates attending the convention, about twenty were members of the court party;[202] according to one report, that group elected such a large majority by announcing in each county that partisans in all the other counties now supported a separation, thus making opposition seem futile.[203] Benjamin Sebastian, John Fowler, Caleb Wallace, Benjamin Logan and his brother John, Harry Innes, and Samuel McDowell were all there, and the latter was again elected president. The remaining fourteen or so members were divided about equally between the country party—with Humphrey Marshall and Robert Breckinridge leading—and the partisans. Partisans, however, had not managed to elect any of their leaders; without the guidance of John Campbell, Samuel Taylor, or Ebenezer Brooks their members seemed powerless. Although they still opposed a separation they remained silent when the vote was taken. Later, when the convention discussed whether this vote should be recorded as "nemine contradicente" or "unanimous," two partisans protested against "unanimous." But they were easily overruled.[204]

201. Johnson, *Kentucky Miscellany*, 12–13.
202. List of members in Collins, *Kentucky,* I, 354; Innes to John Brown, Dec. 7, 1787, No. 473, Ky. Hist. Soc.
203. "A Real Friend" [Taylor], *Ky. Gaz.* (Lexington), Apr. 25, 1789.
204. McDowell to A. Campbell, Sept. 23, 1787, Draper Coll., 9 DD 46; McDowell to Fleming, Sept. 23, 1787, Fleming Papers; Wallace to Madison, Nov. 12, 1787, Madison Papers, VIII.

The convention resolved to accept Virginia's terms as stated in the second enabling act and in a dignified petition prayed that Congress would consent to the separation. They provided for the election of a constitutional convention to meet in July 1788, almost a year hence, to form a plan of government for Kentucky, and finally they set December 31, 1788, as the time when the separation would actually take place. This would be about a year later than the first enabling act had allowed and four years after the first convention. The petition to Congress contained the hint of a threat in the court party's statement of its unwillingness to wait longer than a year for separation. "This separation we anxiously desire to effect in the regular constitutional mode, prescribed in the [Virginia] law under which we act," it read, "but so great are our present strivings, which must grow with our growth and increase with our population, that should we be unsuccessful in this application, we shall not consider ourselves in any manner answerable for the future conduct of our constituents." [205]

When John Brown was appointed to Congress that fall and thus was given the task of presenting the petition to Congress, Harry Innes immediately wrote to explain the threat and to instruct him on how to handle it. "Perhaps Congress will think the idea [of an immediate separation] is held out 'In Terrorem.' I assure you it is not the case, but the decided opinion of five-sevenths of the Convention. I think, therefore it will be well done to deliver your sentiments very freely upon the subject that if we should be compelled to adopt other measures we shall stand justified as Congress could not then plead her ignorance of our intention." [206]

"The Indians have been very troublesome on our frontiers, and still continue to molest us, from which circumstance I am decidedly of opinion that this western country will, in a

205. Littell, *Political Transactions*, 85–86.
206. Innes to John Brown, Dec. 7, 1787, No. 473, Ky. Hist. Soc.

few years, Revolt from the Union and endeavor to erect an Independent Government," Innes wrote in another letter to Gov. Edmund Randolph of Virginia; "I have just dropped this hint to your Excellency for matter of reflection." [207] Caleb Wallace, too, predicted that Kentucky would declare "absolute independence" if Congress refused to make it a state. He explained to James Madison that Kentuckians would argue, first, that "a Freedom from State and Federal obligations would enable us to govern and defend ourselves to advantage"; second, that "we should no longer be in subjection to those who have an interest different from us"; and third, "if we had the power in our own hands the Lands of nonresidents and monopolisers would be subjected to a just partition"—all court party arguments. "The Convention wished to suggest to Congress," he added, "that by granting our request [for a separation] the best remedy will be provided against [absolute independence]." [208]

But it appeared that an absolute independence would not be necessary, for now a constitutional separation seemed a certainty. Even Ebenezer Brooks wrote, "Happily for us all, the resolve of the late convention may have put an end to the controversy." [209] Harry Innes reported to John Brown, "Since the adjournment of the Convention I have not heard a Murmur, and upon a pretty general inquiry I have not heard of any of the discontents bellowing against the measures which were adopted. Brooks I think will say no more, Taylor is silent also." [210] Samuel McDowell concluded, "I am persuaded that at least two thirds of the People at large are for a Separation." [211]

Thus at the end of the fifth convention the court party

207. Innes to Randolph, July 19, 1787, Palmer, ed., *Cal. Va. State Papers*, IV, 321–323.
208. Wallace to Madison, Nov. 12, 1787, Madison Papers, VIII.
209. "A Virginian" [Ebenezer Brooks], *Ky. Gaz.* (Lexington), Oct. 13, 1787.
210. Innes to John Brown, Oct. 14, 1787, J. M. Brown Papers, Yale Univ.
211. McDowell to Fleming, Sept. 23, 1787, Fleming Papers.

had once again, they thought, insured a separate statehood for Kentucky. Since the third convention they had moved from advocating a constitutional separation to threatening immediate separation, still thinking of themselves as representatives of the true interests of Kentucky. With the closure of the Mississippi they had finally been given an issue that they could use to advantage. The people of Kentucky clearly wanted the right to navigate the river; now without fear of popular disapproval the court party could demand that right, insist on it, threaten immediate separation if it were not granted. Although they clearly preferred a legal arrangement that would make Kentucky a member of the American confederation, by now they were willing to consider breaking from the Union if legal measures failed.

4

KENTUCKY AND
THE UNION

IN ITS ISSUE of Saturday, March 1, 1788, the *Gazette* reported the arrival of James Wilkinson in Lexington the
previous Sunday and added that he brought information
about the ice on the Ohio River breaking up. Wilkinson
was no doubt surprised to find the Ohio frozen over, thaw-
ing when the spring flowers should be in bloom, but he
was probably more surprised to see how Kentucky had
changed since his first arrival in December 1783, just over
four years earlier. Then the district had been one great
wilderness; now the forests were being cleared away, and
fields of corn and tobacco were plainly in view. Then in a
hundred square miles there had been hardly half a dozen
buildings other than one-story log cabins; now there were
many frame, stone, and hewn log houses, and even a brick
house had been started in Lincoln County.[1] Then most of

1. This was the Whitley house, still standing near Crab Orchard.
Charles G. Talbert, "William Whitley, 1749–1813," *Filson Club Hist.
Qtly.*, XXV (1951), 101–121, 210–215, 300–316.

Kentucky's two or three thousand people had hidden in forts; now a population of fifty thousand or more lived in the open and pursued a variety of occupations.

Wilkinson must have noticed especially the progress Lexington had made. In 1783 it had been just a few log cabins inside a fort; now it was a thriving village of several hundred people. Its streets were laid out in the most advanced pattern, the gridiron.[2] There were so many of them—ten in all—that some had not even been settled; Main Street was just a horse path, with jimson weeds so high on either side that a hog ten feet off was invisible.[3] But the street's very presence promised future growth for the town. By now Lexington had half a dozen two-story houses, a hewn log courthouse, and a satisfactory, if informal, method of controlling fire: when the alarm sounded each citizen rushed out with his leather bucket full of water.[4] During Wilkinson's absence Lexington had acquired a newspaper, two classical schools,[5] and a dancing master.[6] His merchant competitors had begun to advertise a poetic assortment of goods—

Camblet, Durants Moreens, shallons,
Fustians, Jeans, Corduroys, Plush, half-thicks,
Chintz, Callico, and stampt Muslin,
Silk, cotton, linnen and kenting Handkercheifs,
Black and white Gauze.
Apron Lawn, striped and Irish Linnen,
Worsted, thread and cotton Stockings, . . .
Shoe and Knee Buckles, Pen and Cutteau Knives,
Ivory and horn Combs, mens and wome[n]s crooked ditto.

2. Staples, *Pioneer Lexington.*
3. Shane's interview with Fielding Bradford, *Filson Club Hist. Qtly.,* X(1936), 279–280.
4. Advertisement of Samuel Cooper, *Ky. Gaz.* (Lexington), Dec. 22, 1787.
5. Advertisement of John Filson, *ibid.,* Jan. 19, 1788; advertisement of Isaac Wilson, *ibid.,* Jan. 26, 1788.
6. Advertisement of John Davenport, *ibid.,* Mar. 22, 1788.

Chocolate Muscovado Sugar,
Nutmegs, Cloves, Cinnamon and Ginger,
Indigo, Fig blue, Coperas, Brimstone and Rosin,
Drop-shott and a good Assortment of Castings [7]

—all imported from Philadelphia.

The problem of runaway servants was becoming serious in Kentucky. Most of Wilkinson's friends in the articulate center, as well as a few partisans, were slave owners, and their advertisements for runaways could hardly escape attention. In the *Gazette,* its columns otherwise filled with small, close type, advertisements for escaped servants were illustrated with a small black woodcut to catch the eye of every reader. John Campbell sought Isaac, a small, light, hook-nosed Negro missing the toes of one foot, whom he thought "very artfull and insinuating." [8] Later Caleb Wallace would lose a mulatto lad named Sam Jackson, who like Isaac had lost the toes of one foot and was "very artful"; Wallace warned that "if possible [he] will escape from the taker up." [9] Wilkinson himself had occasion to advertise for his Negro Ben. Ben had a wife at John Fowler's plantation, and Wilkinson thought he was probably lurking about in that vicinity.[10]

Wilkinson may well have been most surprised by the progress made in manufacturing and industry during his absence. There had been household manufactures all along, as in any primitive society; but now manufacturing had begun to diversify. All of the newly established enterprises were small, and most were one-man shops, using local raw materials to make items needed in the area: furs for hats, beef hides for leather goods, hemp for rope and hemp cloth,

7. Advertisement of Tegarden and M'Cullough, *ibid.,* Apr. 12, 1788.
8. Advertisement of John Campbell, *ibid.,* Mar. 15, 1788.
9. Advertisement of Caleb Wallace, *ibid.,* Jan. 24, 1789.
10. Advertisement of James Wilkinson, *ibid.,* Oct. 25, 1788.

rags for paper. Yet they were thriving. One Lexington hatter was already advertising for an apprentice.[11]

It was the members of the court party who were working hardest to encourage these Kentucky industries.[12] Lacking any trade outlet, lacking also any immediate hope of establishing an outlet, they had decided during the preceding year to encourage manufacturing in the district. They had, in effect, added a new facet to their glittering dream of commercial dominance for Kentucky: if they made everything they needed, Kentuckians would import only a few luxuries; then when the river was opened they could export manufactured goods to the whole Southwest and bring into the district far more money than flowed out of it. Thus, the court party reasoned, Kentucky would become wealthy. It was a primitive kind of economics, but it appealed to these eighteenth-century lawyers. Some people even thought seaworthy ships might be built from the great cedars of Kentucky, the makers utilizing Kentucky's infant iron industry, their product serving the additional purpose of transporting other goods down the Mississippi to market.[13]

Even while they were working so hard to open the Mississippi, the court party had been considering the potential benefits of its closure. The first question they had debated in the Political Club was "whether the immediate navigation of the Mississippi River will contribute to the in-

11. Advertisement, *ibid.*, Jan. 26, 1788.

12. In addition to the materials cited on the next few pages, see Thomas B. Craighead to John Brown, May 1, 1787, J. M. Brown Papers, Yale; a letter from Fayette copied in Arthur Campbell's hand (probably from a member of the court party), May 3, 1787, Campbell Papers, Filson Club; Samuel McDowell to William Fleming, Dec. 20, 1787, Draper Coll., 2 U 143, Wis. Hist. Soc.; Harry Innes to John Brown, Feb. 20, 1788, Innes Papers, XXVIII, Lib. of Congress; George Nicholas to Innes, May 1789, *ibid.*, XXII, Pt. i; Nicholas to James Madison, May 8, 1789, Madison Papers, XI, Lib. of Congress. I have not seen any evidence that either the country party or the partisans were deeply interested in manufactures.

13. Crèvecoeur, "Sketch of the River Ohio," 18, Durrett Coll., Univ. of Chicago; extract of a letter from Fort McIntosh, *Pa. Packet* (Phila.), Oct. 31, 1785, Draper Coll., 3 JJ 215–217.

terest of this District or not"; with "immediate" being doubtless the crucial point, they had decided in the negative.[14] George Muter had probably echoed their debates when he wrote James Madison soon after: "This country, in my opinion, must be principally employed in manufacturing their own necessarys, or for ever be a poor one." If "the people could furnish some article of light carriage and high value, such as silk, to exchange for such fine goods as they wished to have and could not conveniently make," he added, "it might be well enough."[15] Caleb Wallace agreed. "I should be more happy if our people were less anxious for this priviledge [of navigation] and more affected with the importance of manufacturing for themselves,"[16] he wrote.

"I have always heard that a country could not flourish without the advantages of trade," Caleb Wallace had written in the *Gazette* as "Abigail Trueheart." "But now I am perfectly reconciled, by the reflection, that though great wealth cannot be amassed, yet by frugality and industry a competency shall certainly be obtained." Aware that money was pouring into the district with every immigrant, the court party foresaw prosperity if no money were drained out for imports or for taxes. "Shall we not be as comfortable and lovely clothed in homespun as in foreign lace and brocade? And shall we not in this way effectually secure the independence of our families and our country?"[17]

The court party was encouraging industry with action as well as with words. "If ever we are a great and happy people, it must arise from our industry and attention to manufactories,"[18] Harry Innes thought. During Wilkin-

14. Dec. 30, 1786, in Speed, *Political Club,* 102–109.
15. George Muter to Madison, Feb. 20, 1787, Madison Papers, VII.
16. Caleb Wallace to James Madison, Nov. 12, 1787, *ibid.,* VIII.
17. "Abigail Trueheart" [Caleb Wallace], *Ky. Gaz.* (Lexington), Nov. 10, 1787.
18. Innes to John Brown, Feb. 20, 1788, Innes Papers, XXVIII.

son's absence he had become copartner in the establishment of a tanyard [19] and had advertised for nine Negroes
to work in it.[20] In September 1787 he, George Muter,
Samuel McDowell, Caleb Wallace, and John Brown, along
with a number of other Kentuckians, had formed the
"Kentucke Society for Promoting Useful Knowledge," [21] an
organization probably intended to inspire manufacturing.
In this they had the cooperation of Thomas Marshall and
Ebenezer Brooks, both men who did not let politics interfere with business.

Involved as he was in the river trade, Wilkinson might
have objected to the court party's plan of self-sufficiency for
Kentucky through manufacturing and especially to their
resolution in the Political Club that "the culture of tobacco
will not be beneficial to the citizens of the District." [22] But
if he did object he said nothing; probably he only found
the idea interesting. None of his friends had argued that
Kentucky ought to survive altogether without commerce;
they had said only that Kentuckians should concentrate on
producing objects they could use if the river remained
closed, objects that might be exported if the river were
opened. Wilkinson would surely have agreed to that. His
Mississippi trade in such farm products as tobacco was only
a superficial commitment, one among his many enterprises.
If the opportunity presented itself, he could carry hats and
cotton cloth as easily as tobacco and lard; in fact, he would
probably have found manufactured products more desirable
than raw materials and foodstuffs for his cargoes, because
they were lighter, less bulky, and more valuable. Thus he
did not protest against the court party's support of manufacturing, and he later invested in one industry himself.[23]

19. Peyton Short to Richard C. Anderson, Apr. 27, 1787, Anderson Papers, Box 1, Va. State Lib.
20. Advertisement of Harry Innes, *Ky. Gaz.* (Lexington), Dec.
15, 1787.
21. Advertisement, *ibid.*, Dec. 1, 1787.
22. Apr. 21, 1787, in Speed, *Political Club,* 129.
23. *Ibid.*, 159–160.

Having seen Lexington's progress, Wilkinson rode on to his plantation. It was a choice piece of fertile land that he had bought from Humphrey Marshall three years before,[24] a series of flat meadows set between two high hills in a curve of the Kentucky River, which Wilkinson called "Frankfort" and his wife wrote "Frankford." It was beautiful but isolated, with only a few slaves and one white tenant family,[25] and Mrs. Wilkinson was lonesome there. "I have looked for my Wilkinson this several Months with the utmost impatience, and now know not where he is, it is impossible for me to describe the torture my mind endures," she had written her father two weeks before. She had been sick but thought "my Jimmys Presence would soon make me well." [26] When he arrived she had much to tell him. She had broken every one of their blue and white china cups and saucers, and could buy at Lexington only common delft and queensware to drink her tea from. Her father had sent some shoes and stockings from Philadelphia that "fitted me delightfully"; some shoes he sent for the children "fitted extremely well all but one Pair which came odd, one was large and the other so small it would not go on there feet." [27] But her husband had other things to think about.

To his friends who were concerned about the prosperity of Kentucky, Wilkinson brought important news. The day he reached Frankfort he hired a man to carry a letter across the Kentucky River to Harry Innes in Danville, forty miles away. Innes received the letter the next evening, aroused the messenger's curiosity by sitting up much of the night writing, and then got up early the next morning to

24. Willard R. Jillson, "The First Landowners of Frankfort, Kentucky, 1774–1790," *Register*, XLIII(1945), 107–120.
25. Shane's interview with Tillery, Draper Coll., 11 CC 275.
26. Ann Wilkinson to John Biddle, Feb. 14, 1788, *Pa. Mag. Hist. Biog.*, LVI (1932), 39–41.
27. Ann Wilkinson to John Biddle, spring 1788, *ibid.*, 42–43.

ride to Wilkinson's plantation. When he arrived he found several men gathered there, but Wilkinson left them drinking in the common hall and took Innes off to a back room.[28] Probably then he told the story of his New Orleans trip.[29]

Wilkinson had traveled south at a leisurely pace, stopping at Natchez to give a pair of his fine horses to a Spanish official there, not arriving in New Orleans until July 2, 1787, three months after his departure from home. Threatened with confiscation of the goods he had sent down from the Mississippi on flatboats, he had told Esteban Miro, the Spanish governor, that he came as a representative of the people of Kentucky and would have a written commission were not Kentucky still a part of Virginia, lacking authority to negotiate with a foreign power. But Kentucky was "on the eve of establishing herself a free and independent state," he had said. Kentuckians were angry at Congress for its willingness to cede their rights to the Mississippi and would turn to some foreign power for protection; they had sent him to New Orleans "to develop if possible the disposition of Spain towards their Country, and to discover, if practicable, whether she would be willing to open a negociation for our admission to her protection as subjects." He had then drawn a dire picture of the consequences for Spain if Kentucky turned to Britain for protection.[30]

Miro had been impressed with the argument, as well he

28. Deposition of Richard Thomas, *Innes* v. *Marshall*, 109, Durrett Coll.

29. Humphrey Marshall hoped Thomas's deposition would suggest that Wilkinson had told Innes the story, but he was never able to establish that point. That Wilkinson did tell Innes at some time before May 1788 (whether or not on this particular night) is now established by James Wilkinson to Esteban Miro, May 15, 1788, Feb. 12, 1789, Gayarré, *Louisiana*, III, 208–212, 223–240.

30. Wilkinson's first memorial, Sept. 5, 1787, enclosed in Miro and Navarro to Valdes, Sept. 23, 1787. These quotations are from the translation published in Shepherd, "Wilkinson and the Spanish Conspiracy," *Am. Hist. Rev.*, IX(1903–1904), 498–503. A more extremely worded translation is published in Bodley, "Introduction" to *Reprints of Littell's Political Transactions, cxix–cxxvii.*

might be, for Louisiana was virtually defenseless at the foot of the river. He had asked Wilkinson to put these ideas in writing. Wilkinson had then composed a long essay that Miro dispatched to Spain for the king's approval; for his own use Wilkinson had retained the copy that he probably showed Innes. As a compensation for his services he had asked and had been granted the privilege of trading down the Mississippi; thus he had opened the river to the people of Kentucky.[31] Innes already knew this and had already advertised that he would purchase "tobacco, tallow, butter, well-cured bacon hams, lard and smoaked briskets of beef" for Wilkinson to take "to a foreign market." [32] In addition Wilkinson had served himself as well as the people of Kentucky by opening the Mississippi. His permit to trade in New Orleans was the only one issued; thus in effect he had a monopoly of the Mississippi trade.

As for the Kentuckians' wish to make some more permanent arrangement with Spain, Wilkinson had requested that they be allowed religious liberty and their own English-speaking government.[33] Promised those concessions, he had taken an oath of allegience to Spain [34] and had agreed to act as a Spanish agent in Kentucky, working for the union of Kentucky with the Spanish colonies in America. Thus in the same stroke that had solved the commercial problems of Kentuckians and the difficulties of his own pocketbook he had also disposed of Kentucky's political situation. And in

31. Wilkinson himself presented the matter in this light. See his first memorial, Sept. 5, 1787, in Shepherd, "Wilkinson and the Spanish Conspiracy," *Am. Hist. Rev.*, IX(1903–1904), 498–503; "A Kentuckian" [Wilkinson], *Plain Tale.*
32. Innes and Horatio Turpin, *Ky. Gaz.* (Lexington), Dec. 15, 1787.
33. Wilkinson's first memorial, Sept. 5, 1787, in Shepherd, "Wilkinson and the Spanish Conspiracy," *Am. Hist. Rev.*, IX(1903–1904), 498–503.
34. Wilkinson's expatriation declaration, Aug. 22, 1787, *ibid.*, 496–497; also in Bodley, "Introduction" to *Reprints of Littell's Political Transactions*, cxxxvii–cxxxix.

this too he had served himself: the governor of Spanish Kentucky was to be James Wilkinson.[35] He had sailed for Philadelphia in September and had spent the winter in the East. Now, while he awaited the king's official approval of the plan to make Kentucky a Spanish colony, he was to sound out Kentuckians. Innes he consulted first, and Innes apparently agreed.[36]

Wilkinson then confided in two other Kentuckians. One was Isaac Dunn, his partner in the Mississippi trade; the other was Alexander Scott Bullitt, a Jefferson County planter. The son of a distinguished Virginia lawyer and judge, Bullitt was a man without profession, a person of great ability that was as yet uncultivated. He was twenty-seven in 1788; he had been in Kentucky four years and had already become well established.[37] During the next few years he would read law in his leisure and begin to drink heavily;[38] as yet he was sober but immature and inconsiderate.[39] Although he had taken little part in Kentucky politics, he was and would remain closer to the country party than to the court party.[40] That Wilkinson chose to confide in him may indicate that members of the country party actually had joined in sponsoring the trip to New Orleans, as he claimed. That Bullitt seemed to approve the Spanish scheme is further support for this suggestion. Wilkinson now wrote Miro that both Bullitt and Innes—a mem-

35. Carondelet to Wilkinson, July 16, 1795, Arthur P. Whitaker, "Harry Innes and the Spanish Conspiracy," *Miss. Valley Hist. Rev.,* XV(1928–1929), 247–248.

36. Wilkinson to Miro, May 15, 1788, Feb. 12, 1789, Gayarré, *Louisiana,* III, 208–212, 223–240. See also Innes to A. Campbell, Sept. 19, 1788, Draper Coll., 9 DD 51.

37. Collins, *Kentucky,* II, 106.

38. Innes to Fleming, July 31, 1790, Fleming Papers; Dorsey Pentecost to Isaac Shelby, Mar. 24, 1793, Misc. Bound MSS, III, Durrett Coll.

39. Anne Christian to Anne Fleming, *ca.* 1787, Fleming Papers, #X14; Rosanne Wallace to Anne Fleming, June 23, 1789, *ibid.*

40. Alexander Scott Bullitt to Edmund Randolph, May 16, 1787, Palmer, ed., *Cal. Va. State Papers,* IV, 284–285; see below p. 187.

ber of each important party—knew the whole plan and could be contacted if anything happened to him.[41]

After confiding his Spanish scheme to Innes, Bullitt, and Dunn, Wilkinson sounded out other Kentuckians very cautiously.[42] The plan of making Kentucky a Spanish colony was probably more than his friends had bargained for when they sent him south; they probably had thought merely of a commercial treaty with Spain or perhaps of an alliance in which Spain gave Kentucky military assistance against the United States.[43] If this is so, it may explain Wilkinson's care in presenting his program. He wrote to Miro that because of circumstances beyond his control [44] "the only feasible plan" was "that of a separation from the United States, and an alliance with Spain, on conditions which could not yet be defined with precision." He hoped, he said, that "when the separation should be brought about, this district being then no longer under the protection of the United States, Spain might dictate her own terms," [45] and thus make Kentucky a Spanish colony.

To his friends in the articulate center (excepting Harry Innes, in whom he had confided fully), Wilkinson presented only the plan of separation from the United States and alliance with Spain. He omitted John Brown, who was attending Congress in New York, and Humphrey Marshall, who was still angry at Wilkinson; [46] all the others—including Thomas Marshall, George Muter, Caleb Wallace, Benjamin Sebastian, Samuel McDowell, and John Fowler—became

41. Wilkinson to Miro, May 15, 1788, Feb. 12, 1789, Gayarré, *Louisiana,* III, 208–212, 223–240. It is difficult to believe that he would have given such specific directions without the consent of the men involved.

42. *Ibid.*

43. See above, p. 125.

44. See below, p. 147.

45. See Wilkinson to Miro, May 15, 1788, Feb. 12, 1789, Gayarré, *Louisiana,* III, 208–212, 223–240.

46. See below, p. 153. If Wilkinson had ever discussed the plan with Humphrey Marshall, Marshall would certainly have revealed it in his many verbal battles with the court party.

confidants of the plan.[47] All expressed a warm interest in it
and discussed "with vehemence" the possibility of a Spanish
alliance.[48] Added to Innes and Bullitt, who secretly favored
union with Spain, and to Wilkinson himself, they were
a group of the most important men in Kentucky. Wilkinson's partner, Isaac Dunn, who also favored union with
Spain, declared in New Orleans that spring of 1788, "[I
have] heard it expressed in various conversations among
the most distinguished citizens of that State: *that the
direction of the current of the rivers which run in front of
their dwellings points clearly to the power to which they
ought to ally themselves.*" [49]

Among the general public Wilkinson usually mentioned
neither alliance nor union with Spain, although it was
rumored that he said to one farmer, "Well Billy, how hard
is it for us constantly to be paying taxes, and to receive no
support; look to the people of Louisiana, they pay no taxes,
and are supported in every thing. Had we no connexion

47. Thomas Marshall, George Muter, Caleb Wallace, and Benjamin Sebastian are specifically mentioned in Wilkinson's letter to
Miro of Feb. 12, 1789, Gayarré, *Louisiana,* III, 223–240. Wallace,
Sebastian, and McDowell are listed in Thomas Marshall's letter to
Nicholas of Apr. 26, 1789, Innes Papers, XXII, as favoring a violent
separation. Sebastian, Wallace, and Fowler are listed in Wilkinson to
Miro, Sept. 18, 1789, as "my confidential friends" who "support my
plan." "Papers Bearing on James Wilkinson's Relations with Spain,
1787–1789," *Am. Hist. Rev.,* IX(1903–1904), 765. Thomas Marshall
and Muter soon changed their minds, but Marshall did support a
violent separation for a time. See the deposition of Wallace, *Innes* v.
Marshall, 26, Durrett Coll. For Wallace's role, see below, p. 165;
for Sebastian, see below, p. 197. Wilkinson was living in the home
of John Fowler at this time (see below, p. 146); it is reasonable to
suppose that Fowler was a confidant of the plan. Samuel McDowell's
involvement is clearly suggested by his handling of the matter in the
case of *Innes* v. *Marshall.* He had often spoken of Brown's letter (see
below, p. 160) as a treasonous one; yet when asked to testify he
denied any knowledge of plans for a violent separation and an
alliance with Spain, no doubt to protect himself. "An Observer"
[H. Marshall], No. 3, pamphlet in Wilson Coll., Univ. of Ky.; deposition of McDowell, *Innes* v. *Marshall,* 67, Durrett Coll.
48. Wilkinson to Miro, Feb. 12, 1789, Gayarré, *Louisiana,* III,
223–240.
49. Dispatch of Miro, June 15, 1788, *ibid.,* 212.

with that *d-m-d* Congress, we should live like them also:
—yes, Billy, we shall never be right until we are clear of
them—and how easy is it?—That Congress won't let us sail
down even our own river—no, they say, twenty-five years
will be soon enough for us to touch it. And how do you think
Billy, you and I are to live for twenty-five years? No, Billy,
it can't be; we must join with Spain, and then we shall have
what we want." [50]

Wilkinson made it known that he had an "exclusive privilege" at New Orleans, as he purchased tobacco to ship down
the river; he stressed the necessity of navigating the Mississippi and hinted that Spain was willing to make a commercial treaty with Kentucky. All that was necessary, he implied,
was the independence of Kentucky from Virginia and
from the Union.[51] He was careful not to cause surprise or
alarm, never stating his own view, always offering the idea
of a commercial treaty as one "recommended by eminent
politicians on the Atlantic coast." [52] Humphrey Marshall
thought "more was meant than a mere traffic in tobacco,"
but he was incapable of destroying the general's popularity.
Most Kentuckians admired Wilkinson for opening the
river and thought of him as a great public servant,[53]
especially when he bought their tobacco for Spanish gold
dollars. Never before in the history of Kentucky, in fact,
had anyone been as popular and as well regarded as Wilkinson was now.

Under such public adulation Wilkinson became more
flamboyant than ever. He had arrived in Kentucky with a
coach, the first ever seen in the district, four black horses to

50. "Kentucky Spanish Association" *Ky. Gaz.* (Lexington), Aug.
21, 1806. See also *ibid.*, Sept. 15, 1806.
51. Marshall, *Kentucky*, I, 283.
52. Wilkinson to Miro, Feb. 12, 1789, Gayarré, *Louisiana*, III,
223–240; Marshall, *Kentucky*, I, 286.
53. Depositions of Thomas Barbee and Christopher Greenup,
Innes v. *Marshall*, 46, 160, Durrett Coll.; Marshall, *Kentucky*, I,
283–284.

pull it, and two black servants to drive it; [54] now he decided
to move to Lexington, and his workmen, led by that master
craftsman Barbary Lake, began building the house that
would be famed for displaying the first glass windows in
that town.[55] While it was under construction Wilkinson and
his family moved in with John Fowler, for the Fowler
plantation was a more convenient center for his mercantile
and political activities, and Mrs. Fowler was a congenial
companion for his wife.[56] Here he entertained as frequently
and lavishly as he had at Frankfort, with wine, beef, and
pudding always ready to serve a chance caller.[57]

This expansive style of living was calculated to promote
talk. A rumor that General Wilkinson was a Spanish subject
soon spread in Kentucky,[58] fostered perhaps by Humphrey
Marshall and buttressed by reports of Wilkinson's New Orleans correspondence. Just a month after Wilkinson reached
Kentucky his friend Harry Innes had hired two young men
to carry Wilkinson's private dispatches to New Orleans;
they returned some six months later to say that Wilkinson's
letters had been locked in a trunk weighted with stones
and that they had been given orders to sink the trunk if
there was any interference. On the return trip, they
said, one messenger had carried in his belt a packet of letters, securely wrapped in oilcloth, from the governor of
New Orleans to Wilkinson and Innes.[59]

There is little reason to doubt that Wilkinson sought both
financial profit and political advancement from his work
for Spain. He was deep in debt and needed a handsome re-

54. Marshall, *Kentucky*, I, 283.
55. Collins, *History of Kentucky*, II, 181.
56. Deposition of Richard Thomas, *Innes* v. *Marshall*, 108, Durrett
Coll.; Stevenson interview, Draper Coll., 11 CC 250; Ann Wilkinson
to John Biddle, Sept. 25, 1789, *Pa. Mag. Hist. Biog.*, LVI(1932) 50–
52.
57. Marshall, *Kentucky*, I, 245.
58. *Ibid.*, 283.
59. Depositions of Thomas Barbee and Richard Thomas, *Innes* v.
Marshall, 43–44, 109, Durrett Coll.; Thomas H. Benton to Joseph H.
Daveiss, Jan. 23, 1811, *Innes* v. *Marshall*, 216, *ibid.*

turn from the Mississippi shipping; the coach-and-four and the new house suggest what he expected. He bought gigantic quantities of tobacco and made such large shipments to New Orleans that Miro soon begged him to desist.[60] Yet he always found time to talk about a commercial treaty with Spain, to work for the independence of Kentucky, and to urge his scheme of alliance with Spain. Even after his shipments spoiled, after the Spanish destroyed his monopoly by opening the river, after the attempt to establish a Mississippi trade had bankrupted him, he continued to work for Spain. Eventually he received a pension, but those underhand payments seem hardly adequate to explain his real interest in the Spanish plan. He let it be known later that he wanted to be the "Washington of the West." [61] His pleasure in the luxurious scale of living which the Spanish connection allowed, it seems, was multiplied by the expectation of political glory to come.

When he surveyed the district after confiding in Bullitt, Dunn, and Innes, Wilkinson found an important change in the political scene. On his departure from Kentucky in April 1787 all the articulate center had been occupied with talk about independence; now they were all talking about the proposed new federal constitution.[62] That document had "inspired some with apprehensions, and others with hopes," he wrote to Miro, "so much so that I saw that this circumstance would be a cause of some opposition and delay." [63] Those who favored the new constitution thought it would insure Kentucky fair treatment as part of the American Union and were now less firmly determined on

60. Whitaker, *Spanish-American Frontier*, 97.
61. *Ibid.*, 96.
62. Innes to John Brown, Feb. 20, 1788, Innes Papers, XXVIII; Wilkinson to Miro, Feb. 12, 1789, Gayarré, *Louisiana*, III, 223–240; Marshall, *Kentucky*, I, 285.
63. Wilkinson to Miro, Feb. 12, 1789, Gayarré, *Louisiana*, III, 223–240.

independence for Kentucky; those who opposed the constitution were expending all their political energy in the opposition. Hardly anyone had time to think about a separation.
It was because of this situation that Wilkinson decided to
abandon his plan for union with Spain and to concentrate
on establishing the independence of Kentucky and an
alliance with Spain.

Wilkinson himself opposed the new federal constitution.
According to rumor, "some antifed in Maryland . . . last
Winter fastened on the Ear of General Wilkinson who was
accidentally there and persuaded him that in case of a new
Government the Navigation of the Mississippi would in-
fallibly be given up." [64] Actually the general was probably
less concerned with the navigation of the Mississippi—
having personally taken care of that problem—than with
bringing Kentucky under Spanish control. He could see
that the new constitution was distracting attention from his
Spanish plan; he could foresee that if the constitution were
adopted its supporters might back the national government
and act as a permanent obstacle to independence and a
Spanish connection. Through such reasoning Wilkinson probably became an opponent of the constitution.

Members of the court party were uniformly opposed to
the new constitution. Both George Muter [65] and Samuel
McDowell [66] had initially favored it, but by the middle of
February 1788 they had joined Innes, Sebastian, Wallace,
Fowler,[67] and Shelby [68] in the opposition. This was before
Wilkinson arrived in Kentucky; he did not create their
position unless he did it by mail. Apparently these men in

64. Hugh Williamson to James Madison, June 2, 1788, Burnett,
ed., *Letters of Continental Congress*, VIII, 746.
65. John Brown to Madison, May 12, 1788, Madison Papers, IX.
66. McDowell to Fleming, Dec. 20, 1787, Draper Coll., 2 J 143.
67. McDowell, Wallace, Muter, Sebastian, Innes, Greenup, Allin,
and Logan to the Court of Fayette, Feb. 29, 1788, Draper Coll., 11 J
182. See also Wallace to Fleming, June 29, 1788, Fleming-Christian
Corres., Grigsby Papers, Va. Hist. Soc.
68. Marshall, *Kentucky*, II, 99.

Kentucky reached the same conclusion as Wilkinson by a completely different process of thought. They were resolved to establish independence, anxious to protect their land-holdings, eager to make Kentucky a center of manufacturing and commerce. The new constitution gave too many powers to the federal government that they had expected to enjoy as a state, most notably the right to try in local courts all land suits between residents and nonresidents and the right to encourage local manufacturing by laying a tax on imports. Harry Innes assumed that land cases would be tried in the East by eastern judges and predicted that Kentuckians would lose nine cases out of ten. "Can we suppose Congress will indulge us with a partial impost when we must otherwise procure all our resources from the Eastward?" he demanded; "we shall be impoverished and the Eastern States will draw all our wealth and emigration [to Kentucky] will totally cease." [69] Caleb Wallace objected that "under this New Government Imports and Exports cannot be taxed nor prohibited without the consent of Congress," [70] thus indicating the intention of the court party to encourage Kentucky manufactures.

Every one of the court party's objections was based on a conviction that the interests of the East and the West were different, so completely opposed, in fact, that the two areas could not cooperate under a strong federal scheme. "The adoption of that Constitution would be the destruction of our young and flourishing country which I shall endeavor to point out concisely to you," Harry Innes instructed his young friend, Kentucky Congressman John Brown. "Our interests and the interests of the Eastern States are so diametrically opposite to each other that there cannot be a ray of hope left to the Western Country to suppose that

69. Innes to John Brown, Feb. 20, 1788, Innes Papers, XXVIII. See also James Breckinridge to John Breckinridge, June 13, 1788, Breckinridge Family Papers, V, Lib. of Congress.
70. Wallace to Fleming, May 3, 1788, Fleming-Christian Corres., Grigsby Papers.

when once that interest clashes we shall have justice done to us." Demanding rhetorically, "Is there an article that the Eastern States can export except Fish oil and rice that we shall not abound in?" he answered, "I say not one. So long therefore as Congress hath this sole power [to regulate commerce] . . . we cannot expect to enjoy the navigation of the Mississippi." [71]

The Mississippi River was probably the deciding argument. Partisans were completely silent on the question of the federal constitution,[72] and most people were as unmoved by this issue as by the matter of statehood. During the previous four years they had risen to a unified public position only once, when a cession of their right to navigate the river was threatened; now the court party used that feeling to create opposition to the federal constitution. McDowell, Innes, Sebastian, Wallace, and Muter, along with Benjamin Logan and two of their other supporters, addressed an open letter to the Fayette County Court denouncing the proposed constitution, arguing chiefly that a new government would certainly give up the Mississippi, and demanding a convention to instruct delegates to the Virginia ratifying convention, which was to be held in Richmond in June 1788.[73] The latter suggestion was perhaps calculated to appeal to partisans, always so concerned about the will of the people, for the court party evidently abandoned the idea of instructions once a majority of antifederalist delegates was elected.

As the federal constitution was opposed by the court party, who already distrusted the eastern states and wanted to establish independence, so it was favored by the country party, who had always tried to strengthen East-West ties, who had supported absolute independence only when it

71. Innes to John Brown, Feb. 20, 1788, Innes Papers, XXVIII.
72. Marshall, *Kentucky*, I, 285.
73. McDowell *et al.* to the Court of Fayette, Feb. 29, 1788, Draper Coll., 11 J 182.

seemed the Mississippi actually might be given up. Thus
the division in the articulate center that had begun in the
question of separation was now perpetuated in a new issue. Members of the country party, seldom disposed to take
part in politics, were generally quiet on the constitution;
few of them ran for seats in the ratifying convention, and
most of those who did ran in a gentlemanly way. Only
Humphrey Marshall, always politically inclined and seldom
able to appear the perfect gentleman, fought hard against
opponents of the constitution for a seat in the ratifying convention. Even in his case it appears that the fight was provoked by the court party.

The enmity between Humphrey Marshall and James
Wilkinson had begun during the elections to the fourth
convention of September 1786 and had continued during
Wilkinson's absence;[74] now Innes as well had incurred Marshall's wrath. Late in 1787 Marshall had written Innes a
letter denouncing Horatio Turpin, Innes's partner in various
land speculations as well as in the tanyard, for spreading
scandal; then, presumably finding his information mistaken,
he had written Innes another letter, apologizing profusely.[75]
But thenceforth the two men were bitter enemies. Wilkinson and Innes were united in their hatred of Humphrey
Marshall; now they apparently attempted to defeat him in
the election for the ratifying convention by spreading
stories of a personal scandalous nature about him. "I am
totally ignorant of having done any thing to deserve the
train of vulgar epithets, too gross to repeat, which have

74. See above, pp. 113–114; Humphrey Marshall, *Ky. Gaz.* (Lexington), Mar. 22, 1788.
75. This letter is apparently no longer extant, for it is not in the
Innes Papers at the Library of Congress. That it was written is well
established, however; see Jordan Harris [James Wilkinson], Apr. 12,
1788, *Ky. Gaz.* (Lexington); Humphrey Marshall, *ibid.*, Apr. 19,
1788; deposition of Christopher Greenup, *Innes* v. *Marshall*, 158,
Durrett Coll. Marshall thought the letter the cause of subsequent
difficulties between himself and Innes. For his apology, see his letter
to Innes, Feb. 7, 1788, Innes Papers, XXII.

been thrown on me by licentious tongues," Marshall complained in the *Gazette,* in a story printed over his own name. "I request those people, I demand it of them, I defy them, to exhibit a charge of the facts against me, which will justify their conduct." [76]

In this article Marshall singled out a Kentuckian named Jordan Harris as one who had especially misused him, and Harris determined to punish him for the contemptuous reference. Equipped with a pair of pistols, he followed Marshall through Lexington the next week, greeted him pleasantly, and then offered him a pistol. Marshall refused; he was after the court party and considered Harris beneath the dignity of a duel. When Harris swore and prepared to fire, he struck Harris's pistol with his stick and dodged the shot. Dismounting from his frightened horse, he then walked toward Harris brandishing his stick, avoided a second shot, and with the stick struck Harris's arm. Harris turned and raced back to town, probably not out of ammunition (as he insisted) after two shots, but from sheer fright. [77]

The physical encounter started a verbal one. Harris sent a formal challenge which Marshall returned unanswered—this being the convention when a gentleman was challenged by someone beneath him—and then published his story in the *Gazette,* denouncing Marshall in the most extreme terms. [78] Marshall answered with his version a week later, prefacing it with a mock apology: "Mr. Harris will excuse me if I have not descended to the scurril[it]y of his pen; he must know that I do not choose to imitate him in anything." [79] But his language, too, was unrestrained. Then he appeared in Lexington carrying the stick he had

76. H. Marshall, *Ky. Gaz.* (Lexington), Feb. 23, 1788. I have edited the punctuation of these passages.
77. Jordan Harris, *ibid.,* Mar. 8, 1788; H. Marshall, *ibid.,* Mar. 15, 22, 1788. In general I follow Marshall's account, which seems more likely than Harris's.
78. Harris, *ibid.,* Mar. 8, 1788.
79. H. Marshall, *ibid.,* Mar. 15, 1788. Marshall's letter was continued to the next week, Mar. 22, 1788.

used to defeat Harris, with a blue ribbon tied on it. James Wilkinson complained, "Truth and honor are I fancy appendanges, which Mr. Marshall wears as he did the cane with the blue ribbon merely for show, and to be laid aside or employed as occasion renders necessary." [80]

Marshall won a seat in the Virginia ratifying convention. Whether it was because he received some antifederalist votes after a dispute between the supporters of John Fowler and the supporters of Samuel McDowell (as Wilkinson insisted),[81] because he promised to vote against the constitution (as Innes later claimed),[82] or because some people actually did favor the constitution will probably never be known. Perhaps it was simply because the blue ribbon on his cane caught the public eye. In any case the court party lost that seat; the *Gazette* that published the last installment in the controversy between Marshall and Jordan Harris also announced Marshall's election.

Now Wilkinson devised a means for destroying whatever popularity Marshall had. Taking up Harris's cause and writing over Harris's name, in the next *Gazette* he promised a series of "small tales, for the diversion of little children, of which *Humphrey Grubbs,* vulgarly called Marshall, was to be the *Hero.*" [83] He warned, "If I should in the course of my enquiries, apply terms of derision or reproach to *Grubbs,* which may be deemed indelicate or illiberal, I trust, they will be ascribed to their true cause, to wit, a regard to propriety, in adapting my language to my subject." [84] Then he called his hero "a wretch who

80. Harris [Wilkinson], *ibid.,* Apr. 6, 1788.
81. *Ibid.,* Apr. 26, 1788.
82. Innes to W. C. Nicholas, June 10, 1807, Innes Papers, XIX. See also George M. Smith, *Ky. Gaz.* (Lexington), Sept. 19, 1795.
83. Humphrey Marshall later claimed that the articles were written by John Coburn, "under the direction and assistance of General Wilkinson"; see *ibid.,* Oct. 23, 1806, and Green, *Spanish Conspiracy,* 66. This description is from Harris [Wilkinson], *Ky. Gaz.* (Lexington), Mar. 29, 1788.
84. *Ky. Gaz.* (Lexington), Mar. 29, 1788.

stands stigmatized to the world, for a liar, coward, and scoundrel," a "Monkey in Mans Cloathes," a "Wolf in sheeps cloathing." [85]

During the next five weeks Wilkinson reminded *Gazette* readers of every Marshall misdemeanor that he could remember or discover, including the double fee,[86] the controversy with John Clark, the letter to Innes denouncing Turpin, and the cane with the blue ribbon.[87] When readers complained that the name of his hero was obscure he pondered, "Strange that among so many Tobacco-planters, the little mischievous, night-working, root gnawing worm, should be totally and entirely forgotten," and explained that "as the little grubbs works in darkness, strikes at the root and feast[s] on the destinction, of the most valuable part of the vegetable creation: so doth Captain Humphrey Marshall deal in deception, insidiously sap the interest of his neighbours, and take delight to maim and mangle the reputation of his fellow citizens." [88]

If there had been any uncertainty in Marshall's feeling about Wilkinson, the series of articles over the signature "Jordan Harris" decided it. Marshall answered on April 5 and again on April 19, denying the truth of the charges, insisting that "it is now utterly in vain for the writer whose works Jordan Harris signs, to pretend to conceal the party of which he is an illustrious member," and threatening to expose the true author if he did not reveal himself. When the series continued to appear over Jordan Harris's name, Marshall prepared a piece exposing Wilkinson and left it with the *Gazette* editor before he departed for Richmond and the ratifying convention.[89] This article was never printed.[90]

85. *Ibid.*, Mar. 22, Apr. 5, 1788.
86. *Ibid.* See above, p. 42.
87. *Ibid.*, Apr. 12, 1788. See above, pp. 41–42, 151, 153.
88. *Ibid.*, Apr. 5, 1788.
89. Advertisement, *ibid.*, Apr. 12, 1788; editorial, *ibid.*, May 10, 1788.
90. The editors' refusal to print the article provoked a small controversy in itself. See "Cato" and "Phileleutheros," *ibid.*, May 10, 1788.

Such an "attack on the character of a private gentleman" required payment, the editors explained.[91] Wilkinson had all along been paying for the privilege of smearing Marshall's character.[92]

While this controversy provoked by the federal constitution was raging in Kentucky, John Brown in New York was wavering between the federalist arguments of his friend James Madison and Harry Innes's antifederalist instructions. "I hope and believe [the new Constitution] will be adopted," he wrote Madison, "[but] I hear nothing friendly is to be expected from that quarter." [93] Madison had asked him to write the Kentucky delegates; he doubted that "any good effect will result from a communication of my Sentiments," but added, "as I am personally acquainted with the men and fully possess their confidence I shall at all events hazard the attempt," and so wrote three of the delegates, including John Fowler.[94] He was more concerned about whether Congress would rule favorably on Kentucky's plea for separation, having waited several months for a quorum to gather to rule on it. "My mind is and for some time has been so irritated that I have avoided writing to my friends from the District now at Richmond," he reported later, "least I might drop something which might have a similar effect upon them. I hope you have a decided majority without them and that the ninth Pillar may be raised in Virginia." [95]

It was not because of the fourteen Kentucky delegates that Virginia became a pillar supporting the new federal constitution. It seemed that their votes would determine whether Virginia ratified and thus whether the nation accepted it; as one Virginian wrote, "The fate of Virginia is

91. Editorial, *ibid.*
92. Green, *Spanish Conspiracy,* 66.
93. John Brown to Madison, May 12, 1788, Madison Papers, IX.
94. *Ibid.;* John Brown to James Breckinridge, June 21, 1788, James Breckinridge Papers, Univ. of Va.; John Brown to Matthew Walton, June 5, 1788, Filson Club. This letter is mistakenly cataloged as being from James Brown.
95. John Brown to James Madison, June 7, 1788, Madison Papers, IX.

thus suspended upon a single Hare." [96] But the Kentucky delegates were generally weak, the most capable Kentuckians having been elected to a convention that was meeting in the district at nearly the same time, and most of them had been influenced by the court party's antifederalism. Only three voted for the new constitution: Robert Breckinridge, who had heard that John Brown favored the constitution and was reassured to have "so respectable a character as Mr. Brown of the same oppinion as myself"; his country party colleague from Jefferson County; and Humphrey Marshall, who had heard that Brown opposed the constitution and had been "abundantly forewarned of the loss of popularity" if he supported it.[97] Ten of the Kentucky delegates voted against it, including John Fowler. One did not vote at all.[98]

Thus the court party dominated the votes of Kentuckians at the Virginia ratifying convention. The occasion was important, not because it showed any change in party strengths —for it did not—but because it showed the determination of Kentuckians to secure their right to the navigation of the Mississippi. Perhaps even more significant, it was the occasion when the enmity between Humphrey Marshall and the court party found public expression and hardened into a solid unchanging hatred. Politics in Kentucky was largely a matter of personal friendships and antipathies; for the next twenty years the enmity between Humphrey Marshall and the court party would shape political contests in the area.

While the ratifying convention in Richmond debated the federal constitution, Kentuckians prepared for the meeting

96. Archibald Stuart to John Breckinridge, June 19, 1788, Breckinridge Family Papers, V.

97. Robert Breckinridge to James Breckinridge, July 2, 1788, Breckinridge-Marshall Papers, Filson Club; John Brown to Matthew Walton, June 5, 1788, also in Filson Club; Marshall, *Kentucky*, I, 287. I have edited the punctuation of the passage quoted. See "Independence," *Palladium* (Frankfort), Sept. 11, 1806.

98. Charles Gano Talbert, "Kentuckians in the Virginia Convention of 1788," *Register*, LVIII(1960), 187–193.

of a state constitutional convention that the fifth convention of September 1787 had called for July 1788. Members of the court party had received word from John Brown, in letters written the previous February, that Congress had assigned their petition for statehood to a special committee and that the committee was preparing a bill for the reception of Kentucky into the Union.[99] They had heard nothing positive since then, but—since it usually took three months for travelers to carry a letter from New York to Kentucky —they had no doubt that the bill had passed. And if Congress refused they had an alternate plan, Wilkinson's scheme of union with Spain. Confident now of separation, once again they asked the advice of their friends on forms of government. James Wilkinson wrote an acquaintance in Virginia,[100] and John Brown requested James Madison to draft a constitution that could be presented to the convention. "I fear," he explained, "that few will be found in that Body who have sufficiently attended to political Subjects to quallify them for the task of framing a good System of Government for that District." [101]

When a "numerous and respectable company of Ladies and Gentlemen" gathered at a Lexington tavern on the fourth of July, probably already established as an occasion for patriotic celebrations, the court party had an opportunity to demonstrate their sentiments. "An elegant entertainment prepared for the occasion" included an ode composed by a Lexington gentleman and sung to the tune of "Rule Britannia" with the chorus "Hail Kentucke! Kentucke, thou shalt be/ For ever great, most blest, and free." Around three o'clock dinner was served; then fourteen toasts were drunk, accompanied by the discharge of fourteen rifles at each interval, and the evening concluded with a ball, "elegance, order and decorum" marking the occasion. The

99. Littell, *Political Transactions*, 27; Bradford, "Notes on Kentucky," *Ky. Gaz.* (Lexington), Mar. 23, 1827.
100. George Nicholas to Wilkinson, Jan. 23, 1788, Nicholas Papers, Durrett Coll.
101. John Brown to Madison, May 12, 1788, Madison Papers, IX.

fourteen toasts and fourteen rifles apparently symbolized the number of states that would be part of the Union after Kentucky's admission; indeed, the first toast was to "The United States of America" and the last to "The Commonwealth of Kentucke, the fourteenth luminary in the American Constellation." Other toasts, however, reflected the alternate plan: "The Western world, perpetual Union, on principles of equality, or amicable Separation"; "The Navigation of the Mississippi, at any price but that of Liberty"; "May the Atlantic States be just, the Western States be Free and both be happy." [102]

Now that a separation seemed imminent and the crucial question was the kind of constitution that would be adopted, the court party was anxious for party divisions to be forgotten. From the first they had considered themselves best qualified to determine matters of governmental policy, but in the course of doing what they thought best for Kentucky they had offended many people. To encourage their own election to this constitutional convention, they urged the people before the April election to abandon party distinctions and vote for the best men. They said, as the court party poet phrased their appeal,

> . . . This once discharge your trust,
> This once dare to be free, dare to be just;
> Follow not blindly with the giddy host;
> But freely vote for him who merits most.[103]

By "the best men" the court party meant those who were best trained and most experienced in the science of government; thus they included country party members in this category, but omitted partisan leaders. Partisans found the omission a grave offense and made it the topic of several campaigns to come.

The court party must have been highly gratified by the

102. *Ky. Gaz.* (Lexington), July 5, 1788.
103. "Sophia Kentuckeana" [William Ward], *ibid.,* May 24, 31, 1788.

election. In Fayette, James Wilkinson received 742 votes and Caleb Wallace, 613, running well ahead of Thomas Marshall, with 493 votes the next delegate.[104] At Danville—now in the recently created Mercer County—Samuel McDowell, John Brown, and Harry Innes were elected, all three running ahead of the two members of the country party who were elected;[105] partisans Ebenezer Brooks and Samuel Taylor were excluded altogether. Benjamin Sebastian and Alexander Scott Bullitt were elected in Jefferson, and in London, Benjamin Logan and Isaac Shelby were chosen. Altogether the court party had at least fifteen of the thirty-five delegates, and perhaps more. The country party elected half a dozen or more members, including Thomas Marshall. Partisans could claim perhaps a dozen members of the sixth convention, but none of them was among that party's leaders.[106]

Meanwhile, in New York, John Brown's mind was "irritated,"[107] as he told James Madison, by Congress's action on the petition sent by the fifth convention of July 1787. He had presented the petition in February and soon after had been able to write home the encouraging news that a committee was drawing up a bill for the district's reception into the Union. But then nothing had been done until June 2, when the committee asked to be relieved from acting on the petition. Their public argument was that it should be referred to the Congress of the new federal government; yet one member from Massachusetts had declared he would rather see the ocean wash the western slopes of the Alleghenies than to see new states created there.[108] Brown

104. *Ibid.*, Apr. 19, 1788. See A. K. Marshall, *Western World* (Frankfort), Oct. 25, 1806.
105. *Ky. Gaz.*, May 3, 1788.
106. Manuscript journal of the sixth convention, Ky. Hist. Soc.
107. John Brown to Madison, June 7, 1788, Madison Papers, IX. See also John Brown to Jefferson, Aug. 10, 1788, Boyd, ed., *Jefferson Papers*, XIII, 494.
108. Littell, *Political Transactions*, 28. See also "An Early Inhabitant," *Ky. Gaz.* (Lexington), July 26, 1806, and "A Kentuckian" [Wilkinson], *Plain Tale*, 7.

wrote home that the jealousy of the eastern states had prevented Kentucky's admission.[109] The event seemed to confirm the suspicions Brown and his court party friends had held of Congress at least since the negotiations with Spain began, suspicions that may well have dated back to the days when they feared Congress might allow a partisan independence to Kentucky.

John Brown knew that Virginia would not consent to Kentucky's separation unless Congress would make her a state, and he was convinced that the eastern states would never allow her to become part of the nation. Assured by Harry Innes that the recently rejected petition was the last one Kentucky would make before declaring her independence of the United States, knowing that Kentucky could not survive as a separate nation, he was in a highly agitated frame of mind when the Spanish ambassador began to cultivate his friendship that June of 1788. Neither Don Diego de Gardoqui nor John Brown knew yet of James Wilkinson's arrangement with Esteban Miro at New Orleans, but Kentucky's need for the New Orleans market was obvious. Gardoqui told Brown that Spain could not give any trade advantages while Kentuckians remained a part of the United States, "artfully insinuating," as he described it later, "that only [they] themselves could remove the difficulty." [110] The suggestion corresponded perfectly with the idea of Kentucky's independence that was already in Brown's mind. On a slip of paper he wrote, "In a conversation I had with Mr. Gardoqui, the Spanish minister, relative to the navigation of the Mississippi, he stated that, if the people of Kentucky would erect themselves into an independent state, and appoint a proper person to negotiate with him, he had an authority for that purpose, and would enter

109. John Brown to George Muter, July 10, 1788, printed in Green, *Spanish Conspiracy*, 171–172.
110. Dispatch of Gardoqui, July 25, 1788, printed in Brown, *Political Beginnings*, 146; in Green, *Spanish Conspiracy*, 106–161.

into an arrangement with them for the exportation of their produce to New Orleans, on terms of mutual advantage." [111] This he enclosed in a letter to Samuel McDowell, who had been president of the previous four conventions, and dispatched it by a special messenger, together with Congress's resolutions on the petition from Kentucky.

A few days later Brown called on Gardoqui to report that he had written home about Gardoqui's suggestion and that he himself was leaving for Kentucky August 1. He would keep Gardoqui informed, he said; he expected that the district would soon resolve on the creation of an independent state and that it would be under a lasting obligation to the Spanish minister. [112] To his mentor, Thomas Jefferson, he wrote, "I am sorry to inform you that from the present complection of affairs there is reason to apprehend that the Connection [between Kentucky and the maritime states] will not be of long duration. . . . There is every reason to expect that immediately on hearing that Congress have refused to receive them they will assume their Independence. Should they take this Step I think it very problematical whether or not they will apply for admission into the new Confederacy. . . . I hope that Kentucky will see the danger and impropriety of breaking off from the Union at this time and that it may still be in the power of Congress to conciliate their minds and to secure their attachment to the Confederacy." [113] He told James Breckinridge, "I pre-

111. This actually is not the original form of the letter, but McDowell's later recollection of what it said, the letter having been "accidentally" destroyed by McDowell's son. Certificate of McDowell, reprinted in "An Observer" [H. Marshall], 29–30, pamphlet in Wilson Coll. McDowell told Humphrey Marshall later that in this letter the objects "were more clearly expressed, than in the letter to Judge Muter." *Ibid.*, 4–5. See also "Kentucky Spanish Association," *Western World* (Frankfort), Nov. 1, 1806.

112. Dispatch of Gardoqui, July 25, 1788, in Brown, *Political Beginnings,* 146.

113. John Brown to Jefferson, Aug. 10, 1788, Boyd, ed., *Jefferson Papers,* XIII, 494–495.

sume Kentucky will proceed to establish her independence as tho she had been admitted and will apply or not to
the New Government as her Interest may dictate. If unanimity prevails in the District perhaps the present disappointment may be productive of good Consequences to that
Country." [114]

"Kentucky must and will be independent," [115] John
Brown declared to a Virginia friend. "In my opinion their
Interest requires that they should assume their Independ-
ence frame a Constitution and proceed to the exercise of
Government and when the New Government is in motion
then to make application to be admitted into the Union if it
should appear advisable," he wrote hastily to a relative in
Virginia; "I have engaged in foreign Negotiations which if
successful will be of great consequence to Kentucky—Am
not at liberty to inform you of particulars at present." [116]
Then he reported the conference with Gardoqui to several
Kentucky friends. To one he said, "We must act for ourselves—assume our independance—frame our Constitution,
and apply to the new Government for admission into the
Union as our interest and Circumstances may dictate. If
we are unanimous and prudent, we have nothing to
fear." [117] And he wrote to another, "Upon a review of the
Situation I am inclined to think they will find it necessary to
assume their Independence and organize their internal Government. This step appears to me to be advisable and necessary to secure unanimity and prevent licentiousness and
cannot have any effect to prevent their application for admission into the Union under the New Government which

114. John Brown to James Breckinridge, June 21, 1788, James
Breckinridge Papers.
115. John Brown to Archibald Stuart, June 25, 1788, Burnett, ed.,
Letters of the Continental Congress, VIII, 757.
116. John Brown to John Smith, July 9, 1788, J. M. Brown Papers,
Yale Univ.
117. John Brown to Col. Steele, June 22, 1788, copied in James
Speed to John Brown, Dec. 31, 1808, Brown Papers, Filson Club.

must require a considerable length of time to bring it about in a Constitutional way." [118]

To a few selected friends he confided the truth of his conference with Gardoqui. Besides McDowell, he wrote to Muter, "In private conferences which I have had with Mr. Gardoqui, the Spanish minister, at this place, I have been assured by him in the most explicit terms, that if Kentucky will declare her independence and empower some proper person to negotiate with him, that he has authority, and will engage to open the navigation of the Mississippi, for the exportation of their produce, on terms of mutual advantage. But that this privilege can never be extended to them while part of the United States." [119] In writing to other, closer friends Brown declared more explicitly that he thought Gardoqui's offer might be well for Kentucky.[120]

118. John Brown to James Breckinridge, Aug. 5, 1788, James Breckinridge Papers.
119. John Brown to Muter, July 10, 1788. This letter was first printed in the *Ky. Gaz.* (Lexington), Sept. 4, 1790; see p. 207 below. By 1806 only one copy of that paper was extant ("Kentucky Spanish Association," *Western World* [Frankfort], Nov. 1, 1806), but in Sept. of that year, it was reprinted from the original letter in the *Palladium*, the *Western World*, and the *Ky. Gaz.* Humphrey Marshall later observed, "There is good ground to believe that Mr. Brown did not consider Col. Muter as one of his confidential friends, and that consequently he was much more reserved to him, than to some others." "An Observer" [H. Marshall], *Western World* (Frankfort), Sept. 13, 1806.
120. "An Observer" [H. Marshall], 18, pamphlet in Wilson Coll.; "Kentucky Spanish Association," *Western World* (Frankfort), Nov. 1, 1806. Whether or not Brown did write other letters similar to those he sent Muter and McDowell later became a political issue. There are only two arguments for the negative position: (1) no such letters are extant, and (2) John Brown stated before the Kentucky legislature, as reconstructed from memorandum notes by his grandson John Mason Brown, that he wrote only to McDowell and Muter. These two bits of evidence are inconclusive. There was good reason to destroy such letters, as McDowell destroyed his and as someone destroyed all copies except one of the *Ky. Gaz.* that printed Muter's letter. Also, John Brown had good reason to deny writing such letters; there is evidence that under similar circumstances other members of the court party perjured themselves, and in any case the statement was reconstructed by John Brown's most loyal supporter, his grandson, from a memorandum note that no longer exists. The

Then he declared to a Kentuckian passing through New York that he had decided "to return home, and, on his arrival, to call for a general assembly of his fellow citizens, in order to proceed immediately to declare themselves independent, and to propose to Spain the opening of a commercial intercourse with reciprocal advantages." [121]

Only one of Brown's missives reached Kentucky during July,[122] the one to Samuel McDowell, which he had sent by special messenger in a packet with the congressional resolution denying Kentucky admission into the Union. McDowell received this bundle of bad news on July 29, 1788, the second day of the constitutional convention.[123] He immediately laid the congressional resolution and Brown's letter out on the table for delegates to read; the slip of paper describing the conversation with Gardoqui he reserved for future consideration.[124] The news that Congress had refused them took the delegates by surprise. Elected to frame a constitution and not for any other action, they soon resolved that their power was at an end. But they did not yet dis-

---

argument that he did write such letters is stronger. See his own statements in the letter to Muter, July 10, 1788, in *Ky. Gaz.* (Lexington), Sept. 4, 1790; to Gardoqui, Sept. 15, 1788, Gardoqui Papers, I, 379–386, Durrett Coll.; and in Gardoqui's dispatch, July 25, 1788, in Brown, *Political Beginnings*, 146. Several Kentuckians later claimed to have seen such letters; see "An Observer" [H. Marshall], 10, pamphlet in Wilson Coll., and the writer of the "Kentucky Spanish Association," *Ky. Gaz.*, Nov. 10, 1806, who spoke of "a copy of a letter from Mr. Brown to General Garrard now in the Possession of Mr. John Waller of Millersburgh, in which Mr. Brown has given his ideas of separation in a much fuller manner than in his letter to Judge Muter."

121. Miro to Valdes, Nov. 3, 1788, Gayarré, *Louisiana*, III, 222.

122. John Brown to Gardoqui, Sept. 15, 1788, Gardoqui Papers, I, 379–386, Durrett Coll.

123. Basic sources for the sixth convention are the manuscript journal, Ky. Hist. Soc.; list of members in Collins, *History of Kentucky*, I, 354–355; "A Farmer" [Harry Innes], *Ky. Gaz.* (Lexington), Oct. 18, 1788; Wilkinson to Miro, Feb. 12, 1789, Gayarré, *Louisiana*, III, 223–240; Littell, *Political Transactions*, 27–29, 94–95; Marshall, *Kentucky*, I, 289–293; George Walker to Innes, June 1814, Innes Papers; depositions in *Innes* v. *Marshall*, Durrett Coll.

124. Deposition of Samuel McDowell, *Innes* v. *Marshall*, 64, Durrett Coll.

band. The second enabling act had now expired, and they were all conscious that the Virginia legislature would have to pass a third enabling act and that another year at least would be lost before Kentucky could establish a constitutional independence.

In a private meeting of his court party friends Mc-Dowell, who was said to favor a violent separation,[125] showed the slip of paper enclosed in the letter from John Brown. Harry Innes, pacing the floor, made some reference to Vermont, which had lately declared independence from New York; then he nodded and said, "It will do; it will do." [126] The information about Brown's conference with Gardoqui soon became known to other members of the convention.[127] Someone noticed that there were now three parties in the convention, one group that opposed separation altogether, another that favored a separation only with the consent of Virginia, and a third group that wanted Kentucky to declare her independence, establish a government, and then—perhaps—apply to the Union for admission.[128] John Brown's letter helped to develop strength for the third group; [129] even Thomas Marshall was saying that Kentucky should establish her independence before applying to the Union for admission.[130]

Although they were now merely private citizens, since their power was at an end, the delegates continued to meet as the "sixth convention." Caleb Wallace rose and moved "that it was the duty of this Convention as the Representatives of the people to proceed to frame a Constitution of Government for this District and to submit the same to their consideration with such advice relative thereto as

125. Ebenezer Brooks to a friend then in Virginia, Oct. 25, 1788, published in *Western World* (Frankfort), Sept. 20, 1806.

126. Deposition of McDowell, *Innes* v. *Marshall*, 64, Durrett Coll.

127. Deposition of James French, *ibid.*, 121–124.

128. Deposition of John Allin, *ibid.*, 186. See also "An Early Inhabitant," *Ky. Gaz.* (Lexington), July 26, 1806.

129. Deposition of French, *Innes* v. *Marshall*, 121–124, Durrett Coll.

130. Deposition of Caleb Wallace, *ibid.*, 26.

emergency suggests." [131] The motion was referred to a committee of the whole so members could speak freely off the
record; there Wallace supported the motion by observing
that Virginia had already given her consent twice to Kentucky independence, and Benjamin Sebastian and probably
James Wilkinson argued that no good could come from a
connection with the eastern states and that Congress in postponing action on Kentucky's petition for statehood was
only deceiving the people.[132] The stammering Harry Innes
spoke almost eloquently in behalf of Wallace's motion.
"Mr. President," he ended a long speech, "when I reflect
on the treatment of the United States to this country, I feel,
I cannot tell how,—I feel, sir, like shedding blood." [133]

James Wilkinson reported to Miro, "The arguments used
were unanswerable, and no opposition was manifested in
the course of the debates. It was unanimously conceded
that the present connection [with Virginia] was injurious
to our interests, and that it could not last any length of
time." Yet, he had to add, "fear and folly prevailed against
reason and judgment." [134] Someone, evidently John Edwards,[135] a strong member of the country party, convinced

131. Minutes of the sixth convention, Ky. Hist. Soc.; Wilkinson to
Miro, Feb. 12, 1789, Gayarré, *Louisiana*, III, 223–240; deposition of
Christopher Greenup, *Innes* v. *Marshall*, 157, Durrett Coll. The
minutes do not say who made the motion, and Wilkinson lists
Sebastian and Innes, as well as Wallace, as supporters. Greenup says
Wallace made the motion in the seventh convention of Nov. 1788,
an error in time, for the minutes of the seventh convention record
no such motion then. See "Cornplanter" [Ebenezer Brooks], *Ky. Gaz.*
(Lexington), Sept. 20, 1788; Draper Coll., 18 CC 159; and George
Muter's statement when he published John Brown's letter of July 10,
1788, in the *Palladium*, Sept. 1806, printed in Green, *Spanish Conspiracy*, 173–175. See also "Kentucky Spanish Association," *Ky. Gaz.*,
Nov. 10, 1806; *Western World* (Frankfort), July 12, 1806, Nov. 7,
1806.
132. Wilkinson to Miro, Feb. 12, 1789, Gayarré, *Louisiana*, III,
223–240.
133. Deposition of French, *Innes* v. *Marshall*, 121–124, Durrett
Coll. See also the deposition of John Allin, *ibid.*, 186.
134. Wilkinson to Miro, Feb. 12, 1789, Gayarré, *Louisiana*, III,
223–240.
135. Deposition of French, *Innes* v. *Marshall*, 121–124, Durrett
Coll.

the convention that Congress had a good enough reason for postponing action on Kentucky's statehood petition. Perhaps Kentucky should wait until the new Congress took office so it could rule on the question of statehood for Kentucky. If the convention was unwilling to wait that long— for a third enabling act, a seventh convention, and a second presentation to Congress—at least they should refer the question to the people of the district. They had been elected as a constitutional convention, and they had no right to take on the authority of a legally elected legislature.

A partisan member, apparently,[136] now suggested that the convention determine the will of the people on the question of statehood by requesting militia captains to poll their companies. The articulate center evidently united to defeat this plan, with Thomas Marshall presenting their case. Whether they feared the will of the people might be against a separation or simply opposed instruction as a general policy is not clear; their arguments suggest both reasons. The officers, they said, "must be able and willing to give every necessary information to the people," a qualification "not necessarily belonging to militia captains," and they "should be perfectly disinterested and impartial, else the votes would not be correctly taken even if correctly formed," a situation "calculated to disappoint every honest man who depended on it for a correct result." Moreover, "such a measure would supersede the necessity of a convention, or deliberative body"; it was "to avoid the manifest mischiefs incident to such a course [that] resort was had to representatives and general assemblies, where all were to hear and be heard preparatory to decision." [137]

136. It was apparently a partisan member because the partisan "Cornplanter" [Brooks] favored the measure later, while writers for both the court party and the country party later opposed it. *Ky. Gaz.* (Lexington), Sept. 20, 1788; "A Farmer" [Innes], *ibid.*, Oct. 18, 1788, and "Poplicola" [James Morrison], *ibid.*, Oct. 11, 1788.

137. Marshall, *Kentucky*, I, 290. Humphrey Marshall drew on Thomas Marshall's notes, no longer extant, to write of the sixth and seventh conventions; it seems reasonable to suppose that the memo-

The committee of the whole devised a resolution, which the convention then accepted unanimously, that a seventh convention should meet the coming November with "full powers to take such measures for obtaining admission of the District as a separate and independent member of the United States of America, and the Navigation of the River Mississippi as may appear most conducive to these important purposes. And also to form a Constitution of Government for the District and organize the same whenever they shall judge it necessary, or to do and accomplish whatever on a consideration of the State of the District may in their opinion promote its interests." [138] So much power had been given to no other Kentucky convention except the abortive one of May 1787; that grant of power we can attribute to the court party. But in one respect the partisans and the country party had laid their mark on the resolution: they had specified that the new state was to be a member of the Union. More important, they had prevented the court party from undertaking a violent separation at this critical sixth convention.

Once again a declaration of independence was postponed, to be resolved certainly in one more convention. Once again the court party planned for a separation. Just as they had seized on the threat to negotiate away their rights to the Mississippi, using it to develop local antagonism toward Congress, so now they used the refusal of Congress to admit Kentucky to the Union. "Our most discerning men are of opinion that Congress will never fail to find an excuse," Caleb Wallace wrote to Virginia; "I wish we were delivered from a State of suspense which In no instance was ever more pernicious than to our infant settlements." [139] Now the court party's plan had become definite. First they would

---

randum notes he quotes here were Thomas Marshall's notes for debate. To make these passages readable I have edited their punctuation.

138. Manuscript minutes of the sixth convention, Ky. Hist. Soc.
139. Wallace to Fleming, Aug. 13, 1788, Fleming Papers.

establish the independence of Kentucky; then they could negotiate both with Spain and with the United States, accepting whichever offer seemed most advantageous. Once they had established independence they could manage their own future.

The controversy over separation broke out in the *Gazette* as soon as the sixth convention was ended. Partisans, thinking the question settled, had been silent an entire year; now again they brought out their arguments for postponing separation indefinitely. Signing himself "Cornplanter," Ebenezer Brooks reiterated the message he had presented as "A Virginian" a year earlier. "A separation on *any terms,* especially without the concurrence of Congress, would be the most *effectual barr* against a free trade through the Mississippi," he thought. Virginia was a "tender ruler," and the connection with her was valuable. Kentuckians could be sure a separation would be expensive, for "the first exertions of our new government will be a *heavy* tax." [140] He offered a complex argument that there would be no military advantage in separation, and finally published a Virginia law against independent governments within the state, a law directed at his former collaborator, Arthur Campbell.[141]

A member of the country party who signed himself "Poplicola" answered "Cornplanter" and managed to balance between the antiseparation of partisans and the violent separation of the court party. As Brooks had done a year before, "Poplicola" wrote a history of the separation movement. Brooks had used that device to argue that separation was against the will of the people, but this country party writer argued that the sheer number of conventions showed

140. "Cornplanter" [Brooks], *Ky. Gaz.* (Lexington), Sept. 13, 1788.
141. "Cornplanter" [Brooks], *ibid.,* Sept. 20, 1788. There is no longer an extant copy of this issue of the *Ky. Gaz.* but see the notes Draper took on it, Draper Coll., 18 CC 159.

"an almost irresistible public sentiment" favoring separation. Yet, he said, "some are determined to oppose." These partisans "convert the ill judged and intemperate propositions of two or three men, in the late [sixth] convention, into a powerful Combination" and "deduce the most terriffic consequences." The object of partisans, he added, was "to defeat a new Convention being called" and thus to delay separation.[142] "Poplicola" was satisfied that a separation would be desirable if it were legal.

Harry Innes, as "A Farmer," now gave the court party's view of the statehood conventions, arguing that strong public support for a separation was revealed in the several conventions' votes on that question—the second (May 1785), third (August 1785), and fifth (September 1787) having been unanimous, and the fourth (September 1786–January 1787) having supported separation by "a majority of more than three to one." He injected a new element into the court party's rhetoric by arguing that the conventions had always been solicitous to get the opinion of the people; the second convention of May 1785, he said, had postponed action because they "feared the good people in general had not sufficient notice," and the sixth convention of July 1788 had unanimously decided to "leave the whole matter again with the people at large." [143]

Although Innes began his history with a rhetoric of concern for the common man—"The nose of the poor has been held to the grindstone of oppression in this District ever since I became a resident"—neither court nor country party had demonstrated any real concern for the condition or the political desires of the people. Working from a premise that the people had a right to choose their repre-

142. "Poplicola" [Morrison], *Ky. Gaz.* (Lexington), Sept. 20, 1788, notes in Draper Coll., 18 CC 161. It is unfortunate that this issue of the paper is no longer extant and that Draper's notes are so brief, for Morrison's article might have provided further information on the obscure early conventions.
143. "A Farmer" [Innes], *Ky. Gaz.* (Lexington), Oct. 18, 1788.

sentatives, all of the old articulate center agreed that those representatives should then determine policy and make decisions without further recourse to popular wishes. The court party had been willing to violate this principle before the Virginia convention to ratify the federal constitution, when they had worked for the instruction of delegates. But in that case a majority of the people had supported their position; ordinarily they could not rely on such strong support. Now Innes argued against the instruction of delegates to the next convention, a plan being urged by partisans. "Popular opinion," he said, was inadequately informed to give adequate instructions; "if the common people, without any, (or perhaps with a *very partial*) representation of the *state of things,* must be called on to decide on *Knotty* and *intricate* points of state *policy,* any man with half a grain of sense, (even the simple Cornplanter) may see that unanimity is not to be expected in *any* public measure whatever." [144]

About the same time James Wilkinson used a controversy with a member of the country party to bring another new element into the court party rhetoric. Introducing the disagreement into the *Gazette,* he signed himself "A Whig" and addressed his opponent as a "late British officer." [145] This theme—the court party's identifying themselves with the "Whigs" who had supported the American Revolution and their opponents with the "Tories" who opposed it—would remain an element of their oratory for many years, although it had little, if any, justification in fact. In this case the man whom Wilkinson called a "late British officer" answered immediately and angrily, under the signature "Civis," that he had fought not against the American cause but for it. Using the partisan arguments against the court party, he added that it was "a favorite maxim with the Whig's friends, that Interest and Policy are the ruling

144. *Ibid.*
145. "A Whig" [Wilkinson], *ibid.,* Oct. 4, 1788.

principles of individuals and States," and that Wilkinson himself "would sacrafice that union [of American states], to the ambitious or interested views of a few individuals." Consequently, he thought, members of the new convention should be instructed by their constituents; they should not be allowed the absolutely unlimited power recommended in the resolutions of the recent sixth convention.[146] Thus this member of the country party had now taken up partisan arguments for instruction.

Just as these newspaper controversialists warmed to their task the court party suffered a blow so staggering as to be almost mortal: they were deserted by George Muter. The loss of Muter was not in itself a serious matter, for he was the party's weakest member even though as chief justice he held the most prestigious position in the district. But the court party's loss was the country party's gain, and with Muter the country party gained a fine piece of ammunition against the court party. Muter had always suffered from a deficit of original ideas, shaping his own opinion from the thoughts of his associates. Now he had moved from Danville to a plantation near Thomas Marshall's Buck Pond and had become a frequenter of the Marshall household. As he talked with the Marshalls, all of whom favored only a legal separation from Virginia, Muter too began to abhor the idea of violent separation. He showed Thomas Marshall the letter he had received from John Brown in which Brown told of his negotiations with Gardoqui; with such proof at hand, Marshall decided immediate action was necessary to prevent violent separation.[147] He wrote and persuaded Muter to publish over his own name a handbill demanding instruction of delegates to the November convention.[148]

Muter's handbill, later published in the *Gazette*, was a

146. "Civis" [James Hughes], *ibid.*, Oct. 11, 1788.
147. Marshall, *Kentucky*, I, 295–298.
148. George Muter, *Ky. Gaz.* (Lexington), Oct. 18, 1788.

turning point in the partisan and country party work toward instruction for delegates to the seventh convention. Because it achieved the instruction, it was also a turning point in the whole separation struggle. Soon after the handbill was circulated, militia officers in Fayette County met and drew up a set of instructions for presentation to delegates when they were elected.[149] These resolutions, which Humphrey Marshall thought "moderate," [150] were not quite along the lines requested by Muter. He would have directed the delegates "not to agree to the forming of a constitution . . . till the consent of the legislature of Virginia, for that purpose, is first obtained—not to agree to make any application whatever to obtain the navigation of the Mississippi, other than to the legislature, and the congress of the United States—to draw up and forward to the assembly of Virginia, a memorial requesting them to alter their acts for the separation of this district from Virginia, that the same may be brought before the congress of the United States, in the manner directed by the federal constitution." [151]

Ebenezer Brooks reported that the "sly politicians" at the muster "had the fortune to reconcile a small number" by "changing only what you will, for what you please.[152] The instructions as finally agreed upon read: "Gentlemen, we the independent electors of Fayette county, reposing special trust and confidence in your wisdom, integrity, and attachment to the weil of this district, have appointed you to represent us in a convention to be held at Danville, on the first Monday in next month, with authority to take such measures for obtaining admission of the district as a separate and independent member of the United States of America, and the navigation of the Mississippi, as may appear most conducive to those important purposes; and also

149. "Brutus," *ibid.*, Oct. 18, 1788.
150. Marshall, *Kentucky*, I, 298.
151. George Muter, *Ky. Gaz.* (Lexington), Oct. 18, 1788.
152. Ebenezer Brooks to a friend then in Virginia, Oct. 25, 1788, *ibid.*, Oct. 2, 1806.

to form a constitution of government for the district." [153]
The actual instructions gave the delegates a free hand in
the Mississippi situation, contrary to Muter's recommendation, and encouraged them to form a constitution, suggesting that separation could take place without the consent of
Virginia and Congress.

Both Muter and Marshall ran in Fayette for the seventh
convention of November 1788. Wilkinson and Wallace were
also running in that county, on a court party ticket and a
platform of independence, but they did so badly that on the
fifth and last day of the election Wilkinson disclaimed
any interest in a violent separation and announced that
he would be guided by the will of the people. He was
elected, but with fewer votes than Marshall, Muter, and
two other members of the country party.[154] Wallace was
defeated, but he declared that seven years hence the people would be convinced he and Wilkinson had been in the
right.[155] Later he said he had "declined a Seat in the Convention" because "if we obtain independence many will be
highly displeased, and if we fail a number equally great will
resent the denial," and he felt that "whatever Sentiment I
should espouse, I should expose myself to censure without
the prospect of doing good." [156] It is certain that he ran in
Fayette, though, so the statement was probably made out
of pride. In Mercer the court party fared somewhat better,
electing three of that county's delegates, sending exactly
the same men to this as to the previous convention, including McDowell, Innes, and Brown. Benjamin Sebastian was
elected in Jefferson, so all the court party was present at the
seventh convention except Wallace and John Fowler. The

153. *Ibid.*
154. Marshall, *Kentucky*, I, 298.
155. Brooks to A. Campbell, Oct. 25, 1788, published in the
Western World (Frankfort), Sept. 20, 1806, quoted in Green,
Spanish Conspiracy, 215.
156. Wallace to Fleming, Nov. 18, 1788, Fleming-Christian
Corres., Grigsby Papers.

country party, however, dominated. Few partisans were elected, and apparently none of their leaders were present.

John Brown, elected in Mercer as a member of the court party, had arrived in Kentucky only a month before. Even though he had negotiated with Gardoqui and had promised to keep him informed of Kentucky developments, Brown had remained dubious of the Spanish scheme. In Pittsburgh, exhausted from a stagecoach trip over muddy roads, without any company except that of his Negro servant, and worried about Kentuckians' reaction to his letters, he had written James Madison, "I am still undetermined what they ought to do in the Business I (in confidence) mentioned to you. I will thank you for your observations upon that Subject." [157] Arriving in Kentucky, seeing the opposition to independence, Brown almost deserted the Spanish scheme—although he did mention it to at least one man [158]—and absolutely refused to speak for it in public,[159] for his initial support of it had been based on Harry Innes's assurances that Kentuckians were on the verge of separation anyway. His hesitation was perhaps increased by Madison's assurance, "I anticipate every political calamity from the event. . . . I cannot but persuade myself that it will by degrees be viewed in all quarters as no less unnecessary than it certainly is critical and hazardous." [160] But James Wilkinson took Brown in hand. They discussed the matter for the first time, and Wilkinson somehow persuaded Brown to stay with the court party.[161]

When the seventh convention met, on November 3,

---

157. John Brown to Madison, Aug. 26, 1788, Madison Papers, IX.
158. This was Christopher Greenup. "Kentucky Spanish Association," *Western World* (Frankfort), July 7, 1806. See the controversy, *ibid.*, July 12 and 19, 1806.
159. Wilkinson to Miro, Feb. 14, 1789, Gayarré, *Louisiana*, III, 240–247.
160. Madison to John Brown, Sept. 26, 1788, in Brown, *Political Beginnings*, 195–196.
161. Wilkinson to Miro, Feb. 14, 1789, Gayarré, *Louisiana* III, 240–247.

1788,[162] the court party still hoped for a separation from the Union. Samuel McDowell was again elected president, an auspicious omen for the party. The same three parties were present.[163] The convention quickly resolved itself into a committee of the whole to consider the congressional refusal to admit Kentucky to the Union, elected Wilkinson chairman, and immediately began to wrangle about whether the committee could consider the navigation of the Mississippi. Thomas Marshall presented a long argument against considering the Mississippi just yet. It was, he said, "an improper mingling of subjects which should be kept as distinct in the consideration," for they were "different in their nature"; the first topic to be considered was whether the application for separation should go to the Virginia legislature; then, when the mode of separation had been determined, the navigation of the Mississippi might arise as a separate topic.[164] He was understandably anxious to prevent Wilkinson's effective oratory on the topic until after the convention had agreed on a legal separation.[165]

Wilkinson, however, immediately countered with an equally long argument for considering the Mississippi at once. It was vital to his cause that the convention consider the possibility of Spanish alliance before deciding on the mode of separation; he said it was vital to Kentucky, for it was not to be presumed that Congress would obtain the

162. Basic sources for the seventh convention are the manuscript minutes, Ky. Hist. Soc.; McDowell to Wilkinson, Nov. 12, 1788, Draper Coll., 33 J 133; John Brown to Madison, Nov. 23, 1788, Madison Papers, X; Wilkinson to Miro, Feb. 12 and 14, 1789, Gayarré, *Louisiana*, III, 223–240, 240–247; Thomas Marshall to Nicholas, Apr. 26, 1789, Innes Papers, XXII; Littell, *Political Transactions*, 29, 32; Marshall, *Kentucky*, I, 316–341; depositions in *Innes v. Marshall*, Durrett Coll.

163. "Kentucky Spanish Association," *Ky. Gaz.* (Lexington), July 22, 1806.

164. Marshall, *Kentucky*, I, 317. Here Humphrey Marshall quotes from Thomas Marshall's notes.

165. See Joseph Crockett to A. K. Marshall, Oct. 3, 1806, printed in the *Western World* (Frankfort), Nov. 1, 1806; A. K. Marshall, *Ky. Gaz.* (Lexington), Oct. 20, 1806.

navigation of the Mississippi for Kentucky. But Kentuckians could obtain it for themselves. The course had been indicated in the previous convention; he would not repeat it now, but every gentleman present would connect it with a declaration of independence, the formation of a constitution, and the organization of a new state, which could "find its way into the union on terms advantageous to its interests and prosperity." He elaborated further and then, having reached his climax, announced that one member of the convention had information of the first importance on the topic. He doubted not that it would be equally agreeable for the gentleman to communicate it and for the members to receive it. He sat down, and everyone turned to look at John Brown.[166]

Brown, under pressure from Wilkinson but still hesitant about the Spanish scheme, rose and said briefly "that he did not think himself at liberty to disclose what had passed in private conferences between the Spanish minister, Mr. Gardoqui, and himself; but this much in general, he would venture to inform the convention—that, providing we are unanimous, everything we could wish for, is within our reach." [167] Then he sat down. Thomas Marshall caught his eye with a look of disapproval; Wilkinson, expecting more from Brown, was caught unprepared but recovered himself quickly and rose to continue his oration. He had, he said, some knowledge of the subject himself. Ever desirous of sharing his knowledge as well as his mercantile profits for the general good, with the consent of the convention he would read an essay on the subject of "the navigation and commerce of the Mississippi." Then, hardly waiting for the

166. Marshall, *Kentucky*, I, 318. Either Humphrey Marshall had Thomas Marshall's notes to work from, or he had heard the story often. His version is far too vivid, and far too plausible, to be entirely the product of his own imagination.

167. John Brown to Madison, Nov. 23, 1788, Madison Papers, X; Thomas Marshall to George Washington, Feb. 12, 1789, printed in Green, *Spanish Conspiracy*, 250–253.

convention's consent, he produced a manuscript of fifteen or twenty pages and read it aloud, handing each page to Sebastian as he finished. Members of the country party heard with alarm that the essay was addressed to the Spanish intendant of Louisiana and gathered from what Wilkinson had already said that he had presented this composition to the Spanish governor during his 1787 trip to New Orleans.[168] Someone noticed that there were blank spaces on some pages, as if some passages had been omitted in copying the document,[169] and the clerk noted that Wilkinson did not turn in to him a copy of the paper, as was customary.[170]

Now members of the country party brought in two petitions asking that a "manly and spirited Address be sent to Congress to obtain the Navigation of the River Mississippi"; John Edwards, seconded by Thomas Marshall, moved that an address be sent to Virginia requesting a separation; and Joseph Crockett brought in petitions against violent separation signed by some three or five hundred Kentuckians.[171] Wilkinson, a member of the committee to draw up the address to Virginia, was overwhelmed by this evidence of public opposition to absolute independence. He wrote the address in a style "best calculated to excite the passions of our people; and convince them that Congress has neither the power nor the will to enforce their claim" to the Mississippi; then, he thought, "if Congress does not support them . . . not only will all the people of Kentucky, but also the whole world, approve of our seeking protection from another

168. Marshall, *Kentucky*, I, 319–322.
169. "An Observer" [H. Marshall], 28, pamphlet in Wilson Coll.
170. Testimony of Thomas Todd, *The Report of the Select Committee, to Whom Was Referred the Information Communicated to the House of Representatives, Charging Benjamin Sebastian, One of the Judges of the Court of Appeals of Kentucky, with Having Received a Pension from the Spanish Government* (Frankfort, 1806), 22.
171. Marshall, *Kentucky*, I, 328–329; deposition of Joseph Crockett, *Innes* v. *Marshall*, 175, Durrett Coll.

quarter." [172] Even Marshall and Muter had agreed that they would support a Spanish alliance if this application failed. Wilkinson was certain the application to Congress would fail, for he had been informed by John Brown of the eastern states' jealousy of the West; consequently he could write the application in confidence that it would be rejected and that Kentucky would inevitably be led to a Spanish alliance.[173]

Thus the seventh convention, given full power to do whatever "might benefit the people of Kentucky," expected by the court party to establish Kentucky as a state independent of Virginia and the Union, did nothing more than petition Virginia for a third act enabling a separation and petition Congress for the navigation of the Mississippi. Wilkinson thought it a politic postponement, as he wrote his Spanish friends at New Orleans, for another refusal would justify Kentucky in the eyes of the world. But in fact he was fighting major obstacles. Muter had left the court party, and Brown threatened to leave; McDowell was lukewarm; Fowler was not involved in politics; Wallace had been defeated in Fayette. Now he was reduced to Innes and Sebastian for dependable supporters. Moreover, he had heard no answer to his memorial, written in September 1787, which had been read to this seventh convention of November 1788 and sent on by Miro to the king of Spain. As yet he had nothing to promise his supporters; in fact, he did not yet even know whether the king of Spain supported his project of making Kentucky a Spanish colony.

John Brown, who always found it difficult to make up his mind, was in the throes of indecision over the Spanish scheme. In New York he had been under pressure from Gardoqui, on the one hand, and from James Madison, on

172. Wilkinson to Miro, Feb. 14, 1789, Gayarré, *Louisiana*, III, 240–247.
173. Wilkinson to Miro, Feb. 12, 1789, *ibid.*, 223–240.

the other; now in Kentucky he was appealed to by Wilkinson in behalf of the scheme, but he was also aware of the popular feeling against it. He wrote to James Madison, announcing the decision of the seventh convention to appeal once again to Virginia for a separation: "I need not observe that this measure puts an end to the subject which employed our confidential conversation. I always entertained doubts respecting the expediency of it but when on my return I found the District in a state of Political distraction I was fully convinced that at present it was not only improper but impracticable." [174] But to Gardoqui he wrote: "The political business of this country has been concluded according to the hopes I expressed to you personally. . . . We have little hope of this new state, and I think that in a very short time there is a possibility that the inhabitants of this country will accept unanimously the advantageous offer that you are so generously giving them." [175]

Wilkinson, however, was clever enough to provide for just the kind of uncertainty that John Brown was showing. He persuaded Brown, Benjamin Sebastian, Harry Innes, and Isaac Dunn to petition Gardoqui for a grant of sixty thousand acres of land on the Yazoo and Mississippi rivers.[176] This Wilkinson intended, as he wrote Miro, as "a recompense for the aid they had afforded me" [177] and "a place of refuge for myself and my adherents, in case it should become necessary for us to retire from this country,

174. John Brown to James Madison, Nov. 23, 1788, Madison Papers, X.
175. John Brown to Gardoqui, Dec. 17, 1788, Gardoqui Papers, IV, 402–405, Durrett Coll.
176. Petition to Gardoqui from James Wilkinson, Benjamin Sebastian, John Brown, and Isaac Dunn, Jan. 15, 1789, ibid., V, 59–66. Harry Innes's name does not appear on this copy of the petition, but Wilkinson stated in a letter to Miro, Feb. 14, 1789, ibid., III, 240–247, that Innes had signed it.
177. Wilkinson's second memorial, Sept. 17, 1789, William R. Shepherd, ed., "Papers Bearing on James Wilkinson's Relations with Spain, 1787–1789," Am. Hist. Rev., IX(1903–1904), 751–764.

in order to avoid the resentment of Congress." [178] Most important, the petition was designed by Wilkinson as a means "of engaging my political associates in Kentucky in some interesting affair likely to show up their principles and opinions, which would serve as a guaranty of their faithfulness whenever tested or jeopardized." [179]

The petition to Gardoqui had hardly been signed before John Brown was elected to the new Congress, representing Kentucky as a member of the Virginia delegation. (Wilkinson claimed that he had been offered the position but had declined "because my presence in Kentucky was very necessary for our purposes.") John Brown wanted to withdraw from the Spanish scheme, arguing that it was incompatible to hold a seat in Congress while negotiating with Spain, but Wilkinson was able to draw "a lively picture," as he described it, of "the Terrible spectacle that would accompany disunion [of the Spanish conspirers], treachery, and dejection of mind." After what Wilkinson called "some difficulty," Brown agreed to attend Congress as a spy for Spain, reporting all developments regularly to Wilkinson.[180] The petition to Gardoqui had been a wise move on Wilkinson's part. He had doubtless threatened to expose Brown if he did not remain faithful to the Spanish plan.

When in July 1788 the old Congress had refused to admit Kentucky to the Confederation, Virginians realized that the second enabling act, which provided for Kentucky to become a state on January 1, 1789, would expire before Congress could consent and therefore before Kentucky's statehood could be accomplished. Consequently the Virginia legislature had passed a third enabling act during its fall 1788 session. This new act stated that Kentucky could

178. James Wilkinson to Esteban Miro, Feb. 12, 1789, Gayarré, *Louisiana*, III, 223–240.

179. Wilkinson's second memorial, Sept. 17, 1789, Shepherd, ed., "Papers on Wilkinson's Relations with Spain," *Am. Hist. Rev.*, IX (1903–1904), 751–764.

180. *Ibid.*

become a state at any time after November 1, 1790, provided Kentucky assented to the terms of the law in a convention to meet on July 20, 1789, and provided the United States Congress consented before September 1, 1790. In addition to the same provisions made in the two previous enabling acts, the new law demanded that Kentucky pay a part of the domestic as well as the public debt of Virginia, and that all Kentucky land grants for a certain length of time had to be approved by the Virginia legislature before they would be valid.[181]

With an eighth convention scheduled to meet on July 20, 1789, the controversy over separation continued in the *Gazette*. One partisan, signing himself "Valerius," argued that the advocates of separation merely hoped to gain offices. He was foolish enough to add that he would never lay down his pen until the struggle was ended [182] and thus made himself a target for the court party poet, who wrote,

> Here lies, in this obscure condition,
> Valerus [sic] that great Politician:
> Who having just took up his pen,
> Death bid him lay it down again.[183]

In all, there were four answers to "Valerius." [184] Although all but one of them were better written than the original article, none bore as much weight as the article by "Valerius." "Valerius" took up his pen again just before the elections to the convention, still opposing a separation, urging the people to vote, and insisting that under a separate state the taxes would not be lower nor the laws more wholesome.[185]

181. Hening, ed., *Statutes*, XV, 788–791.
182. "Valerius," *Ky. Gaz.* (Lexington), Nov. 15, 1788.
183. "Hezekiah Stubblefield" [William Ward], *ibid.*, Jan. 24, 1789.
184. "Hezekiah Stubblefield" [Ward], *ibid.*, Nov. 29, 1788 (Draper Coll., 18 CC 195, 197), Jan. 24, Feb. 21, 1789; "A Layman," *Ky. Gaz.*, Dec. 13, 1788 (Draper Coll., 18 CC 201), Jan. 24, 1789; "Rantampann Manfolderoltomminy," *Ky. Gaz.*, Jan. 24, 1789; "Incognitus," *ibid.*, May 23, 30, 1789.
185. "Valerius," *ibid.*, May 2, 1789.

The most important article published in the *Gazette* that spring was by partisan Samuel Taylor, "A Real Friend to the People," opposing separation in answer to Harry Innes's pro-separation article by "A Farmer." Taylor's opponents insisted that he had "given a lawyer a guinea to write, and the printer ten Dollars to publish" it;[186] whether or not that was so, the article was well written and persuasive. Innes wrote in "the common place stile of aristocratic advocates," Taylor said; Innes's concern for the poor put him "in mind of a driver so seeing his ass nearly sinking under his load" who "out of pity to the poor animal—mounts and gives him the spur to keep up his spirits." Taylor recounted the history of the previous statehood conventions, insisting that the general public had never favored statehood, demanding rhetorically, "Has any gentleman ever yet told his constituents previous to his election that if they chose him he would consider them in favor of the separation? . . . Is not the unequal division of our landed property naturally calculated to promote an aristocracy? . . . Has there not been frequent overtures and even an actual attempt made to usurp a government independent of the general Union?"[187]

Except for the answers to "Valerius," the court party was silent before the eighth convention. Fearing that Congress would accept a petition for admission to the Union, they quietly threw their support to the partisans who opposed separation,[188] even though—as Thomas Marshall said to a newcomer in the district—"I have heard several of these Gentlemen speak in convention with great contempt both of the number and abilities of that party." John Brown argued that the provisions of the new enabling act were un-

186. "A Friend to Truth," *ibid.*, Apr. 18, 1789.
187. "A Real Friend to the People" [Samuel Taylor], *ibid.*, Apr. 25, 1789.
188. Thomas Marshall to George Nicholas, Apr. 26, 1789, Innes Papers, XXII; Levi Todd to Edmund Randolph, May 27, 1789, Palmer, ed., *Cal. Va. State Papers*, IV, 630; Wilkinson's second memorial, Sept. 17, 1789, Shepherd, ed., "Papers on Wilkinson's Relations with Spain," *Am. Hist. Rev.*, IX(1903–1904), 751–764.

acceptable; Marshall thought he simply wanted to continue as the only western representative in Congress, to be looked upon "as the Oracle of Western Politicks, and every thing respecting this Country be directed principally by him." In that situation, Marshall realized, he would "have it in his power to take *special care* of his own interest and that of his particular friends." [189] Accused of wanting a total separation, Brown and his friends insisted that they merely wanted to set in motion the new government without waiting for the further assent of Congress and the Virginia legislature.[190]

The eighth convention, scheduled to decide whether Kentucky would accept Virginia's terms for a separation as laid out in the third enabling act, met on July 20, 1789,[191] only a week after Kentuckians suffered the most terrible storm that most of them had ever seen. The sky was illuminated most of the night with an incessant blaze of lightning, and the corn and other grains were severely damaged,[192] but no one seems to have considered the storm a portent of good or evil to come. The members of the convention were an undistinguished lot; one visitor to the district who heard them debating thought there were "no able speakers among them," [193] and another observer put it even more strongly. "The folly of the District was fully represented," he said. "Dullness the offspring of Ignorance presided during the whole session save when an inroad was made on her dominion by the noisy, pert impertinence of Sam Taylor." [194]

Only one member of the court party was elected to the

189. Thomas Marshall to Nicholas, Apr. 26, 1789, Innes Papers, XXII; Nicholas to Madison, Nov. 2, 1789, Madison Papers, XII.
190. Nicholas to Madison, May 8, 1789, Madison Papers, XI.
191. Sources for the eighth convention are the manuscript journal of proceedings, Ky. Hist. Soc., and James Brown to John Preston, Sept. 3, 1789, Draper Coll., 5 QQ 122.
192. Ky. Gaz. (Lexington), July 18, 1789.
193. Diary of Joel Watkins, July 23, 1789, 23, Durrett Coll.
194. James Brown to John Preston, Sept. 3, 1789, Draper Coll., 5 QQ 122.

convention; that was Samuel McDowell, who was promptly and unanimously selected once again as president. Of the forty-four remaining members of the convention, only twenty-four had served in previous conventions, and of those twenty-four, five had first served in the fateful seventh convention.[195] The members spent a week considering the third enabling act and finally resolved "that the terms now Offered by Virginia . . . are materially altered, from those formerly offered and agreed to on both sides; and that the said Alternation of the terms is injurious to and inadmissable by the people of this District." The resolution passed by a vote of 25 to 13, with Thomas Marshall's son James and other members of the country party voting in the affirmative, and Samuel Taylor, John Campbell, and their partisan supporters in the negative.

Partisans had apparently reached a point where they opposed anything advocated by either party of the old articulate center. They opposed a separation from Virginia, but they also opposed the country party's complaint against the terms of separation, a complaint that would certainly have the effect of delaying separation. Immediately after the eighth convention ended, Samuel Taylor and his supporters got up a petition to the Virginia legislature complaining against the action of the convention, for which they were able to get several hundred signatures. The convention had met "under the strongest conviction," they said, "that it was not the will of the good people of said District that the same should be erected into an independent state," for "a separation may injoure us until time shall be no more." "A new Government here," they added, "will be clothed with no national power and . . . will only serve as one of Pharos lean kine to devour our liberty, whilst it can be of no security to our property." The convention, partisans insisted, had voted a protest against the terms of

195. This conclusion is reached by comparing the roll with those of the first, second, third, fifth, sixth, and seventh conventions. No roll is extant for the fourth convention.

separation when they should in good conscience have voted straightforwardly against a separation; now "the smallest alteration may be thought to san[c]tify the prosecution of a separation after cloaking their designs with a ficticious zeal for the public good." [196]

Partisans were still largely a group of men who owned little or no land. Of the 429 men who made decipherable signatures to the petition, 320 owned no land at all, and an additional 46 owned only 1,400 acres or less, the standard holding for early settlers, leaving only 63 of the 429 who had large holdings. More than half of the 429—278 men —had signed no previous petition; this suggests that they were newcomers to the district. Among the 63 men who had large holdings there were the inevitable land speculators—three of them had patented more than a hundred thousand acres each. Thus partisan policy was still determined, as it had been all along, by a few large landowners who feared to lose their property through excessive taxation if the old articulate center came into power in a new state.[197]

While the eighth convention was meeting and the partisan petition was being circulated in Kentucky, James Wilkinson was in New Orleans again. He took advantage of his presence there to write a second memorial to the Spanish authorities and to beg pensions for his supporters and his potential supporters in Kentucky. For Harry Innes, Benjamin Sebastian, John Brown, Caleb Wallace, and John Fowler, whom he marked "my confidential friends" who "support my plan" of making Kentucky a Spanish colony, he asked one thousand dollars annually. For Benjamin Logan, Isaac Shelby, and one other "man of influence" he asked eight hundred dollars each; these, he said, "favor

196. Petition to Virginia, summer 1789, Va. State Lib., also No. 58 in Robertson, ed., *Petitions,* 121–122.

197. Jillson, *Land Grants.* It must be remembered, however, that this measures only the land patented under Virginia, not land purchased from some other person.

separation from the United States and a friendly connection with Spain." For Alexander Scott Bullitt—"a man of ability and fortune, but very changeable; still he will be of use to our cause"—he asked one thousand dollars; for Humphrey Marshall—"a villain without principles, very artful, and could be troublesome"—he asked six hundred.[198] Wilkinson returned to Lexington by land with, it was said, six thousand dollars in Spanish silver and with a companion who enjoyed demonstrating his ability to pick up a sack containing two thousand dollars in silver.[199] It was a performance not calculated to remain unknown.

Wilkinson did not know it yet, but any real threat from his Spanish conspiracy was at an end. Kentucky was no closer to being a state than it had been at the end of the first convention in December 1784, but neither was it closer to being a Spanish colony. The work of partisans to prevent statehood had cancelled out the work of the court party for an absolute independence from the United States and a Spanish connection, leaving the conventions to do nothing at all or to steer a middle course. The first (December 1784), second (April 1785), fourth (September 1786–January 1787), and sixth (July 1788) conventions had done nothing but recommend the election of additional conventions; the third (August 1785), fifth (July 1787), seventh (November 1788), and eighth (July 1789) conventions had petitioned for statehood and membership in the Union. Partisans had dominated the first convention; the court party had directed the second through the fifth conventions; and the country party had controlled the sixth, seventh, and eighth conventions. Now they would remain in control until Kentucky became a state.

198. Wilkinson to Miro, Sept. 18, 1789, Shepherd, ed., "Papers on Wilkinson's Relations with Spain," *Am. Hist. Rev.*, IX(1903–1904), 764–766.

199. Daniel Clark, *Proofs of the Corruption of Gen. James Wilkinson* (Philadelphia, 1809), 15. Actually it was $7,000 that Wilkinson brought to Kentucky. Jacobs, *Tarnished Warrior*, 99, 100.

5

STATEHOOD ACCOMPLISHED

KENTUCKY was host to a number of distinguished visitors during the 1790s. Among them was Harry Toulmin, who first visited Kentucky in 1793. A free-thinking English cleric, Toulmin was seeking a place in a country that tolerated a variety of religious and political opinions, where he might raise his family and leave them in a situation to provide for themselves. He was also collecting information about the United States for a group of friends in Lancashire, England, who wanted to emigrate to America.[1] A careful observer, orderly, literate, outspoken about his liberalism in religion and his republicanism in politics, Toulmin had become a friend of James Madison and Thomas Jefferson in Virginia and carried letters of introduction from them.[2] In Kentucky he found himself congenial companions among members of the court party, the Kentucky friends of Madison and Jefferson.

1. Harry Toulmin, "Comments on America and Kentucky, 1793–1802," ed. George B. Toulmin, *Register,* XLVII(1949), 3; Isaac J. Cox in *DAB* s.v. "Toulmin, Harry."
2. Thomas Jefferson to John Breckinridge, Oct. 25, 1793; James Madison to John Breckinridge, Nov. 19, 1793, both in Breckinridge Family Papers, IX, 10, Lib. of Congress.

When Toulmin first arrived in Kentucky he visited the farm of Thomas Marshall, Jr., in Mason County, a fine piece of level land in a hilly but rich part of the district to which Marshall had moved two years earlier. The farm consisted of a thousand acres, which Marshall meant to divide into three parts, his twenty-two Negroes being too many to work a single farm. When Toulmin was there Marshall had fifty acres cleared from the virgin state of the land two years before. Of this he kept four and a half acres for pasture and meadow, planting one and a half acres in flax and the remainder in Indian corn mixed with kidney beans and pumpkins. In keeping with his family's lack of interest in the Mississippi trade, he planted no tobacco, seeking instead to make his farm as self-sufficient as possible. "It is peculiarly difficult for a man of property to hire a laborer," Marshall told Toulmin; "he must humor him a good deal, and make him sit at the same table with him."[3] Conscious of his own social position, like all the members of the court and country parties, Marshall no doubt disliked eating with his laborer almost as much as eating with one of his Negroes.

After being at Thomas Marshall's farm, Toulmin visited the estate of Alexander Scott Bullitt in Jefferson County, the same Colonel Bullitt to whom James Wilkinson had confided his plan to make Kentucky a Spanish colony, and whom Wilkinson had later found "a man of ability and fortune, but very changeable." Bullitt had only 500 acres in his plantation, but he had fully 150 cleared, fenced, and cultivated. Unlike Thomas Marshall and other members of the country party, he gave a large part of his land to the growing of tobacco; this may explain his interest in the opening of the Mississippi. He had, all told, forty-five Negroes, among them two spinners, a carpenter, a gardener, and other craftsmen; only fourteen—eight males and six females —were laboring hands. Bullitt's total annual income,

3. Toulmin, *Western Country*, 78–89.

figured in cash, came to £683 3s. 8¾d.; his plantation was doubtless one of the most important agricultural establishments in the district.[4]

When Toulmin visited Lexington he found it still a log village, with several farms in town, a number of large, hewn log buildings, and only a few brick houses.[5] To an outsider it probably looked primitive, but Mrs. Wilkinson could report that the society was good there, much preferable to that in the country. "I put John and James to School," she wrote to her father in Philadelphia; "the man is a Poor Simple looking Simon but he told me he was taught by Anthony Benezet of Philadelphia which Prejudiced me in his favor, and I Concluded he could not learn them bad Pronunciation." "At any rate," she thought, "it was better than running about the Streets."[6] In addition to schoolmasters, Lexington could boast, as one proud citizen put it, of "nailers, copper-smiths, tin-men, silver-smiths, watch and clock-makers, stocking-weavers, brewers, bakers, distillers, cabinet-makers, carpenters, saddlers, etc. etc. with a long train of other useful mechanics and manufacturers."[7] It was "the greatest place for dealing I ever saw," another visitor reported.[8]

It was not the crafts but the manufacturing which Toulmin found most interesting. "Kentucky is at present too much in a state of infancy for manufactures to have arrived at any considerable growth," he wrote; "it is probable, however, that no part of the United States would afford greater encouragement to the mechanics and the manufacturers of useful articles of almost every description." Toulmin noted, as others had done before him, that Ken-

4. *Ibid.*, 84–88.

5. Autobiography of Gen. James Taylor, 7, Durrett Coll., Univ. of Chicago.

6. Ann Wilkinson to John Biddle, May 18, 1789, *Pa. Mag. Hist. Biog.*, LVI(1932), 46–50.

7. "Artifex," *Ky. Gaz.* (Lexington), Aug. 4, 1792.

8. Journal of Needham Perry, 1794, Draper Coll., 14 CC 1–9, Wis. Hist. Soc.

tucky was capable of producing virtually every raw material that might be used in the manufacture of any useful article. (He even thought the district could grow cotton, an error, since the growing season even in the southern part is too short for that crop.) The distance of Kentucky from Europe and the east coast made prices of imports almost prohibitive, thus laying a natural high tariff on importations and offering a strong encouragement to locally manufactured products.[9]

For the benefit of his friends in England, Toulmin listed the most important manufactured products of Kentucky. They were leather, hemp, flax, wool, cotton, iron, other metals—copper, lead, tin, brass, and silver—wood products, paper, gunpowder, salt, sugar, manufactures from fruit, grain, and seeds—such as cider, brandy, whiskey—linseed oil, flour, starch, tobacco products, earthenware, hats, soap, and candles.[10] Many of these items were manufactured at home, but more and more independent factories were being established.[11] More and more, too, these items were appearing in the market, coarse fabrics being already "a drug in all the stores."[12] It occurred to Toulmin, as his friends in the court party had realized earlier, that ships might be built in Kentucky, their sails and rigs made by the hemp and iron industries, and the completed ship used to transport other manufactured products to New Orleans.[13]

Another visitor to Kentucky, at the same time, described its products in a slightly different way.

9. Toulmin, *Western Country*, 95.
10. *Ibid.*, 95–109.
11. See, for instance, Thomas Hart to Isaac Shelby, Oct. 15, 1793, Shelby Papers, II, Lib. of Congress; Thomas Hart to William Blount, Dec. 23, 1793, T. J. Clay Papers, 1st Ser., II, Lib. of Congress; William A. Leavy, "A Memoir of Lexington and its Vicinity," *Register*, XL(1942), 118–119.
12. Toulmin, *Western Country*, 97. See also Isaac Shelby to Thomas Hart, Aug. 24, 1791, Shelby Papers, Wilson Coll., Univ. of Ky.
13. Toulmin, *Western Country*, 97.

Here is found all the variety of soil and climate necessary to the culture of every kind of grain, fibrous plants, cotton [the same error Toulmin had made], fruits, vegetables, and all sorts of provisions. The upper settlements on the Ohio produce chiefly wheat, oats, barley, rye, Indian corn or maize, hemp and flax. The fruits, are apples, pears, cherries, peaches, plumbs, strawberries, rasberries, currants, gooseberries and grapes; of culinary plants and vegetables, there are turnips, potatoes, carrots, parsnips, cymbiline or squash, cucumbers, pease, beans, asparagus, cabbages, brocali, celery and sallads; besides which there are melons and herbs of every sort. The provisions consist of beef, pork, mutton, veal, and a variety of poultry, such as ducks, Muscovy ducks, turkeys, geese, dunghill fowls and pidgeons. The superfluous provisions are sold to the emigrants who are continually passing through those settlements. . . . Some   considerable   quantity   of spirits distilled from rye, and likewise cyder, are sent down the river to a market, in those infant settlements where the inhabitants have not had time to bring orchards to any perfection, or have not a superfluity of grain to distil into spirits. The beef, pork, and flour are disposed of in the same way. The flax and hemp are packed on horses and sent across the mountain to the inland towns of Pennsylvania and Maryland, and . . . in a few years when grazing forms the principal object of those settlers, they will always find a market for their cattle at Philadelphia, Baltimore, and Alexandria.[14]

There was more talk about the manufacture of cotton products than about any other industry in Kentucky. The court party had in 1789 formed the Kentucky Society for Promoting Manufactures (probably a descendant of the

14. Imlay, *Description of the Western Territory*, 88–89.

Kentucke Society for the Promotion of Useful Knowledge, for the membership was much the same), with James Wilkinson, John Brown, Harry Innes, and Samuel McDowell, among others, as members.[15] By the fall of 1789 the society had imported machinery from Philadelphia and raw cotton from Franklin (Tennessee) to the south and had begun to manufacture cloth and stockings. The company had bought a three-acre plot in Danville to serve as a garden for the factory workmen and had constructed several stone buildings to house them. The machinery was to consist of one carding machine, two spinning machines, and three or four looms each for cloth and stockings. "We hope that Kentucky manufactures will considerably reduce foreign importations into the whole Western country," one member of the company wrote; "we even expect to be in a position to supply the Spanish settlements on the Mississippi much cheaper than they are supplied from Europe." [16]

To encourage local manufacturing and keep currency from being drained out of the district, several members of the court party had joined with several partisans in July 1789, during the eighth convention, to pass an agreement against the use of "foreign luxuries." [17] According to the agreement no member was to drink any hard liquor, except Kentucky-produced whiskey, or any wine, except that made in Kentucky; nor was he, to purchase linen for more than a piastre or any woolen for more than thirty shillings. One could purchase in Baltimore or Philadelphia for one piastre what might cost three in Kentucky, for the prime object of the agreement was to prevent the draining out of currency, not to prevent elegant living. Members foresaw, however, that if they avoided the appearance of luxury, their in-

15. Kentucky Manufacturing Society, *Ky. Gaz.* (Lexington), Oct. 21, 1789; Speed, *Political Club*, 159–160.

16. Barthélemi Tardiveau to Crèvecoeur, Aug. 24, 1789, Oct. 7, 1789, in Rice, *Tardiveau*, 31–34, 35–38; George Nicholas to John Brown, Nov. 2, 1789, No. 715, Ky. Hist. Soc.

17. *Ky. Gaz.* (Lexington), Aug. 29, 1789.

feriors might have less incentive also to purchase luxury items. "If the men who are first in wealth and position do not display insulting luxury," they explained, confident of their own standing in society, "their inferiors will be less tempted to deck themselves out in frippery which would only show up their silly vanity, and the acquisition of which is surely burdensome to their pocketbooks." [18]

Humphrey Marshall, as unconcerned as other members of the country party about the Mississippi trade, thought the association against the use of foreign luxuries was "unquestionably a lump from the leven of Spanish intrigue." Such a measure, he thought, could only increase the distress of the people and "thereby prepare them for the more easy inflammation on the subject of the Mississippi navigation." The Mississippi was not Kentucky's only opening for exportation, he pointed out; where imports were admitted, exports would find a way out to pay for the imports. The result of prohibiting imports, he thought, could only be to diminish exports and thus to increase the difficulty.[19] Marshall's economics was as primitive as that used by members of the court party, but it brought him to a different conclusion. Somehow, every time the issue was raised, the country party managed to emphasize the Philadelphia-Kentucky trade rather than that between Kentucky and New Orleans.

Members of the court party were uniformly confident that Kentucky promised to become a center for manufacturing everything that the West might need. Toulmin asked one of them "what articles are raised in the State of Kentucky, in a greater abundance than can be consumed there?" "I answer," his informant said, "were it asked what articles *can be* 'raised in the state of Kentucky in a quantity' greater than the domestic consumption, the question could be more

18. Tardiveau to Crèvecoeur, Aug. 25, 1789, in Rice, *Tardiveau,* 31–34.

19. Marshall, *Kentucky,* I, 351–352.

readily answered, as there is scarcely a production of the earth, without the torrid zone, which might not be raised there in far greater quantity than the demands of the inhabitants, were a sufficient spur given to their industry." Pressed to answer the question as asked, he went on, "The articles in general which have as yet been exported are tobacco . . . ; hemp; flour; salted beef and pork; bacon; an inconsiderable quantity of whiskey, barley, corn, butter and cheese, and hogs' lard" [20]—all of them objects of home production. Manufacturing was growing in Kentucky, but it had not yet reached a point of exporting goods from the district.

The court party's dream of self-sufficiency and wealth for Kentucky through local manufactures and their exportation required the use of the Mississippi River. That is at least part of the reason why the party concentrated so on America's right to use the river. "I am only a friend to that [federal] union as I think it may be serviceable to my country," one member wrote to James Madison, after a long discourse on the advantages being offered to Kentucky by Great Britain and Spain, "and if I find that the powers of government are either with held from us, or perverted to our destruction then I should be compelled with my country-men, however reluctantly, to look out for other anchoring ground." [21] John Brown speculated on the consequences of a British seizure of New Orleans in a letter to Harry Innes: "The monop[o]ly of Trade—discouragement to manu-factures—introduction of Fact[i]ons . . . and probable separation of the western Country from the Atlantic States: are consequences as obvious as only require to be mentioned to be seen." [22] And a man at Louisville hinted, in a letter to

20. Toulmin, *Western Country,* 109–111.
21. George Nicholas to James Madison, Dec. 31, 1790, Madison Papers, XIII, Lib. of Congress.
22. John Brown to Harry Innes, July 10, 1790, Innes Papers, XIX, Lib. of Congress.

the East, "Nothing will separate this western territory from the Union, but wrong measures at home." [23]

Though the members of the court party had taken pains to keep secret their lack of devotion to the Union, there was still some talk in Kentucky about a Spanish conspiracy. Late in December 1790 an itinerant appeared in Louisville and declared, under oath to Thomas Marshall, that Miro had told him confidentially that John Brown, Harry Innes, Benjamin Sebastian, and James Wilkinson each had a colonel's commission in the services of Spain. His report, according to Wilkinson, was "too absurd to carry any weight with men of understanding, [but] has had considerable influence over the ignorant and inferior orders of society." [24] The rumor spread and was perhaps the inspiration of a writer for the *Kentucky Gazette* who declared, "I hear a whisper going about, buzzing the most fatal, poisonous and deadly sentiment that ever entered the human heart. That it would be best for us to secede, to revolt from the union!" [25]

Actually the court party was no longer actively working to bring about a formal connection between Kentucky and Spain. The Spanish government had made that unnecessary by opening the Mississippi River to American use in the spring of 1789.[26] This event had utterly destroyed any hope of success that James Wilkinson's plan of attaching Kentucky to Spain might have had, for that plan was based on the idea that Kentuckians as a whole, like the court party in particular, would give up their national allegiance to gain the use of the river. The opening of the river, added to the strengthening of the national government, had caused Wilkinson to change his plans from independence for

23. Letter from a man at Louisville, Mar. 14, 1790, *Md. Jour.* (Baltimore), May 18, 1790, Draper Coll., 3 JJ 485.
24. James Wilkinson to Esteban Miro, Dec. 17, 1790, Corbitt Papers, Filson Club; James O'Fallon to Miro, Dec. 17, 1790, Pontalba Papers, Filson Club.
25. "The Disinterested Citizen," *Ky. Gaz.* (Lexington), Dec. 11, 1790.
26. Whitaker, *Spanish-American Frontier,* 101–102.

Kentucky and a Spanish alliance to a policy of encouraging emigration from Kentucky to the Spanish colonies.[27] The Spanish conspirators were still working—"My attention to this affair takes up the greater portion of my time," Benjamin Sebastian wrote Wilkinson; "on principle, I am as much attached to the interests of Louisiana as any one of the subjects of his Catholic Majesty,"[28] and Wilkinson wrote to Miro, "Harry Innes is friendly to Spain and hostile to Congress, and I am authorized to say that he would much prefer receiving a pension from New Orleans than from New York"[29]—but they were no longer attempting to attach Kentucky to Spain.

With Wilkinson and the court party no longer working for a Spanish connection and with the partisans who had opposed separation quiet,[30] the ninth convention had met on July 26, 1790, and ratified Virginia's terms of separation.[31] The court party was once again conspicuous by its absence; only its supporters Isaac Shelby and Benjamin Logan were among the delegates. Not even Samuel McDowell, president of every previous convention except the first, was present; in his absence George Muter had been elected president, thus demonstrating the strength of the country party. One Kentuckian had written, "I from my knowledge of the Representation, fear there will be scarcely wisdom sufficient in the House to methodize the business: as the representatives here chosen, are so far from being the most enlightened Characters that on the

27. Wilkinson's second memorial, Sept. 17, 1789, in Shepherd, ed., "Papers on Wilkinson's Relations with Spain," *Am. Hist. Rev.*, IX(1903–1904), 751–764; Wilkinson to Miro, Jan. 26, 1790, Gayarré, *Louisiana*, III, 277–280.

28. Sebastian to Wilkinson, Jan. 5, 1790, *Gayarré, Louisiana*, III, 275–276.

29. Wilkinson to Miro, Jan. 26, 1790, *ibid.*, 277–280.

30. George Nicholas to Madison, May 3, 1790, Madison Papers, XIII; Nicholas to John Brown, Dec. 31, 1790, No. 715, Ky. Hist. Soc., published in Huntley Dupre, ed., "Three Letters of George Nicholas to John Brown," *Register*, XLI(1943), 6.

31. Basic sources for the ninth convention are the manuscript journal at Ky. Hist. Soc. and Marshall, *Kentucky*, I, 360–362.

contrary they are frequently from the lowest order of the people." [32] It had taken the convention only two days to resolve "that it is expedient for, and the will of the good people of the District of Kentucky that the same be erected into an Independent State" as specified in Virginia's fourth enabling act, passed the previous fall.[33] The resolution had passed by a vote of 24 to 18, with country party members Alexander Scott Bullitt, George Muter, James Marshall, Humphrey Marshall, and John Edwards in the affirmative, and with Samuel Taylor and his partisan friends in the negative. Kentucky's fate was finally settled. She would become a state, and a member of the American Union, on June 1, 1792.

"At present, all our politicians seem to have fallen asleep," Wilkinson wrote to Miro early in 1790. "Buoyed up by the privilege of trade which has been granted to them on the Mississippi, the people think of nothing else than cultivating their lands and increasing their plantations." [34] Kentucky was indeed politically sleepy during 1790, chiefly—as Wilkinson remarked—because there was no event to stir the people and their leaders. The parties still existed, however, lying dormant, ready to awaken at the next sound of battle. As another member of the court party put it, "The parties seem to rest on their arms; perhaps the proceedings of the next session of the Virginia assembly may set them in motion." [35]

By far the most important party in the district was the court party, an offshoot of the old articulate center, which had tried to speak for the whole people of the district.

32. Samuel Terrill to Garritt Minor, July 7, 1790, Terrill-Carr Papers, Univ. of Va.
33. Hening, ed., *Statutes*, XIII, 17–21.
34. Wilkinson to Miro, Jan. 26, 1790, Gayarré, *Louisiana*, III, 277–280.
35. George Nicholas to John Brown, Nov. 2, 1789, No. 715, Ky. Hist. Soc.

Weakened by the loss of George Muter and the impending defection of Samuel McDowell to the country party, it consisted now of James Wilkinson, John Brown, Harry Innes, Caleb Wallace, Benjamin Sebastian, and John Fowler. Almost all graduates of the College of William and Mary and almost all trained in the law, the members of this party were distinguished chiefly by the intensity of their interest in government. All friends with Thomas Jefferson and James Madison, they anticipated for Kentucky such a government as Jefferson and Madison had planned for Virginia, even asking those two statesmen to draft a constitution for their use. For Kentucky they dreamed of a commercial dominance over the western world; they expected to see Kentucky-made products shipped to the settlements up the Mississippi, to the Spanish colonies in America, and even to Europe. To make this dream real, they had brought Kentucky to the verge of statehood to give her the power of regulating imports and control over the grants of her own land; they had opposed the new federal constitution because it threatened Kentucky's nearly accomplished independence, and they had considered leaving the Union and undertaking a Spanish connection to gain a free use of the Mississippi River.

The court party had no formal organization and no discipline except that imposed by Wilkinson when he threatened to expose the Spanish connection; it was simply a coalition of personal friends and relatives, some of whom held office in the Virginia government of the district, all of whom aspired to office in the new state. As members the old articulate center had done, its representatives considered themselves the most capable spokesmen for the people of Kentucky and potentially their most able rulers. By 1790 the party had developed its own rhetoric, a rhetoric of the written word, for none of them except Wilkinson was gifted as a public speaker. Members of the party spoke of themselves as whig champions of American independence, announcing their support of every landless farmer in the district. Their policy, they claimed, was to make more land available by placing a tax on all land and thus ruining absentee landlords and the largest landowners. Actually, only the party faithful stood to profit much from the party's policies; they were interested primarily in making themselves the owners and governors of the new state.

In 1789 the court party was augmented by a new member—George Nicholas, one of a distinguished Virginia family of lawyers and jurists and an outstanding lawyer and legislator in his own right. Although he was only thirty-six in 1789, people already referred to him as "Old Nicholas" because of his disproportionately large bald head.[36] He was so fat that James Madison is said to have laughed "till the tears came into his eyes" when Nicholas was described as "a plum pudding with legs to it."[37] Nicholas had been a classmate of Harry Innes's at William and Mary, had fought in the Revolution, and had risen to the rank of colonel before the war was over. In the Virginia legislature he had cooperated with James Madison in the struggle to disestablish the English church in Virginia. As a member of the Virginia ratifying convention he had fought hard for the acceptance of the new federal constitution; yet when he migrated to Kentucky he immediately fell in with those who had not supported it.[38] Nicholas quickly became known as the best lawyer in the district.[39] He built a fine brick house in Lexington and established a plantation about

36. Robert Wickliffe, Sketch of George Nicholas, 12, Carter-Smith Family Papers, Univ. of Va.

37. Hugh Blair Grigsby, *The History of the Virginia Federal Convention of 1788* . . . (Virginia Historical Society, *Collections*, New Ser., IX[Richmond, 1890]), 79.

38. Thomas P. Abernethy in *DAB* s.v. "Nicholas, George"; Richard H. Caldemeyer, The Career of George Nicholas (unpubl. Ph.D. diss., University of Indiana, 1951); Nicholas Papers in the T. J. Clay Papers and in the Durrett Coll.; Nicholas letters in the Breckinridge Family and Madison Papers.

39. John T. Mason to John Breckinridge, Feb. 1, 1793, Breckinridge Family Papers, IX.

five miles from Danville, which earned a reputation as one of the most extensive in Kentucky. Visitors to it were intrigued by the diversion of a spring from its natural course so that it watered a large area of meadow and then turned a water wheel that carried two pairs of millstones, for the grinding of wheat.[40]

In Kentucky, Nicholas adopted all of the court party's positions: he wanted independence for Kentucky;[41] he insisted on Kentucky's right to the Mississippi River;[42] he even gave himself up to the dream that Kentucky would be a center of manufacturing and commerce. He told Harry Innes that he would make personal sacrifices to promote industry in Kentucky, for the future of the district depended on it; keeping his word, he soon became involved in two losing enterprises, the Danville cotton factory and the iron furnace in Bourbon County.[43] Like some other members of the court party, he also invested heavily in lands.[44] "A man of uncommon firmness and inflexible perseverance,"[45] as a friend put it, he had certain fixed notions of good government—chiefly the idea that the purpose of government is the protection of liberty and property, and that the best means of insuring liberty is a strong government[46]—and he was a tireless worker for their accomplishment.

Although it gained a strong adherent in Nicholas, the court party was soon to lose James Wilkinson, who was

40. David Meade to Ann Meade Randolph, Sept. 1, 1796, William Bolling Papers, Duke University.
41. George Nicholas to John Brown, Dec. 31, 1790, No. 715, Ky. Hist. Soc., published in *Register*, XLI(1943), 6–8.
42. Nicholas to Madison, Dec. 31, 1790, Madison Papers, XIII.
43. Nicholas to Harry Innes, May 4, 1789, Innes Papers, VIII, Lib. of Congress; Speed, *Political Club*, 159–160; Nicholas to John Brown, Nov. 2, 1789, No. 715, Ky. Hist. Soc.; J. Winston Coleman, Jr., "Old Kentucky Iron Furnaces," *Filson Club Hist. Qtly.*, XXXI (1957), 227–242.
44. Caldemeyer, Nicholas, 41–43.
45. James Brown to John Brown, Oct. 20, 1790, J. M. Brown Papers, Yale Univ.
46. Caldemeyer, Nicholas, 49.

about to leave Kentucky forever. Wilkinson invested too
heavily in tobacco during the summers of 1790 and 1791,
and his shipments to New Orleans were plagued with misfortune. One of his boats sprang a leak and sank; three
ran aground in the Kentucky River and could not be sent
down the Mississippi with the others; and, of 591,000
pounds that he sent south in 1790, only 262,000 passed the
royal inspection. His shipment of some 400,000 pounds in
1791 was equally disastrous, leaving him deep in debt to a
host of creditors. On October 22, 1791, by the recommendation of George Nicholas and John Brown [47] he was
given a commission as lieutenant commander in the regular
United States Army. With a military future in mind, he
departed from Kentucky early in 1792, leaving his papers
with Harry Innes, who would settle his affairs. All his
property was put on the market, and it proved enough to
satisfy the creditors.[48] "I am unfortunate and distressed," he
wrote Innes, "but I have ever deserved the Character of a
Man of honor." [49]

During 1790 the court party was rapidly changing from
a group of men in the service of Virginia to the same group
of men in the federal service. Because they were of all men
in Kentucky the least loyal to the Union, it was curious that
most of the federal appointments in Kentucky went to
members of the court party or their supporters. (President
Washington, who knew of the Spanish plan and was eager
to foil it, wanted to cement those people to the Union.)
John Brown, himself a member of the federal Congress, had
recommended his close friend Harry Innes as judge for the
federal district of Kentucky,[50] and his recommendation
had been accepted. Innes had been made judge (Humphrey
Marshall thought he took the position for the salary [51]), and

47. Nicholas to Madison, Sept. 16, 1791, Madison Papers, XIV;
John Brown to Innes, Apr. 13, 1792, Innes Papers, VIII.
48. Jacobs, Tarnished Warrior, 105–107.
49. Wilkinson to Innes, Feb. 29, 1792, Innes Papers, XXIII, Pt. i.
50. John Brown to Harry, Sept. 23, 1789, Innes Papers, XIX.
51. Marshall, Kentucky, II, 78.

John Brown's brother James had been appointed district attorney.[52] When James Brown quickly resigned the office, George Nicholas was appointed in his place, and Samuel McDowell, Jr., was made federal marshal.[53] As collector at the port of Louisville, Peyton Short, the business partner of James Wilkinson, was established, but when he resigned a country party supporter, Richard Taylor, was installed in his place.[54] It was to these federal offices that Wilkinson attributed, perhaps correctly, the downfall of the Spanish conspiracy.[55]

Unlike members of the court party, the members of the country party hardly thought of themselves as a party at all. They were just a group of men—the Marshall family, George Muter, Alexander Scott Bullitt, Robert Breckinridge, John Edwards, and Joseph Crockett—who happened to coincide in opinion and who happened to work together during the summer and fall of 1788 to prevent Kentucky from making a "violent separation" from the Union. Now that the crisis was over, some of them would support the court party. Many of the members of the country party were surveyors, planters at heart, and almost all of them held large quantities of land, which they were anxious to secure under a stable government. They possessed a strong loyalty to the Union; they were uninterested in the Mississippi River trade and interested instead in East-West trade routes. They considered themselves among the "best men" in the district —among the most capable and most qualified to govern— but they lacked the determination to govern that directed the actions of the court party. They had developed no rhetoric of their own and little party organization.

The most distinctive things about the country party were,

52. James Brown to John Brown, Nov. 29, 1790, J. M. Brown Papers.
53. *Ky. Gaz.* (Lexington), Jan. 2, 1790.
54. Tobias Lear to Richard Taylor, Feb. 11, 1790, Washington's letterbook No. 7, 264, Washington Papers, Lib. of Congress.
55. Wilkinson to Miro, Jan. 26, 1790, Gayarré, *Louisiana*, III, 277–280.

first, that it revolved around a single family, the Marshalls, and second, that its politics were based on personal animosity. There was a valid differentiation in belief between the country party and the court party—the difference between attachment to the American Union and indifference to it—but in practice the differences between the two parties had always seemed to be prompted by personal hatred. In particular Humphrey Marshall stood at sword's point with the court party. He had become a bitter enemy of James Wilkinson's in August 1786, when Wilkinson had defeated him for a seat in the fourth convention, and he had earned the wrath of Harry Innes late in 1787 or early in 1788 by writing the letter denouncing Innes's partner, Horatio Turpin. He had withstood the slanders that the court party privately circulated about him and the torrent of public abuse that Wilkinson had poured on his head; now he and his cousin James M. Marshall ran afoul of John Brown and his brother in the congressional election of 1790.[56] An announcement which John Fowler inserted in the *Gazette* the next year shows how the controversy continued: "Thomas Marshall, jun, having informed Maj. John Crittenden that I had said to him on some distant occasion 'that the said Crittenden was a rascal;' I think it my duty to declare that this information is a malicious fals[e]hood, in my opinion invented to answer electioneering purposes."[57] It would be many years before this personal flavor left Kentucky politics.

Partisans were the group most conscious of themselves as a political party, for they most often found themselves fighting against the ruling party. John Campbell, Samuel Taylor, Ebenezer Brooks, and their friends formed a party that actually did speak for the great majority of men in the district, those landless farmers whose major goal was the acquisition of a few acres to cultivate. These men had risen

56. See below, pp. 206–207.
57. John Fowler, *Ky. Gaz.* (Lexington), May 14, 1791.

in one great passion at the closing of the Mississippi, not because they dreamed of sending manufactured goods down, but because they expected to export their own farm products. They, like the court party, wanted to open the river, but unlike the court party they thought their hope lay in the federal Union. They had favored statehood when it seemed that they might upset the system of Virginia land grants by becoming a state through the Union, but they had opposed statehood ever since Virginia's claim to Kentucky had been confirmed by Congress. Virginia, they argued, was "a tender ruler"; a new state would only mean new taxes and perhaps a new system of land grants, which might destroy the claims that they had managed to make. This party, led by a few men who had tremendously large landholdings, was supported by hundreds who, like the majority of men in the district, held no land at all.[58]

In the late 1780s the partisan group had been strengthened by the arrival of a lawyer who did not immediately align himself with the court party. Only twenty-three when he settled in Kentucky in 1789, James Brown was already a graduate of William and Mary. Although an acquaintance described him as "a Young Man of exceeding good Character and Abilities," [59] he was actually never outstanding as a Kentucky lawyer, and as a person he lacked the brilliance and coolness of temper that belonged to his brother John. He was devoted to his brother, and handled both his business and his political affairs while John Brown was absent from Kentucky in Congress, but he early manifested a political temperament that was alien to his brother's position. In particular he was opposed to slavery and was always ready to work for its abolition. Soon after arriving in the

58. The available evidence suggests that the majority of Kentuckians were landless. See "A Real Friend to the People" [Samuel Taylor], *ibid.,* Aug. 15, 1789; "A Plan for Supporting the Civil List," *ibid.,* June 2 and 9, 1792; Toulmin, *Western Country,* 80.

59. George Mason to Thomas Marshall, Oct. 16, 1789, T. J. Clay Papers, 1st Ser., II.

district he made a name for himself by defending a slave charged with burning a fodder house,[60] the kind of case that the more outstanding lawyers would never have undertaken. As the years passed he associated himself more and more with the beliefs of the partisan group; in general, however, he did not like the leaders. Soon after his arrival he spoke of "the noisy, pert impertinence of Sam Taylor" in the eighth convention,[61] and he did not find his friends among the partisans. Yet his liberal convictions seem to have strengthened the partisan position, especially their opposition to slavery, although he never found his situation incompatible with support for his more conservative brother.[62]

James Brown's extreme devotion to his brother showed up in the congressional election of 1790, while John Brown was out of the district representing Kentucky in Congress. James undertook the job of developing support for his brother against his opponent, James M. Marshall, the son of Thomas Marshall. James Marshall had heard about the letter that John Brown had written George Muter on July 10, 1788, describing the overtures made by Gardoqui and announcing that a total separation from Virginia and the Union was necessary to develop the Spanish connection; in campaigning for the congressional seat he spoke often of this letter as an argument against continuing John Brown in Congress. James Brown heard the talk and denied categorically that his brother had ever written such a thing. Soon he had challenged James Marshall to a duel for lying, and only the publication of the letter prevented a public slaughter. George Muter, appealed to by James Marshall, was at first reluctant to make the letter public;

60. Shane's interview with Benjamin Allen, Draper Coll., 11 CC 67–69, also in *Filson Club Hist. Qtly.*, V(1931), 63–98.
61. James Brown to John Preston, Sept. 3, 1789, Draper Coll., 5 QQ 122.
62. Melvin J. White in *DAB* s.v. "Brown, James"; James Brown Papers, Lib. of Congress; J. M. Brown Papers.

after the business of a total separation was at an end, as he said, he had "avoided as much as possible, making it the subject of conversation," for he was reluctant to lower his standing with members of the court party any further. Pressed to use it to avert the duel, however, he consented to the publication, and the letter appeared in the *Gazette* of September 4, 1790, for the whole world to see John Brown's involvement with Spain.[63]

Despite the publication of his letter to Muter, John Brown won the election by a large majority. Reports of the election show the role of parties then in Kentucky. "You got all the Votes in Madeson Mercer and Jefferson," Benjamin Logan informed him, "but two in each County Mr. James Marshal got and his intrust was but half as good in Lincoln . . . for he got but one vote in Lincoln which was his Uncle Billey."[64] James Brown wrote to "mention the Names of those who were most active at your late Election. . . . Mr. Innes your heart will say must not be neglected. Col. Nicholas is really a valuable man. . . . He is becoming extremely popular, and his exertions at the late Election were such as discovered him to be a warm friend on whom you may safely rely. . . . In Fayette Gen. Wilkinson [who had not yet left Kentucky] still continues to possess the confidence of the people and convinced me, by his successful exertions on your behalf that he is much the most influential character in that County. . . . In Jefferson you have a

63. Deposition of Christopher Greenup, *Innes* v. *Marshall*, 161, Durrett Coll.; letter from George Muter, *Palladium* (Frankfort), Sept. 1806, in Green, *Spanish Conspiracy*, 173–176. By 1806, when it was desired to reprint the letter of John Brown to Muter, all copies of the 1790 *Ky. Gaz.* in which it was originally published had been destroyed except a single copy in the possession of Alexander Scott Bullitt. Green, *Spanish Conspiracy*, 177. By now even that one copy is no longer extant. "Franklin," *Ky. Gaz.* (Lexington), Sept. 15, 1806, suggests that the enmity between the Browns and the Marshalls went back to 1786, though I have discovered no evidence for it.

64. Benjamin Logan to John Brown, Sept. 27, 1790, J. M. Brown Papers. See also Nicholas to Madison, Dec. 31, 1790, Madison Papers, XIII.

warm friend where you did not expect one In Col. John Campbell. He is an intelligent old fellow, and very fond of your humble servant." [65] Partisans, then, had united with the court party to reelect John Brown to Congress, and the country party was not sufficiently organized to promote the candidacy of James Marshall.

"Let me know what effect the exertions of my Woodford [County] FRIENDS have had to lessen the confidence of the people of Kentucke in me," [66] John Brown wrote to Harry Innes during the election, referring to the bitter enmity that had developed between himself and the Marshall family. But once the election was over and he had safely won it, he proposed to his brother James that peace be made with that family. Insisting that his hatred for "every branch of that hostile family" had thoroughly subsided, James Brown still refused to consider any compromise. "The haughty insolent behaviour of this whole family, and the dishonest practices of some of them, have given offence to many Characters of influence here," he explained. "On the friendship of these you may calculate with certainty. . . . By compromising with the Marshalls we might disaffect these useful friends: whilst the reconciliation would be so cold and incomplete as to afford us no security for their future good conduct." [67] Thus personal animosity still dominated politics in Kentucky.

With the statehood question settled and with James Wilkinson out of politics, Kentucky was quiet during most of 1790 and 1791. Except for the election race between James M. Marshall and John Brown, observers might almost have thought political parties were dead. Certainly if parties had been dead no one would have been happier than the members of the court party. Having succeeded in bringing

65. James Brown to John Brown, Oct. 30, 1790, J. M. Brown Papers.
66. John Brown to Harry Innes, June 18, 1790, Innes Papers, XIX.
67. James Brown to John Brown, Jan. 10, 1791, J. M. Brown Papers.

Kentucky to statehood, they were eager for political distinctions to vanish so the "best men" could rule. By the
"best men" they meant, of course, themselves. But under-
neath the calm, the same old parties remained. The court
party was still resolved to make Kentucky a center for
commerce and manufacturing, still determined to open the
Mississippi for a free Kentucky trade; the country party was
still interested in East-West trade routes; and the partisans
still feared the efforts of the other two parties and were
determinedly loyal to the federal government. And the
hatred between the court party and the Marshall family
still existed.

As the year 1790 came to an end, as the ninth convention
accepted Virginia's terms of separation, and as Congress
approved Kentucky's petition for admission into the Union,
the leaders in Kentucky began to think once again about a
constitution for the new state. Members of the court party,
always interested in problems of government, had been
thinking about a constitution since the statehood conventions
had begun late in 1784. Having little confidence in the
ability of the people to govern themselves wisely, yet convinced theoretically that all power stems from them, they
were confronted with the problem of drawing up a plan of
government in which the people would elect their representatives, but in which the representatives would not be
guided by every passing fancy of the electorate. They
thoroughly distrusted "the idea and caprice," as James
Wilkinson had said in a different context, "that guides the
greater part of those whose imagination is trained by habit
and education to wander at will, without order or philosophy, not listening to reason or philosophy, until personal
misfortune or public calamity forces them back into a sane
way of thinking." [68]

In 1787 the Political Club had debated various consti-

68. Wilkinson to Miro, Sept. 17, 1789, Corbitt Papers.

tutional points, and the members had offered several suggestions for protecting the government from the whims of the general public. To limit the power of the electorate over their representatives, they resolved that elections should be held biennially rather than annually; [69] to limit the right of suffrage to those who had a definite interest in the well-being of the community, they resolved that there should be some qualification "other than freedom" for voting. [70] A bicameral legislature was desirable, they agreed, probably in order that the upper house could protect property interests; when a legislative act was contrary to the constitution, the judge ought to govern his decision by the permanent constitution rather than by the more temporary law. [71] In keeping with their theory that power derives from the people, they resolved that representation in the legislature should be by population and not by counties as in the Virginia legislature and the statehood conventions. [72] The Political Club's suggestion that some property qualification should be placed on suffrage was a markedly conservative one in a place like Kentucky, where everyone was accustomed to voting without question [73] and where limitations—if there were any—were agreed on informally by the various candidates, county by county, at the time of the election. [74]

Several times members of the court party had asked James Madison's advice on a constitution for Kentucky, and twice at least Madison had written a lengthy list of recommendations. Favoring a government of three parts, between which there was to be as absolute a separation as possible, he suggested various devices for protecting the

69. Speed, *Political Club*, 115, 118.
70. *Ibid.*, 125.
71. *Ibid.*, 139, 130.
72. *Ibid.*, 114.
73. Marshall, *Kentucky*, I, 197–198.
74. See the petition of John Waller, Oct. 28, 1789, Bourbon County Legislative Petitions, Va. State Lib.

government from the fickleness of the people. The most important was the establishment of an upper house in the legislature, the members of which would be elected every sixth year by voters who could meet a property qualification, thus forming a branch that could protect the rights of property and "withstand the occasional impetuosities of the more numerous [lower] branch," which would be elected annually without suffrage restrictions. In Madison's scheme the executive was to consist of a president—how elected he did not specify—and a council of state chosen by the people. Appointments to the judiciary were to be divided between the executive and the legislature; judges were to be protected from the whims of the public by being given life tenure during good behavior and a liberal salary so fixed that it could not be altered during their lifetimes.[75]

Once George Nicholas had moved to Kentucky, the court party had a member who had his own opinions about the constitution. Nicholas was less frightened of the people than his friends, more anxious to protect property from usurpation, and more fearful of conspiracy in the government. Like Madison he favored a bicameral legislature, the lower house to be chosen directly by the people, the upper to be selected by electors chosen by the people. The senate he thought necessary because "the factions and [the] unanimity of a single legislative body would be equally dangerous to the people"; it was to be given a broad character by choosing senators from the state at large rather than from a given district, and by giving the senators a long term it was to be protected from the "sudden and violent passions" of the people at large. The executive was to be elected by the people directly, as the best guarantee that he would be chosen for merit and ability, "without any undue influence from wealth, family, or faction"; he was not to be chosen by

75. Madison to Caleb Wallace, Aug. 23, 1785, Madison Papers, V; Madison to John Brown, Oct. 1788, *ibid.*, X; another copy in Misc. Bound MSS, Durrett Coll.

the legislature because that would open a door to "factions, intrigue, and corruption." A single executive was preferable because a plural one might lay a basis for "an artful cabal" able "to distract and enervate the whole system of administration." As for the judiciary, the judges were to be appointed by the governor, but the legislature was to have the right of impeachment; they were to be as independent as possible, holding office during good behavior and enjoying salaries high enough to remove the temptation of secret bribes. The basis for suffrage was to be broad, with every man who served in the militia and paid taxes enjoying the right to vote; otherwise an aristocracy would be created, Nicholas thought.[76]

Early in 1791 members of the court party and the country party began to present in the *Gazette* their plans for a constitution. The most cogent series was by "The Disinterested Citizen," probably George Nicholas himself, for this writer proposed much the same kind of government that Nicholas advocated. "The Disinterested Citizen" stressed the importance of laying barriers between the three departments of the government; otherwise, he said, the legislature would usurp the power of the other two branches. He favored a bicameral legislature, the lower house to be chosen by the people at large, the upper house to be selected by those who could meet some property qualification. "Two houses secure our freedom," he said; "if there was but one house a majority of its members would be good and ignorant." The members of the upper house were too likely to be independent of the people, but the members of the lower house "by their mistaken zeal and indiscretion . . . and by that passion and hurry so incident to a multitude, [are too apt] to overturn ransack and confuse the settled and established regulations of a political society." Thus "The Disinterested Citizen," like other members of the

76. Nicholas to Wilkinson, Jan. 23, 1788, Nicholas Papers, Durrett Coll.; Caldemeyer, Nicholas, 51–68.

court and country parties, distrusted the ability of the general public to govern itself wisely.[77]

Meanwhile partisans were forming their own plans for the new constitution.[78] Convinced that government stems from the people and should be responsive to the wishes of the people and satisfied that the annual elections were too corrupt to be conclusive, partisan leaders had in the past been consistently interested in "taking the sense of the people," as they put it, to determine what action the statehood conventions should take. In the sixth convention of July 1788, for example, they had recommended polling the people through the militia companies, for almost every adult male in the district was a militia member. Now they began forming county committees, composed of representatives from each militia company, to discuss the wishes of the people for their government.[79] Committees met in at least five of the nine counties in the district—Madison, Mercer, Mason, Fayette, and Bourbon—and then a joint meeting was held in Harrodsburg by representatives from three of the county committees. Comparing their proceedings, they found almost perfect agreement among the different counties' recommendations.[80]

The Bourbon County committee, probably somewhat more extreme than the others, made six recommendations for the new constitution: that the legislature be unicameral; that immoral men "ought to be excluded from all places of

77. "The Disinterested Citizen" [George Nicholas?], *Ky. Gaz.* (Lexington), Dec. 11, 1790, Mar. 5 and 12, July 2, Oct. 22 and 29, and Dec. 31, 1791, and Feb. 25, 1792.

78. These writers can be identified as partisans by their disgusted references toward the statehood movement. "H. S. B. M." wrote, "Was it the mind and will of a majority of the people, that we should separate from the State of Virginia at this time, if the sense of the people had been fairly taken by district elections, and committees?" *Ibid.*, Dec. 24, 1791. See also the article by the Bourbon County committee, *ibid.*, Feb. 11, 1792.

79. Fayette County committee, *ibid.*, Sept. 17, 1791; Bourbon County committee, *ibid.*, Oct. 15, 22, 1791, Feb. 11, 1792.

80. "H. S. B. M.," *ibid.*, Dec. 24, 1791.

power and trust"; that the people should have the right to elect their own militia officers; that there should be free suffrage by ballot; "that a simple and concise code of laws be framed, adapted to the weakest capacity"; and that all uncultivated land and other property should be taxed.[81] All of these suggestions were designed to take power away from the lawyers and large landowners of the court and country parties and put it into the hands of the people at large. Many partisans, including Samuel Taylor, also favored an emancipation of slaves, either immediate or gradual, and wanted an inexpensive government.[82] They disliked lawyers in particular; the concise code of laws that they recommended was designed to "happily supercede the necessity of attorneys, pleading in our state." [83] "The fewer Lawyers and Pick pockets there are in a country, the better chance honest people have to keep their own," [84] wrote one partisan, and another complained, "If lawyers should ever again get into the house of assembly, no doubt but the laws will be intricate and difficult, perplexed and entangled, and hard to be understood; for as the[y] expect to be often engaged in either sides of the question, those kind of laws best answers their purpose." [85]

The county committees themselves soon became objects of controversy, with the court and country parties opposing

81. Bourbon County committee, *ibid.*, Oct. 15 and 22, 1791.
82. "Philip Philips," *ibid.*, Nov. 26, 1791; "Brutus Senior," *ibid.*, Mar. 10, 1792. Most of the controversy over slavery was evidently in the issues of July 30 to Sept. 10, 1791, of which there are no longer any extant copies. See "Little Brutus," *ibid.*, Dec. 17, 1791, writing against "Cornplanter," who had opposed slavery. See also "Philanthropos" [David Rice], *Slavery Inconsistent with Justice and Good Policy* (Lexington, 1792). Rice can be identified as a partisan by his signature on the 1789 petition opposing statehood. The controversy over expense, like that over slavery, was in the lost issues of the *Ky. Gaz.* but see the answer of "Felte Firebrand" to someone who advocated economy, *ibid.*, Nov. 12, 1791.
83. Bourbon County committee, *Ky. Gaz.* (Lexington), Oct. 15, 1791.
84. "Salamander," *ibid.*, Dec. 24. 1791.
85. "H. S. B. M.," *ibid.*, Jan. 7, 1792.

them as determinedly as the partisan group favored them.[86] "That the county committees and the general convention should both engage in the work [of making a constitution], is too great an absurdity to escape the notice of any man," [87] one member of the articulate center pointed out; another tried to turn the argument the other way by declaring, "It is now to be determined whether we will give our unbiased votes as becomes Free-men, or submit to have our choice directed by Committees and vote only as they shall direct." [88] Partisans, however, conceiving that elections were corrupted by "flattery" and "grog," [89] made plans for continuing the committee system as a permanent part of the government. The corruption could be overcome, they thought, if the county committee did the work of recommending candidates before the election. The members of the committee were also to instruct the county's representatives, to petition the legislature, and to preside at elections.[90] Someone even suggested that the constitution should be submitted to county committees for their approval, and that the committees might be given a veto on laws passed by the legislature.[91] Partisans as usual were trying to cure governmental evils by putting power closer to the hands of the people.

Harry Innes gave the court party's reaction to partisan plans. "The people of Kentucky are all turned Politicians from the highest in Office to the Peasant," he wrote. "The Peasantry are perfectly mad; extraordinary prejudices and without foundation have arisen against the present Officers

86. In addition to the articles cited below, see "Felte Firebrand," *ibid.*, Nov. 12, 1791; "A. B. C.," *ibid.*, Dec. 3, 1791; "X. Y. Z.," *ibid.*, Jan. 14 and Feb. 18, 1792.
87. "A. B. C.," *ibid.*, Oct. 8, 1791.
88. "A Citizen," *ibid.*, Dec. 17, 1791.
89. "Address to the freemen," *ibid.*, Oct. 15, 1791; "H. S. B. M.," *ibid.*, Nov. 19, 1791.
90. Bourbon County committee, *ibid.*, Feb. 11, 1792.
91. "H. S. B. M.," *ibid.*, Nov. 19, 1791; see also the answer of "A. B. C.," *ibid.*, Dec. 3, 1791.

of Government—the Lawyers and the Men of Fortune—
they say *plain honest Farmers* are the only men who ought
to be elected to form our Constitution. What will be the end
of these prejudices it is difficult to say, they have given a
very serious alarm to every thinking man, who are determined to watch and court the temper of the people." [92]

And the court party did court the people. Just as they
had done in the elections before the sixth convention of
July 1788, which was supposed to be a constitutional convention, the court party urged that parties be forgotten and
the "best men" elected. The members of the convention
"ought to be men of INTEGRITY—of WISDOM—and who
have a COMMON INTEREST with us," one man wrote. "If
a set of novices should find means to push themselves
forward, they will only be able to establish, under the name
of a constitution, a collection of absurdities expressed in
unintelligible language, which will produce misery at home
and disgrace abroad. Designing men may possibly Insnare
us; but ignorant men even of the best intentions, like an
Ignis Fatuus will most certainly lead us astray." [93] Pre-
tending to be an unlearned Irishman, one wit reported a
conversation about lawyers from the meeting of county
committees at Harrodsburg: "Squire [Samuel] T[aylor]
put some cunning questions and col [George] N[icholas]
answered them, and one question was if lawyers were
necessary in courts, and col. N[icholas] said they were a
necessary evil, and he said too they had done a grate dele
of good . . . that unless larned men and lawyers too go
to the legislature we shall have ten lawyers to ware there is
now one and proved it to squire T[aylor]. . . . Now col.
N[icholas] is a grate reasoner and he said if unlarned men
go to the legislater to make laws, they could not understand
them when they had made them, and it would take all the

92. Innes to Thomas Jefferson, Aug. 27, 1791, Jefferson Papers,
LXVI, Lib. of Congress.
93. "A. B. C.," *Ky. Gaz.* (Lexington), Oct. 1, 8, 1791.

larned men and all the squires in court to make it out." [94]

The county committees' campaign against "great men" was apparently successful, for the members of the convention from counties where committees were organized were notably undistinguished. The country party elected Alexander Scott Bullitt, Robert Breckinridge, John Edwards, and Samuel McDowell; the court party elected Benjamin Sebastian, George Nicholas, Caleb Wallace, and supporters Benjamin Logan and Isaac Shelby; the partisans sent John Campbell, Samuel Taylor, and—as Taylor's colleague from Mercer County—Jacob Froman, among others.[95] (Humphrey Marshall remarked that "Mr. Taylor, a shrewd and . . . a crude politician, had his perfect contrast in the simplicity and ignorance of Jacob Froman.") [96] A few of the other members had served in the statehood conventions, especially in the eighth and ninth conventions which were so largely made up of undistinguished men, but at least a third of the forty-five members had had no experience in government at all. Presumably most of them were partisans, pledged to an economical government that would protect the people from the wiles of lawyers and large landowners. "I hope the deliberations of the Kentucky Convention will terminate more favorably than you seem to apprehend," John Brown wrote to Harry Innes after the election; "it would be a circumstance truly humiliating, if at this day when the subject of Government is so fully understood, Kentucky actuated by motives of niggardly economy, should adopt a bad form of Government rather than incur the necessary expenses of a good one." [97]

Despite the numerical superiority of partisans in the

94. "Philip Philips," *Ky. Gaz.* (Lexington), Nov. 26, 1791.

95. MS journal of the First Constitutional Convention of Kentucky, held in Danville, Kentucky, Apr. 2 to 19, 1792, Ky. Hist. Soc.; published by the State Bar Association of Kentucky (Lexington, 1942), *v–vi.*

96. Marshall, *Kentucky,* I, 395. To make it readable I have edited the punctuation of this quotation.

97. John Brown to Innes, Apr. 13, 1792, Innes Papers.

constitutional convention, the sessions were dominated by George Nicholas of the court party.[98] This was perhaps made possible by the pains Nicholas had taken to make himself popular among the people.[99] The convention elected as president Samuel McDowell, who had been president of seven of the nine statehood conventions; some petitions from the county committee of Bourbon County were read, and on the second day the convention resolved itself into a committee of the whole to begin its work. Nicholas opened the deliberations with a carefully prepared speech, designed perhaps to awe inexperienced partisans.

> Met as we are for framing a constitution or permanent form of government for this infant state, we are about to be engaged in the most interesting and important undertaking that can be entrusted to the deputed wisdom and virtue of any society. Man is employed in his noblest avocation when prescribing laws for his own government. . . . It is an occasion which fills me with feelings of exultation and pride, which language is inadequate to express. But they are feelings that will meet kindred emotions in the bosom of every one who hears me, when I tell you that it is the pride and exultation of an American citizen, in the exercise of that great right, the free exercise of which we have atchieved for ourselves and our posterity. . . .[100]

He then presented to the convention a series of resolutions, intended as a framework on which the constitution could be built. Providing for a government of three fully separated departments, with a bicameral legislature and free manhood suffrage, the resolutions were much the same as Nicholas

98. Marshall, *Kentucky*, I, 414.
99. "Philip Philips," *Ky. Gaz.* (Lexington), Nov. 26, 1791; Marshall, *Kentucky*, I, 395.
100. Speech of George Nicholas, Nicholas Papers, 20–23, Durrett Coll.

had advocated in his articles by "The Disinterested Citizen." He defended them himself, and they were adopted much as he had presented them.[101]

Only two points seem to have merited much discussion in the constitutional convention. One was the question of what court should have original (or first) jurisdiction over land claims. In the Virginia system the district court had original jurisdiction, but that arrangement allowed each claimant to the land to start a suit and permitted each suit a further appeal to the supreme court of the state, thus slowing any final ruling in the case.[102] Nicholas found that of around four hundred suits about land that had been brought before the district court of Kentucky in ten years, judgment had been given in only twenty-seven. Fourteen had been decided by the death of one of the parties, 40 had been dismissed because of an outside agreement, and 314 cases were still pending.[103] "I have it much at heart to see some plan adopted by which the land disputes may be specially decided," he had written to Alexander Scott Bullitt. "I think it may be done and in such a way as will do equal justice, and with more satisfaction to the parties than the present circuitous one can possibly give." [104] What Nicholas proposed was that local courts be bypassed and original jurisdiction be given to the supreme court of the state, with only one suit for each piece of land contested.[105] Finding that he had failed to state this plan when running for a seat in the convention, Nicholas resigned to let the voters decide the issue, confident no doubt that he would be supported by those who would be voting in a hastily

101. Note in Nicholas's hand, *ibid.*, 87; Caldemeyer, Nicholas.
102. Nicholas to Alexander Scott Bullitt, Aug. 19, 1792, William Marshall Bullitt Coll., Filson Club.
103. George Nicholas, "Courts," Nicholas Papers, 120, Durrett Coll.
104. Nicholas to Alexander Scott Bullitt, July 30, 1791, Bullitt Coll.
105. Note that Humphrey Marshall opposed original jurisdiction, Marshall, *Kentucky*, II, 26.

arranged election. He was indeed reelected and returned to the convention to engraft his plan of original jurisdiction on the constitution.[106]

The other point that was much discussed in the convention was the question of slavery.[107] Many partisans were in favor of emancipation—George Nicholas said that they had been "clamorous on that subject, as well in the convention as out of it." One of them introduced a resolution providing for gradual emancipation without compensation to slaveowners, and another made a long speech supporting the resolution.[108] In return Nicholas introduced and got the convention's approval for a resolution protecting slave owners from emancipation without their consent and without full compensation to them. Toward the end of the convention Samuel Taylor moved that the resulting article of the constitution respecting slavery be expunged, and a roll-call vote was taken on the question.[109] The vote was related, but not perfectly, to party membership. Of the ten members of the convention who can definitely be identified as partisans (by their vote against statehood in the eighth or ninth convention or by their signing of the petition against statehood), six voted to expunge the article and four voted to keep it. Of fourteen who can be identified as members or supporters of the court or the country party, nine voted to preserve the article, three voted to expunge it, and two did not vote. The vote was also related to land ownership, as these figures show: [110]

106. Journal of the First Constitutional Convention, 3; Marshall, *Kentucky*, I, 395; Caldemeyer, Nicholas, 73.
107. Hubbard Taylor to Madison, Apr. 16, 1792, Madison Papers, XV.
108. Nicholas to Madison, May 2, 1792, *ibid.;* David Rice, *Slavery Inconsistent with Justice and Good Policy, Proved by a Speech Delivered in the Convention, Held at Danville, Kentucky* (Philadelphia, 1792).
109. Journal of the First Constitutional Convention, 10.
110. Jillson, *Land Grants.* It must be remembered that this measures only land patented under Virginia, not land purchased from another patenter.

Voted to Retain Article on Slavery	Land Ownership	Voted to Expunge Article on Slavery
5	0 acres	5
1	1–1400	5
10	1400–10,000	4
10	Over 10,000	2

The vote was related to the ownership of slaves about as directly as to the ownership of land.[111] Those who wanted to protect slavery and to keep the article won, by a vote of 26 to 16. Some of those who voted for slavery, however, would have favored a prohibition on the importation of slaves, if such a plan had been presented to the convention.[112]

The constitution as adopted was just what the court and the country parties had planned for. About the only concessions to partisan desires were the provisions that all elections be by ballot and that sheriffs, coroners, and some militia officers be elected by the people. Free suffrage was provided for, but that was a desire of the articulate center as well as of partisans. The legislature was not made unicameral, immoral men were not excluded from office, and a simple code of laws was not provided for. The taxation of uncultivated land was ignored, slaves were not emancipated, and the people were not protected from lawyers and other extravagant "great men." The articulate center had succeeded in protecting slavery and in giving the supreme court original jurisdiction over land suits. They had protected the interests of property, too, by providing that

111. Joan W. Coward, in preparing a doctoral dissertation for Northwestern University tentatively entitled The Kentucky Constitutions of 1792 and 1799: The Formation of a Political Tradition, has constructed a chart showing the relation of slave ownership to the vote on slavery. The labor that it took to make the chart was immense. She shows a rough correlation between slaveholding and the vote, but an imperfect one, and attempts to explain the inconsistency.

112. Hubbard Taylor to Madison, Apr. 16, 1792, Madison Papers, XV.

the senate and the governor be chosen by electors. No property qualification was specified for membership in the senate, but "notwithstanding *all* have a right to vote and to be elected, the wealthy will nineteen times out of twenty be chosen," as George Nicholas said; "I will give up my opinion as soon as I see a man in rags chosen to that body." [113]

Nicholas wrote to James Madison, "We have formed our government which I believe you will think is not the worst in the Union." [114] Caleb Wallace hoped William Fleming "will not think [it] contemptable, though perhaps you may think it has some very popular features." [115] Samuel McDowell was more positive. "I think we will have a tolerable good constitution," [116] he wrote during the convention; after the constitution was finished he concluded, "Upon the whole I think it one of the Best in America." [117]

113. Nicholas to Madison, May 2, 1792, *ibid.*
114. *Ibid.*
115. Wallace to William Fleming, May 28, 1792, Fleming-Christian Corres., Grigsby Papers, Va. Hist. Soc.
116. Samuel McDowell to Andrew Reid, Apr. 18, 1792, Otto A. Rothert, ed., "Samuel McDowell's Letters to Andrew Reid . . . ," *Filson Club Hist. Qtly.*, XVI(1942), 176–177.
117. McDowell to Arthur Campbell, May 21, 1792, Draper Coll., 9 DD 69.

CONCLUSION

THE INAUGURATION of the new state government, on June 4, 1792, was an occasion for pompous ceremonies in Kentucky. Isaac Shelby, whom the electors had chosen governor almost unanimously,[1] and who had modestly kept them waiting several days for his decision because he "conceived his walk through life had not quallified him to fill [the office] with real advantage to his country or honour to himself,"[2] left his Lincoln County farm on June 3 to make the trip to Lexington, which was to be the center of government until a permanent capital was established. Passing through Danville, the city that had served as a capital for almost ten years, he received a congratulatory address and gave an address in reply; from there he was escorted to Lexington by a detachment of cavalry. Arriving in Lexington, he was met by the county lieutenant with more cavalry. His arrival was the occasion for a parade of cavalry and

1. "Coriolanus" [Humphrey Marshall], *Ky. Gaz.* (Lexington), Aug. 25, 1792.
2. Autobiography of Isaac Shelby, 26, Durrett Coll., Univ. of Chicago.

light infantry, a speech by the chairman of the trustees of Lexington, and another speech by Shelby.[3]

Kentucky politics did not end with the beginning of the new state government; in fact the new government only provided the occasion for a new episode of politicking, marked by the same parties, as bitter as ever. The same three groups would continue in Kentucky for at least two dozen more years, traceable in the voting of the General Assembly. In 1792 no one dreamed what the confused political picture of the years to come would be like, with the Democratic Societies, the 1796 race for the gubernatorial seat, the Kentucky Resolutions, the new constitution of 1799, and the resurrection of Spanish conspiracy charges in 1806. About the only thing anyone could have predicted was the continuing enmity between the Marshall family and the court party. By 1792 that had been a stable factor in Kentucky politics for six years, perhaps the single most determining factor, and it would continue to be important for many more years. Only that could have been forecast by participants. The remainder was too completely influenced by unsuspected outside events to have been predicted by anyone.

Kentucky history has been written as if Kentucky were a one-party area from the time of its settlement until the relief war and the Old Court–New Court struggle in the early 1820s. It is assumed that all settlers were liberal patriots during the American Revolution. During the prestatehood period attention is centered on those who wanted a separation, and during the early years of statehood interest is focused on the Republican Party. Actually there was much more variety in Kentucky politics than these monolithic accounts suggest. There were never fewer than two parties there, and during most of the early years three distinct parties were in operation.

3. *Ky. Gaz.* (Lexington), June 9, 1792; Autobiography of James Taylor, 8, Durrett Coll.; Marshall, *Kentucky*, 2, 1.

The discovery that there were tories in Kentucky during the American Revolution is completely new. Most of those who have written on Kentucky during that period have been so influenced either by local pride or by Frederick Jackson Turner's thesis of frontier liberalism that they have over-looked the possibility of conservative political sentiments on the frontier. In fact Kentucky seems to have served, during its frontier period, partly as a catchall for men who were undesired in the more settled colonies, including those whose political sentiments made them undesirable. Thus, the area apparently received a flood of refugees from the backwaters of the southern states, where toryism was the popular po-litical sentiment in opposition to coastal patriotism. In Kentucky loyalism seems to have been the same kind of frontier protest against the East Coast that it was in North Carolina. Some settlers, discontented with the Virginia land laws and the lack of defense provided by Virginia, ap-parently took the political position opposite to that popular in Virginia, and thus became loyalists instead of patriots.

Toryism in Kentucky did not last long, and it had no apparent enduring effects, but it is significant both as an expression of dissatisfaction with the rule of Virginia and as an expression of frontier conservatism. It reinforces a suggestion, which has been made by other writers, that the frontier liberalism hypothesized by Turner was no absolute sentiment, but a position of reaction against the coastal regions of the state. Certainly it is the proof positive that frontiersmen were not necessarily liberal.

Of the three parties that eventually developed in Ken-tucky, the most interesting is the group that the other two parties called "partisans." Beginning as a group of landless settlers chiefly from Pennsylvania and North Carolina, partisans opposed the Virginia claim to Kentucky, upholding instead the congressional claim and hoping that Congress would annul the Virginia land grants and redistribute the land of Kentucky more equitably. For five years partisans worked for separate statehood under Congress, trying to bypass Virginia. When it became apparent that Congress would not make Kentucky a state because it had recognized Virginia's claim, and when the court party began to take over the separation movement and work for statehood through the authority of Virginia, partisan leaders one by one turned against any separation and declared a desire to remain a part of Virginia. They were motivated, it seems, chiefly by an unwillingness to allow their political opponents to take control of Kentucky.

Partisans opposed a separation until 1790, when it became obvious that Kentucky would become a state despite their efforts to the contrary. They continued to exist as a political party at least for the first decade and a half after Kentucky became a state. Using a rhetoric of appeal to the common man, partisans declared that the great majority of Kentuckians did not want a separation, because of the extra taxes that would doubtless be imposed on them if Kentucky became a state. They denounced the other two parties as "aristocratic." After statehood became a certainty, they worked for a government close to the people—one that would consist of a unicameral legislature with representatives elected by all free men voting by ballot—and a state in which the laws would be so simple that the average man could understand them without having to rely on aristocratic lawyers. Partisans also wanted an emancipation of slaves, either gradual or immediate, without compensation to slaveowners, and they advocated a tax on uncultivated land. The most important item in their program, however, was the county committee, designed to discover the true will of the people and instruct their representatives accordingly. If they had had their way, the county committee would have been written into the constitution, to continue meeting along the same lines begun during the controversy over the state constitution.

Both of the two remaining parties had a common origin

in the group of bright and ambitious young men whom Virginia sent west as the surveyors and the district court of Kentucky. In Kentucky these young men formed an articulate center of a diverse society; as the upholders of Virginia's authority in Kentucky, they spoke for Virginia and worked for the establishment of Virginia's claim to the lands of Kentucky. They consistently opposed the statehood through Congress that partisans tried to establish.

Considering themselves the top rung of Kentucky society, the members of the articulate center believed themselves the proper rulers of Kentucky and expected to govern the new state just as the Carters and the Lees had governed Virginia—as an impartial public service. They shared with partisans a conviction that governmental power stems from the people, but they firmly believed that, once the people had elected representatives, those representatives should rule without further recourse to public wishes. In the opinion of the articulate center, the best trained and most experienced men could do better for the people than they could do for themselves. Consequently, they ordinarily opposed the instruction of delegates to legislature or convention; instructions could only tend to make unanimity impossible, limit the bargaining power of representatives, and tie their hands so that nothing would be accomplished.

Even though these men in the articulate center shared certain convictions about the nature of government, they eventually split into two distinct parties. Of these two parties, the most important was the group that came to be called "the court party" and later formed the nucleus of the Republican Party in Kentucky.[4] Most of the members of

4. The alignment of court and country parties with the developing national Republican and Federalist Parties is described in the closing chapter of my doctoral dissertation (Yale University, 1964). That material I omitted here because the end of the statehood struggle and the beginning of the new state government seemed the most logical place to stop one book and start another. For anyone who is interested, the dissertation is available on microfilm.

the court party were trained in the law, and the party comprised both the judges and the lawyers of the district court in Kentucky. Although they shared a number of political convictions, the essence of their organization was their common interests, their long-standing friendship, and their kinship within the Preston family.

Convinced by the long distance between the capital of Kentucky and the capital of Virginia and by the mountainous barrier between the two areas that the western settlements must be separate politically from the Atlantic states, the court party worked hard to make Kentucky a separate state. Originally they planned to make Kentucky a state through the consent of Virginia, intending that the Virginia land grants be guaranteed and that any partisan redistribution of the land be prevented. Later, as they realized what might be done with the uncultivated lands of nonresidents and as Virginia insisted on a free use of the Ohio River, they began to think in terms of a separation without the consent of Virginia. Still later, they began to consider the possibility of a separation from the United States as well as from Virginia and began to think of foreign aid, either British or Spanish, in the case of a revolution against the United States. They apparently sent James Wilkinson to New Orleans to negotiate with the Spanish for aid, and they eagerly embraced the idea of a Spanish connection that he proposed when he returned to Kentucky.

The court party's conviction that the West must be politically distinct from the East was reflected in their attitude toward the new federal constitution, designed to tighten federal control over the states. Their conviction that the eastern states would dominate the Union and that those states' jealousy of the West would prevent justice from being done, either in the case of land suits or in gaining the navigation of the Mississippi, led the members of the court party to oppose the constitution and eventually brought ten of the fourteen Kentucky representatives in the Virginia ratifying convention to vote against it. This was one case in which they were willing to forego their strong conviction against instructions for delegates, for they were assured that public opinion was behind them.

The court party's conviction that Kentucky must be separate from the East extended to economics as well as politics. They dreamed of making Kentucky a center of commerce and manufacturing to serve the whole Southwest and worked to make the dream a reality. Their conviction that Kentucky must manufacture her own necessities was frequently repeated in their letters to the East and in the newspaper articles that they wrote; in addition, they personally invested in manufacturing enterprises. It was their belief that, if money continued to be drained out of Kentucky for trade with the eastern states, the area would be impoverished, whereas if Kentucky could manufacture everything she needed and then export some of the products of her factories, she would be enriched, with no money leaving the district but with funds pouring in. (Their unwillingness to have money flow out of the district for taxes is another reason they advocated separate statehood.)

Thus the court party from the beginning was suspicious of the eastern states, opposed a strong federal union, and was unwilling to trust the fate of Kentucky to the action of those states which they distrusted. It was no wonder the court party members in the federal Congress opposed the strong economic measures advocated by Alexander Hamilton and joined James Madison in the opposition. They had been friends of Madison's all along and might have been expected to support him on that ground alone, but in addition they were instinctively opposed to any plan that would strengthen the national government. They were ready in 1788 and 1789 for the Kentucky Resolutions of 1798 and 1799.

The other party that arose out of the old articulate center, called the "country party" in opposition to the "court party," later became the Federalist Party, although it was much less interested in politics than the court party. The members did, however, have some convictions that were essentially political, and on two occasions they found themselves compelled to act on them. Most of the members of the country party had been surveyors and thus had acquired great quantities of land in Kentucky. With these large landholdings they were slower than the members of the court party in coming to favor a separation for Kentucky; no doubt they feared the loss of their lands in some such redistribution as partisans advocated. Once Virginia had passed an enabling act guaranteeing her grants of land in Kentucky, they began to favor a separation.

The country party was as convinced of the essential unity of the American nation as the court party was of the discreteness of East and West. This showed up in its unwillingness to undertake a separation except with the consent of Virginia and with a previous statement from Congress that the new state would be admitted to the Union. It appeared, too, in the attitude of members of the country party toward the new, stronger, federal constitution; they heartily favored it and voted for it in the Virginia ratifying convention. When it became apparent that the court party was thinking of separating from the Union as well as from Virginia, members of the country party were aroused to an intense political activity to avoid that possibility. They circulated handbills, wrote newspaper articles, got up petitions, and ran for membership in the convention. By such an effort they were able to prevent an absolute or "violent" separation in the critical seventh convention of November 1788.

Once they gained control of the statehood movement, the country party continued to be politically active. They controlled the movement until separation was accomplished, leading the district down the middle path of legal action, avoiding both the antiseparation sentiments of partisans and the desire of the court party for an absolute separation. In the new state they continued to act as a political party, supporting at times measures that encouraged land specu- lation, but at other times acting in the interest of partisan small farmers. In fact, in the new state the country party and the partisans often took a common stand on political questions, in opposition to the court party. In the federal Congress members of the country party supported the measures of Alexander Hamilton that tended to strengthen the national government; thus they continued to think in terms of the unity of the nation and the importance of a strong national government.

The Federalist and Republican parties in Kentucky were remarkably similar in origin and in social status. Despite their differences in attitudes toward the West, they had a common idea about the nature of government. Sharing a conviction that they alone were suitable to govern the state, they both looked down on the abilities and interests of partisans. Their government, they thought, was one in which the best-qualified men would deliberate impartially (without thought of personal interest) and would then do what was best for the people of the state, whether or not the people wanted it done. In establishing the government of the new state Federalists and Republicans were able to cooperate because they did share this common idea. Al- though they seldom worked together at other times, they were able to cooperate on the writing of constitutions be- cause they agreed on the nature of government.

The views of the Republican Party were unlike the ideology of Thomas Jefferson, which the members professed to accept. Though they did believe that governmental power rests with the people at large, in fact they had little respect for popular desires. Certainly they did not share with Jefferson the idea that the people, if informed, could do no wrong. In the view of the Kentucky Republican Party, the people at large could never be sufficiently impartial to know what was best for the community; it was essential that the rights of property be protected from their attacks. Too much democracy, in the eyes of Republicans, was a mistake, for the people were incapable of establishing any policy and then following it through. Nor were Republicans interested in establishing a community dominated by small farmers, as Jefferson was. The small farmer was the very man they distrusted as partial; they worked instead to establish manufactures to make the community self-sufficient and they wanted to put the manufacturer and large property owner in control of the state.

That all three Kentucky parties were established by 1785, with their views clearly defined at that time, suggests that the date ordinarily given for the origin of parties in the United States is mistaken. Most recent writers have abandoned the old idea that the national parties were simply groupings of local parties welded together on a national level; the preferred view now is that parties first developed on the national level, out of the struggle over Hamilton's economic proposals and the fight over the Jay Treaty, that they began to develop in 1792 and were fully grown by 1795.[5] According to these recent writers, the parties then filtered down to the state level after their origin in the federal Congress. But their earlier existence in Kentucky and the fact that Kentucky's members of Congress voted, after their admission in 1792, according to the positions they had previously taken in state politics, proves that in one state at least parties did operate on the state level before they developed in Congress. It suggests that historians might look back to the states for the origin of the positions taken in Congress on Hamilton's economic proposals.

Thus the three parties in Kentucky suggest a national

5. Joseph Charles, *The Origins of the American Party System* (Chapel Hill, 1956); Noble E. Cunningham, Jr., *The Jeffersonian Republicans: The Formation of a Party Organization, 1789–1801* (Chapel Hill, 1957).

political situation that has not yet been explored. One historian has indicated his belief that a two-party system developed in the United States because the national administration took strong measures and definite united opposition was necessary to counter it.[6] Another writer, however, has suggested that a full-blown two-party system did not exist until a whole generation raised under the very tentative early party system came to power.[7] The three-party situation in Kentucky, which lasted for many years, at least until 1816, indicates that no two-party ideal was fixed in the minds of Kentuckians. A multi-party system could have emerged, had not the national situation and the necessity for local groups to make a national alliance eventually dictated the death of the third party. The existence in 1788 of four rather inspecific parties in five states and three in one,[8] and the famous threefold division during the American Revolution (as described by John Adams), reinforce this idea.

Very little attention has been given to the opposition to separation in Kentucky. The only other historian who has written about it has assumed that it was a movement of conservative large landowners who feared the loss of their lands through heavy taxation, and he has used this theory to prove that the small farmers—whom he assumes favored separation—actually were the "liberal" democrats that his mentor, Fredrick Jackson Turner, asserted them to be.[9] In fact the apparently "conservative" opposition to statehood came from the "liberal" small farmers who were otherwise

6. Lisle A. Rose, *Prologue to Democracy: The Federalists in the South, 1789–1800* (Lexington, 1968), 5.

7. Michael Wallace, "Changing Concepts of Party in the United States: New York, 1815–1828," *Am. Hist. Rev.*, LXXIV (1968–1969), 453–491.

8. Forrest McDonald, *We the People: The Economic Origins of the Constitution* (Chicago, 1958), chap. 2. McDonald's material on Virginia is so inaccurate that I hesitate to draw on him for information, however.

9. Barnhart, *Valley of Democracy*.

the democrats of the frontier, working to make government a direct function of the people, and the "liberal" movement for statehood came from the "conservative" landowners who were working for separation in order to protect the status quo. The attitudes of Kentuckians toward separation and statehood simply do not fit into the neat categories of "liberal" and "conservative" that frontier historians have devised.

The existence of a third party in early Kentucky politics comes as a surprise. Humphrey Marshall intimated that there were three parties operating, and one member of the sixth convention of July 1788 related specifically that three groups existed in that convention, but later historians have failed to take these suggestions seriously. Actually the third party—the group called "partisans"—had a firm and definite existence from 1779 on. Like the members of the other two parties, its members changed their position on the statehood question around 1785, but the leaders of the party and the kind of person they represented (the small farmer) remained the same; thus the continuity of the party cannot be questioned. This party, the group that opposed statehood, was the most democratic in the state, in the sense of working to bring government closer to the people. Their work makes the other two parties—even the Republicans, who have traditionally been considered liberals —seen very conservative indeed. The Federalists more often cooperated with partisans than the Republicans did; consequently in Kentucky the Federalists can be considered more liberal than Republicans.

Thus Kentucky was an area where there were three parties instead of the traditional two, where the liberal small farmers adopted an apparently conservative policy of opposing statehood, where Federalists were more liberal than Republicans. Whatever else may be said about Kentucky politics, it was not conventional.

BIBLIOGRAPHY

KENTUCKY history is almost as old as Kentucky is. The system of claiming lands established by the Virginia legislature in 1779—that families who had settled in Kentucky before January 1, 1778, and had either lived there a year or raised a crop of corn were entitled to claim four hundred acres [1]—insured an interest in the history of the early settlements in Kentucky. When the court of land commissioners visited Kentucky in the winter of 1779/1780 they took depositions from early settlers to help establish claims. These settlers continued to write down their recollections in depositions and letters for thirty years and more, as long as lawsuits over land ownership persisted.[2] These writings are now, of course, valuable sources for the historian of the frontier.

Once the *Kentucke Gazette* began publication, in the midst of the statehood struggle, there was another practical incentive for the study of Kentucky history. During its first two years the *Gazette* printed four long histories of the

1. Hening, ed., *Statutes,* X, 35–50.
2. These papers are to be found in almost every collection of manuscripts of early settlers and early lawyers. See, for instance, the interesting letter of Isaac Shelby to Thomas Lewis, May 12, 1798, Shelby Papers, III, Lib. of Congress.

statehood struggle, all designed to prove some political point. Ebenezer Brooks wrote as "A Virginian" to show how, as the court party's reasons for a separation diminished, it worked harder and harder to achieve it;[3] both James Morrison of the country party ("Poplicola") and Harry Innes of the court party ("A Farmer") contended that the sheer number of statehood conventions, as well as the near unanimity in each, showed an overwhelming popular support for separation;[4] and finally Samuel Taylor as "A Real Friend to the People" argued that only those aristocrats who billed themselves as "the trusty few" wanted separation, while the common people continuously opposed such a move.[5] These political histories give an invaluable picture of the early statehood conventions, in addition to showing the course of political controversy over statehood.

Personal controversies often provoked the resurrection of past events in the *Gazette;* most politicians did not hesitate to bring out even the most scandalous occurrences to confound their opponents. The most spectacular controversy, though it was but one of many, was the dispute between James Wilkinson and Humphrey Marshall,[6] in which Wilkinson aired every disreputable facet of Marshall's past that he could learn about, giving future historians many clues about Marshall that they would not otherwise possess. It is only a pity that the editors of the *Gazette* declined to print Marshall's attack on Wilkinson,[7] for it presumably would have given equally interesting suggestions about Wilkinson's past.

Thus Kentuckians began to argue about their history almost as soon as they made it, long before Kentucky was a populous community with leisure for the social sciences. Depositions and old letters were published in the news-

3. *Ky. Gaz.* (Lexington), Sept. 1, 1787.

4. *Ibid.*, Sept. 20, 1788, Oct. 18, 1788. There is no longer a copy of the *Ky. Gaz.* for Sept. 20, 1788, extant, but see Draper's notes on the article by "Poplicola," Draper Coll., 18 CC 161.

5. *Ky. Gaz.* (Lexington), Apr. 25, 1789.

6. Jordan Harris [James Wilkinson], *ibid.*, Mar. 22, 29, Apr. 5, 12, 26, 1788.

7. Editorial, *ibid.*, May 10, 1788.

paper, and chronicles were composed so soon after the event that they are primary as well as secondary sources. Since the quarrels were local, the chroniclers were natives. When more scholarly historians have taken up the topic, they too have often been influenced by contemporary social questions or occasionally by contemporary academic disputes. These influences have almost always been local; thus the historians, like the chroniclers, have been natives. Kentucky history has seldom been touched by foreign hands. And the present study is no exception!

It is easy to see the influence of party on the chroniclers, and the historians have proved many of their statements inaccurate. Yet the chroniclers are frequently followed, in their general outline and interpretation of events, by the very historians who dispute their facts so hotly. This has given Kentucky history, as written by Kentuckians, an asp-like quality. It expands in length, rather than in breadth, and its curves are so often entangled with current politics that the written history is almost as interesting a topic as the lived history.

I. SOURCES

So biased is all the historical work on the early history of Kentucky that it is necessary to go to the sources to find out what really happened. And of sources there is a great wealth; for this study I have examined materials in twenty different libraries, some containing many collections.

Curiously enough, virtually all of the extant papers belonged to members of the court party. It is no wonder historians have thought Kentucky universally a Republican state. I have found only three collections of papers of Kentucky Federalists; of those two are small and belong to a period later than this study covers: the manuscripts of Samuel and Joseph Hamilton Daveiss (two boxes, Filson Club) and the personal papers, miscellaneous, of the Short family (one box, Library of Congress). The only useful Federalist papers that I found were those of Alexander Scott

Bullitt in the William Marshall Bullitt Collection (fourteen reels of microfilm, Filson Club); of those, only a half-dozen letters were useful. The papers of Humphrey Marshall were still extant at the middle of the last century, in the attics of two houses in Frankfort,[8] but they have vanished since then, destroyed in part, it is said, by descendants who were embarrassed by his atheism.[9] No papers of John Edwards, Joseph Crockett, or Thomas Marshall remain (although Humphrey Marshall used the papers of Thomas Marshall when he wrote his *History of Kentucky*); the papers of John Marshall, which would doubtless have included letters from his father, Thomas Marshall, have also largely vanished.

Of partisans I have found only scraps: the July 7, 1790, letter from Samuel Terrill to Garritt Minor in the Terrill-Carr Papers (University of Virginia) and two bits of paper in the William Calk Papers (University of Kentucky) recording the meetings of one county committee shortly after statehood. This deficit is less surprising than that of Federalist papers, for partisans were generally poorly educated and consequently less likely to value manuscripts. Samuel Terrill was an exception; his handwriting and grammar suggest that he had some education, but at the time he wrote he was landless, although he was soon to acquire a thousand acres.[10]

NEWSPAPERS AND UNPUBLISHED PAPERS

American Antiquarian Society, Worcester, Mass. *The Western World* (Frankfort).

Duke University Library, Durham, N.C. William Bolling Papers.

Filson Club, Louisville, Ky. Breckinridge-Marshall Papers, Orlando Brown Papers, William Marshall Bullitt Collection (microfilm), Arthur Campbell Papers, Samuel and Joseph Hamilton Daveiss Papers, Pontalba Papers, Isaac Shelby Papers, Todd Family Papers, translations of James Wilkinson letters by D. C. and R. D. Corbitt.

8. Shane's interview with Louis Marshall, Draper Coll., 16 CC 271.
9. Quisenberry, *Humphrey Marshall*, 19.
10. Jillson, *Land Grants*, 244.

Houghton Library, Harvard University, Cambridge, Mass. *The Western World* (Frankfort).

Kentucky Historical Society, Frankfort, Ky. Papers of John Brown, Harry Innes, Samuel Hopkins, George Nicholas, Isaac Shelby, and James Wilkinson; manuscript minutes of the sixth, seventh, eighth, ninth, and tenth conventions.

Lexington Public Library, Lexington, Ky. *Kentucky Gazette* (Lexington).

Library of Congress, Washington, D.C. Breckinridge Family Papers, James Brown Papers, Campbell-Preston-Floyd Papers, Thomas J. Clay Papers (including some papers of George Nicholas's), Harry Innes Papers, James Madison Papers, Preston Family Papers (microfilm), Isaac Shelby Papers.

Massachusetts Historical Society, Boston. Timothy Pickering Papers, Samuel Shepherd Diary.

National Archives, Washington, D.C. Papers of the Continental Congress.

Pennsylvania Historical Society, Philadelphia. Gratz Collection.

Presbyterian Historical Society, Philadelphia. Shane Collection.

University of Chicago, Chicago. Durrett Collection, including Gardoqui Papers, Depositions in the case of *Innes* v. *Marshall,* John Lewis Papers, George Nicholas Papers, Miscellaneous Bound Manuscripts, and Isaac Shelby Papers.

University of Kentucky, Lexington, Ky. Samuel M. Wilson Collection, including the papers of John Bradford, John Breckinridge, Henry Clay, Thomas Hart, and Isaac Shelby; papers of the Brown family, Buckner Thruston, William Calk, the Hart family, Charles Scott, the Shelby family, Isham Talbott, and Hubbard Taylor.

University of Virginia, Charlottesville, Va. James Breckinridge Papers.

Virginia Historical Society, Richmond, Va. Fleming-Christian Correspondence in Hugh Blair Grigsby Papers, Preston Family Papers.

Virginia State Library, Richmond, Va. Legislative petitions, Richard C. Anderson Papers.

Washington and Lee College, Lexington, Va. William Fleming Papers.

Western Kentucky State University, Bowling Green, Ky. Benjamin Sebastian Papers (photostats).

Wisconsin Historical Society, Madison. Draper Collection, including the Boone Papers, Clark Papers, Kentucky Papers, King's Mountain Papers, Preston Papers, Tennessee Papers, and Virginia Papers. (All available on microfilm at the University of Kentucky and the Filson Club.)

Yale University, New Haven, Conn. John Mason Brown Collection.

PETITIONS

Since I attach considerable importance to the petitions sent from Kentucky to Virginia and to the Continental Congress, I list here the ones I think significant, with their locations, if I found them, and any references to them. Those that are starred are statehood petitions.

1. Petition to Virginia, summer 1779 (read Oct. 14, 1779). Virginia State Library. Also No. 6 in James Rood Robertson, ed., *Petitions of the Early Inhabitants of Kentucky to the General Assembly of Virginia, 1769 to 1792,* Filson Club Publications, No. 27 (Louisville, 1914), 45–57. Asking land grants.
2. Petition to Virginia, summer 1779. Draft in Campbell-Preston-Floyd Papers, Library of Congress. Protesting land laws.
3. Petition to Congress, read 1780. Papers of the Continental Congress, Ser. 48, 245, National Archives. Asking permission to move across the Ohio into enemy territory.
*4. Petition to Congress, May 15, 1780 (read Aug. 24, 1780). Papers of the Continental Congress, Ser. 48, 237. Also in Theodore Roosevelt, *The Winning of the West* (New York, 1889–1896), II, 398–399. Asking separate statehood.
*5. Petition to Congress, fall 1781. Referred to in three

letters to Levi Todd, Aug.–Sept. 1806, Draper Collection, 16 CC 39–44. Asking separate statehood.

6. Petition to Virginia, Dec. 1781. Referred to in No. 24 in Robertson, ed., *Petitions,* 78–79. Asking for a district court.

*7. Petition to Congress, spring 1782 (read Aug. 27, 1782). Referred to in *The Papers of Charles Thompson, Secretary of the Continental Congress* (New-York Historical Society, *Collections,* XI [New York, 1878]), 145–150; Worthington C. Ford, ed., *Journals of the Continental Congress, 1774–1779* (Washington, 1904–1937), XXIII, 532; Benjamin Harrison's message to the Virginia General Assembly, Draper Collection, 10 S 78; John Donelson to Arthur Campbell, Apr. 20, 1782, Draper Collection, 9 DD 34; S. Clarke to Benjamin Harrison, Nov. 30, 1782, William P. Palmer *et al.,* eds., *Calendar of Virginia State Papers . . . (1652–1869)* (Richmond, 1875–1893), II, 384–385. Asking separate statehood.

8. Petition to Virginia, spring 1782 (read May 30, 1782). Miscellaneous legislative petitions, Box D, #748, Virginia State Library. Asking that the right of navigating the Mississippi not be ceded to Spain.

*9. Petition to Virginia, spring 1782 (read May 30, 1782). Virginia State Library. Also No. 15 in Robertson, ed., *Petitions,* 62–66. Referred to in John Donelson to Arthur Campbell, Apr. 20, 1782, Draper Collection, 9 DD 34. Asking separate statehood.

10. Petition to Virginia, spring 1782. Virginia State Library. Also No. 24 in Robertson, ed., *Petitions,* 78–79. Asking to stay part of Virginia.

11. Petition to Virginia, spring 1782 (read June 1, 1782). Virginia State Library. Also No. 16 in Robertson, ed., *Petitions,* 66–68. Asking revival of the ancient cultivation law.

12. Petition to Virginia, fall 1782. Referred to in No. 17 in Robertson, ed., *Petitions,* 68–69 (see immediately below). Asking repeal of the law establishing a district court in Kentucky.

13. Petition to Virginia, spring 1783 (read May 21,

1783). Virginia State Library. Also No. 17 in Robertson, ed., *Petitions,* 68–69. Asking that the court law be allowed to stand; requesting other laws.

14. Petition to Congress, spring or summer 1783 (read Sept. 27, 1783). Papers of the Continental Congress, Ser. 41, V, 97. Referred to in Ford, ed., *Journals of the Continental Congress,* XXV, 625. Asking a land grant.

*15. Petition to Congress, fall 1783 (read Jan. 2, 1784). Papers of the Continental Congress, Ser. 41, V, 101–102. Referred to in Ford, ed., *Journals of the Continental Congress,* XXVI, 3; delegates to the governor of Virginia, Feb. 20, 1784, Edmund C. Burnett, ed., *Letters of Members of the Continental Congress* (Washington, 1921–1936), VII, 446; Walker Daniel to Benjamin Harrison, May 21, 1784, Palmer *et al.,* eds., *Calendar of Virginia State Papers,* III, 584–588. Asking separate statehood.

*16. Petition to Virginia, fall 1783. In *Maryland Journal* (Baltimore), Dec. 19, 1783. This petition seems to have originated in Kentucky, even though it is better written than any other in this series except No. 13 above. Asking separate statehood.

17. Petition to Virginia, spring 1784 (read June 5, 1784). Virginia State Library. Also No. 23 in Robertson, ed., *Petitions,* 76–77. Asking that circuit courts be established.

18. Petition to Virginia, fall 1785 (read Nov. 29, 1785). Miscellaneous legislative petitions, Box F, #1414, Virginia State Library. Against a separation.

19. Petition to Virginia, fall 1786 (read Nov. 17, 1786). Miscellaneous legislative petitions, Box G, #1579. Virginia State Library. Asking that the right of navigating the Mississippi not be ceded to Spain.

20. Petition to Virginia, fall 1786 (read Nov. 15, 1786). Referred to in George Muter to James Madison, Sept. 23, 1786, Madison Papers, VI, Library of Congress; *Journal of the House of Delegates of the Commonwealth of Virginia* (Richmond, 1827), 41. Asking

an extension within which Congress could act to admit Kentucky to the Union.

21. Petition to Virginia, winter 1786 (read Jan. 10, 1787). Referred to in *Journal of the House of Delegates,* 136; George Muter to James Madison, Feb. 20, 1787, Madison Papers, VII; "A Farmer" [Harry Innes], *Kentucke Gazette* (Lexington), Oct. 18, 1788; "A Real Friend to the People" [Samuel Taylor], *Kentucke Gazette,* Apr. 25, 1789. Against a separation.

22. To Virginia, summer 1789. Virginia State Library. Also No. 58 in Robertson, ed., *Petitions,* 121–122. Against a separation.

PUBLISHED SOURCES

Abernethy, Thomas P., ed. "Journal of the First Kentucky Convention, Dec. 27, 1784–Jan. 5, 1785." *Journal of Southern History,* I (1935), 67–78.

Clark, George Rogers. *George Rogers Clark Papers,* ed. James Alton James. 2 vols. Illinois State Historical Library, *Collections,* VIII, XIX (Springfield, Ill., 1912–1916), Va. Ser., III, IV.

Gratz, Bernard and Michael. *B. and M. Gratz, Merchants in Philadelphia, 1754–1798; Papers of Interest to Their Posterity.* . . . Jefferson City, Mo., 1916.

Hening, William Waller, ed. *The Statutes at Large; Being a Collection of All the Laws of Virginia.* . . . 13 vols. Richmond, 1819–1823.

Innes, Harry. "The District of Kentucky 1783–1787 as Pictured by Harry Innes in a Letter to John Brown," ed. G. Glenn Clift. *Register of the Kentucky Historical Society,* LVI (1956), 368–372.

Jefferson, Thomas. *The Papers of Thomas Jefferson,* ed. Julian P. Boyd. 17 vols. Princeton, 1950—.

Journal of the First Constitutional Convention of Kentucky Held in Danville, Kentucky, April 2 to 19, 1792. Lexington, 1942.

Madison, James. *The Papers of James Madison,* ed. William

T. Hutchinson and William M. E. Rachal. 5 vols. Chicago, 1962—.

———. *The Writings of James Madison,* ed. Gaillard Hunt. 9 vols. New York, 1900–1910.

Nicholas, George. "Three Letters of George Nicholas to John Brown," ed. Huntley Dupre. *Register of the Kentucky State Historical Society,* XLI (1943), 1–10.

Palmer, William P. *et al.,* eds. *Calendar of Virginia State Papers . . . (1652–1869).* 11 vols. Richmond, 1875–1893.

Rice, David [Philanthropos]. *Slavery Inconsistent with Justice and Good Policy.* Lexington, 1792.

———. *Slavery Inconsistent with Justice and Good Policy, Proved by a Speech Delivered in the Convention, Held at Danville, Kentucky.* Philadelphia, 1792.

Robertson, James Rood, ed., *Petitions of the Early Inhabitants of Kentucky to the General Assembly of Virginia, 1769 to 1792.* Filson Club Publications, No. 27. Louisville, 1914.

Speed, Thomas. *The Political Club, Danville, Kentucky, 1786–1790: Being an Account of an Early Kentucky Society from the Original Papers Recently Found.* Filson Club Publications, No. 9. Louisville, 1894.

Wilkinson, Ann Biddle. "Letters of Mrs. Ann Biddle Wilkinson from Kentucky, 1788–1789," ed. Thomas R. Hay. *Pennsylvania Magazine of History and Biography,* LVI (1932), 33–55.

Wilkinson, James. First memorial. In "Wilkinson and the Beginnings of the Spanish Conspiracy," by William R. Shepherd. *American Historical Review,* IX (1903–1904), 490–506.

———. Letters. In *History of Louisiana,* by Charles E. A. Gayarré, III, 167–311. 4 vols. New York, 1854–1867.

———. "Letters of General James Wilkinson." *Register of the Kentucky State Historical Society,* XXIV (1926), 259–267.

———. "Letters of General James Wilkinson, addressed to Dr. James Hutchinson, of Philadelphia." *Pennsylvania*

Magazine of History and Biography, XII (1888), 55–64.

———. "Papers Bearing on James Wilkinson's Relations with Spain, 1787–1789," ed. William R. Shepherd. *American Historical Review,* IX (1903–1904), 748–766.

———. "Wilkinson's [First] Memorial and Expatriation Declaration." In *Reprints of Littell's Political Transactions in and concerning Kentucky, and Letter of George Nicholas to his Friend in Virginia, also General Wilkinson's Memorial,* by William Littell, ed. Temple Bodley, pp. *cxix–cxxix.* Filson Club Publications, No. 31. Louisville, 1926.

INTERVIEWS, JOURNALS, AND NARRATIVES

Allen, Benjamin. Interview. Draper Collection, 11 CC 67–79. Also in "John D. Shane's Interview with Benjamin Allen, Clark County," ed. Lucien Beckner. *Filson Club History Quarterly,* V (1931), 63–98.

Austin, Moses. "A Memorandum of M. Austin's Journey. . . ." *American Historical Review,* V (1899–1900), 518–542.

Boone, Daniel. "Life and Adventures of Colonel Daniel Boone: The First White Settler of the State of Kentucky." *Magazine of History,* XLV (1930), 205–277.

Bradford, Fielding. Interview. Draper Collection, 13 CC 211. Also in *Filson Club History Quarterly,* X (1936), 279–280.

Butler, William O. Interview. Draper Collection, 15 CC 41–47, 55–66.

Calk, William. "The Journal of William Calk, Kentucky Pioneer," ed. Lewis H. Kilpatrick. *Mississippi Valley Historical Review,* VII (1920–1921), 363–377.

Clinkenbeard, William. Interview. Draper Collection, 11 CC 54–66. Also in "Reverend John D. Shane's Interview with Pioneer William Clinkenbeard." *Filson Club History Quarterly,* II (1927–1928), 94–128.

Collins, Josiah. Interview. Draper Collection, 12 CC 64–78, 97–110.

Cresswell, Nicholas. *The Journal of Nicholas Cresswell,* ed. Samuel Thornely. New York, 1924.

Crèvecoeur, Hector St. John de. "Sketch of the River Ohio and of the Country of Kentucky." Durrett Collection, University of Chicago. Trans. from *Lettres d'un Cultivateur Américain,* III. Paris, 1787.

Darnaby, Mr. and Mrs. Interview. Draper Collection, 11 CC 164–167, 179.

Dewees, Mary Coburn. *Journal of a Trip from Philadelphia to Lexington in Kentucky.* . . . Crawfordsville, Ind., 1936.

Foley, Elijah. Interview. Draper Collection, 11 CC 133–135. Also in *Filson Club History Quarterly,* XI (1937), 252–259.

Gist, Christopher. "Col. Christopher Gist's Journal." In *First Explorations of Kentucky,* ed. J. Stoddard Johnston. Filson Club Publications, No. 13. Louisville, 1898.

Graham, Sarah. Interview. Draper Collection, 12 CC 45–53. Also in "Rev. John Dabney Shane's Interview with Mrs. Sarah Graham of Bath County," ed. Lucien Beckner. *Filson Club History Quarterly,* IX (1935), 222–241.

Hedge, John. Interview. Draper Collection, 11 CC 19–23. Also in "John D. Shane's Interview with Pioneer John Hedge, Bourbon County," ed. Otto A. Rothert. *Filson Club History Quarterly,* XIV (1940), 176–181.

Humphrey, David C. Interview. Draper Collection, 16 CC 272–296, 318–321.

Kemper, Jeptha. Interview. Draper Collection, 12 CC 127–133. Also in "John D. Shane's Notes on an Interview with Jeptha Kemper of Montgomery County," ed. Lucien Beckner. *Filson Club History Quarterly,* XII (1938), 151–162.

Leavy, William A. "A Memoir of Lexington and Its Vicinity. . . ." *Register of the Kentucky State Historical Society,* XL (1942), 107–131, 253–267, 353–375, XLI (1943), 44–62, 107–137, 250–260, 310–346.

McBride, William. Interview. Draper Collection, 11 CC 257–263.

Marshall, Louis. Interview. Draper Collection, 16 CC 239–247, 271.

Nourse, James. "A Journey to Kentucky in 1775." *Missis-*

sippi Valley Historical Review, XIX (1925), 212–238, 251–260, 351–364.

Perry, Needham. "Diary of a Trip Westward in 1794." Draper Collection, 14 CC 1–9. Also in *Filson Club Historical Quarterly,* XXII (1948), 227–247.

Richardson, Marcus. Interview. Draper Collection, 12 CC 124–127, 154–156.

Scott, Patrick. Interview. Draper Collection, 11 CC 5–9, 17–18.

Shelby, Isaac. Autobiography. Durrett Collection.

Stevenson, James. Interview. Draper Collection, 11 CC 247–251.

Tandy, James B. "Reminiscences of James Bledsoe Tandy." *Register of the Kentucky Historical Society,* LIII (1955), 101–114.

Taylor, James. Diary. Durrett Collection.

Thompson, Andrew. Interview. Draper Collection, 12 CC 235–236.

Trabue, Daniel. Mememorandom [sic] made by me D Trabue in the year 1827 of a Jurnal of events from memory and Tradition. Draper Collection, 57 J 3–150.

Walker, Felix. *Memoirs of the Late the Hon. Felix Walker, of North Carolina . . . ,* ed. Samuel R. Walker. New Orleans, 1877.

Washington, George. *The Diaries of George Washington, 1748–1799,* ed. John C. Fitzpatrick. 4 vols. Boston, 1925.

Wilkinson, James. *Memoirs of My Own Time.* 3 vols. Philadelphia, 1816.

II. SELECTED SECONDARY BIOGRAPHICAL MATERIALS

Bakeless, John. *Master of the Wilderness: Daniel Boone.* New York, 1939.

Bodley, Temple. *George Rogers Clark: His Life and Public Services.* Boston, 1926.

Brown, Orlando. *Memoranda of the Preston Family.* Frankfort, Ky., 1842.

Bullitt, Emily M. "Cuthbert Bullitt: One of the Founders of Louisville." *Filson Club History Quarterly,* XXIV (1950), 137–141.

Caldemeyer, Richard H. The Career of George Nicholas. Unpublished Ph.D. dissertation, University of Indiana, 1951.

Clark, Daniel. *Proofs of the Corruption of Gen. James Wilkinson.* Philadelphia, 1809.

Dunn, C. Frank. "Captain Nathaniel G. S. Hart." *Filson Club History Quarterly,* XXIV (1950), 28–33.

Fackler, Calvin M. "Walker Daniel, the Founder of Danville: One of Kentucky's Almost Forgotten Pioneers." *Filson Club History Quarterly,* XIII (1939), 134–146.

Fowler, Ila Earle. *Captain John Fowler of Virginia and Kentucky: Patriot, Soldier, Pioneer, Statesman, Land Baron and Civic Leader.* Cynthiana, Ky., 1942.

Goff, John S. "Mr. Justice Trimble of the United States Supreme Court." *The Register of the Kentucky Historical Society,* LVIII (1960), 6–28.

Green, Thomas Marshall. *Historic Families of Kentucky. With Special Reference to Stocks Immediately Derived from the Valley of Virginia. . . .* Cincinnati, 1889.

Hardin, Bayless. "The Brown Family of Liberty Hall." *Filson Club History Quarterly,* XVI (1942), 75–87.

Harrison, Lowell H. "John Breckinridge of Kentucky: Planter, Speculator, and Businessman." *Filson Club History Quarterly,* XXIV (1960), 205–227.

———. *John Breckinridge: Jeffersonian Republican.* Filson Club Publications, 2d Ser., No. 2. Louisville, 1969.

Jacobs, James Ripley. *Tarnished Warrior, Major-General James Wilkinson.* New York, 1938.

Jillson, Willard R. "Squire Boone: A Sketch of His Life and an Appraisement of His Influence on the Early Settlement of Kentucky." *Filson Club History Quarterly,* XVI (1942), 141–171.

Martin, Vernon P. "Father Rice, the Preacher Who Followed the Frontier." *Filson Club History Quarterly,* XXIX (1955), 324–330.

Mason, Kathryn H. "The Career of General James Ray,

Kentucky Pioneer." *Filson Club History Quarterly*, XIX (1945), 88–114.

————. "The Family and Fortune of General James Ray, Pioneer of Fort Harrod." *Register of the Kentucky State Historical Society*, XLIII (1945), 59–68.

Quisenberry, A. C. *The Life and Times of Hon. Humphrey Marshall*. Winchester, Ky., 1892.

Rice, Howard C. *Barthélemi Tardiveau: A French Trader in the West*. Baltimore, 1938.

Talbert, Charles Gano. *Benjamin Logan, Kentucky Frontiersman*. Lexington, 1962.

————. "William Whitley, 1749–1813." *Filson Club History Quarterly*, XXV (1951), 101–121, 210–215, 300–316.

Tapp, Hambleton. "Colonel John Floyd, Kentucky Pioneer." *Filson Club History Quarterly*, XV (1941), 1–24.

Whitsitt, William H. *Life and Times of Judge Caleb Wallace.* . . . Filson Club Publications, No. 4. Louisville, 1888.

III. WORKS ON THE KENTUCKY FRONTIERSMEN

There are, to the best of my knowledge, only seven truly important books on the Kentucky frontiersmen. Each considers the early history of Kentuckians in relation to the uniqueness of the whole American nation. It is interesting to note that, of the six writers able to take an overview of the Kentucky frontier, only one is a Kentuckian. Here I list these works in the order of their publication.

Roosevelt, Theodore. *The Winning of the West*. 4 vols. New York, 1889–1896. In my opinion this is the best narrative of the frontier ever written. In 1889 almost all manuscripts were still in private hands; yet Roosevelt discovered nearly everything on Kentucky that I have found with the help of modern bibliographic guides, and his documentation is so clear that I can follow his references through all the intervening changes in ownership and cataloging. Roosevelt managed to digest an enormous quantity of material, mastering personalities as well as events; he organized his knowledge so skillfully that the outline is unobtrusive and then told his story beautifully. His facts are remarkably accurate, especially since he wrote in a day before typewriters, note cards, and research assistants were conventional. I could quarrel only with his idea that the pioneers were of a single type and his conviction that Scotch-Irish stock is responsible for frontier achievements. Even those ideas I would dispute hesitantly, knowing that Roosevelt's realization of the similarity of the several frontiers is more important than any picayune distinction amongst frontiersmen and that his knowledge so far surpassed mine that he may be right after all. Roosevelt rediscovered the early separation movement, neglected since Humphrey Marshall had written two paragraphs on it, and gave his discovery to the Kentucky historians.[11] They continued to ignore it, however, perhaps because it did not fit the conventional scheme of events.

Turner, Frederick Jackson. *The Frontier in American History*. New York, 1920. Especially "The Ohio Valley in American History," an address given in 1909. It is Turner rather than Roosevelt who is considered the fountainhead of frontier history, although his knowledge of the frontier was less complete. Certainly he dealt more in ideas than Roosevelt did; he saw the American nation as unique and the frontier as the source of American peculiarity. Turner's language, however, is inexact, and one is never certain whether he thought it was the existence of a half-settled body of land in the West that influenced national policy or whether he supposed frontier conditions so changed the people that the whole nation was finally transformed—or both, or neither. Turner's imprecision was a virtue as well as a deficiency, for it has stimulated more discussion and investigation than any clear statement ever could have.

11. Brown, *Political Beginnings*, 59.

Whitaker, Arthur P. *The Spanish-American Frontier, 1783–1795: The Westward Movement and the Spanish Retreat in the Mississippi Valley.* Boston, 1927. Although this, Whitaker's first volume, is dedicated to Frederick Jackson Turner, it is less concerned with the origin and peculiarity of frontier democracy than with its effect on the manifest destiny—as he sees it—of the American nation to expand into an occupation and control of the Mississippi valley. To him frontiersmen were men who lived in the future and who would trample any international agreement to insure the prospect of commerce down the Mississippi. The product of careful investigation in an area hitherto untouched by American historians, this volume is essential to the study of the pre-Mississippi frontier.

Abernethy, Thomas Perkins. *Western Lands and the American Revolution.* New York, 1937. This work is, in part, an attack on the Turner thesis. By suggesting that it was eastern land speculators rather than the pioneers who influenced national politics, Abernethy seems to undercut Turner's work; but his suggestion actually strikes down only half of Turner's idea while it offers support for the other half. Abernethy, like Roosevelt, read an enormous quantity of manuscripts; that fact, added to the ingenuity of his original idea, makes his book very valuable. However, his prose is usually hard to read, and his chronological chaptering makes it difficult either to follow any particular matter or to grasp the whole. Although he gives his last four chapters, almost seventy-five pages, to western statehood movements after 1784, and most of that to Kentucky, he does not show any clear relation between land speculation and the second Kentucky statehood movement.

Abernethy, Thomas Perkins. *Three Virginia Frontiers.* Baton Rouge, 1940. In three short, undocumented, but clearly written essays Abernethy explores some implications of his *Western Lands.* In the essay on Kentucky he suggests that there were actually two frontiers coexisting side by side, one of pioneers and another of aristocrats. Jeffersonian democracy, he says, was not liberal. The aristocratic minority, finding their landholdings in danger, had to prove their trustworthiness to the pioneer majority; this they accomplished by declaring democratic ideals. As interesting and as plausible as this assertion is, it cannot be taken at face value because it is not backed with specific instances.

Barnhart, John D. *Valley of Democracy: The Frontier versus the Plantation in the Ohio Valley, 1775–1818.* Bloomington, 1953. Barnhart is an avowed neo-Turnerian, writing in opposition to Abernethy. Curiously enough, he adopts Abernethy's concept of parallel frontiers and its prerequisite economic distinction between aristocrats and pioneers. He implies that democracy originated in the economic frustrations of pioneers; where Turner attributed pioneer egalitarianism to a unique social influence of the frontier, Barnhart gives it a cause not peculiar to the frontier. Thus Barnhart unwittingly does as much to destroy Turner's thesis as Abernethy unwittingly did to support it. Barnhart's basic idea is a good one, for he finds many similar patterns in the several Ohio valley statehood movements. He is the only historian to depart from the chroniclers in treating the Kentucky statehood conventions and the only one to give careful attention to the 1792 Kentucky constitutional convention, analyzing members' economic status in relation to their vote and searching out origins of the resulting constitution. Barnhart makes a serious mistake in his treatment of the Kentucky statehood conventions, however. The action that he considers liberal and attributes to radical pioneers was actually accomplished by conservative landowners. It seems to me that this mistake weakens the whole of his argument.

Moore, Arthur K. *The Frontier Mind: A Cultural Analysis of the Kentucky Frontiersman.* Lexington, 1957. Moore explores the idea of the West as a paradise,[12]

12. This idea was first investigated by Henry Nash Smith, in *Virgin Land: The American West as Symbol and Myth* (Cambridge,

attempts to establish Kentucky as a focal point of the myth, and suggests that pioneers were looking for the easy life of Eden when they went to Kentucky. This, he says, explains much of their subsequent political behavior. Moore's treatment of the pioneers is based chiefly on travelers' accounts, an unreliable source at best. As a result his thesis is inadequately established; nevertheless parts of it are probably valid.

IV. THE SPANISH CONSPIRACY

The Spanish conspiracy, so called, has been one of the most persistent questions in early Kentucky history. Actually it was not at all a conspiracy of the Spaniards, but— as Arthur P. Whitaker describes it—"the frontier intrigue with Spain." [13] It is a story that has been told over and over again, but it is so important a part of the Kentucky Republican complexion that to omit it would distort any picture of the origin of that party. I offer below a list only of major documents and historical accounts, not differentiating primary from secondary. Virtually all of the material on the Spanish conspiracy is by native Kentuckians.

John Brown to George Muter, July 10, 1788. Printed in the *Kentucky Gazette,* Sept. 4, 1790; reprinted in the *Gazette,* the *Palladium,* and *The Western World* in September 1806. The revelation of the Spanish conspiracy began when George Muter was pressured into publishing this letter during the 1790 contest between John Brown and James M. Marshall for John Brown's seat in the federal House of Representatives. The letter described Brown's interview with Gardoqui, in which Gardoqui said that "if Kentucky will declare her independence and empower some proper person to negotiate with him, that he has authority, and will engage

Mass., 1950). I have omitted his book from this list because he deals almost exclusively with outside images of the frontiersmen, rather than with the men themselves and their own images.

13. Whitaker, *Spanish-American Frontier,* 90.

to open the navigation of the Mississippi, for the exportation of their produce, on terms of mutual advantage. But that this privilege can never be extended to them while part of the United States." This is the most basic document in the history of the Spanish conspiracy.

Marshall, Humphrey. "An Observer—A Voice in the West —and the Legislative Proceedings in the Case of Judge Innes." Reprinted from *The Western World*. Frankfort, 1806. Pamphlet in the Wilson Collection, University of Kentucky. Humphrey Marshall resurrected the old charges of Spanish conspiracy in 1806, during a political campaign designed to oust Republican leaders from their positions. He based his accusation against Benjamin Sebastian on recent evidence suggesting that Sebastian received a Spanish pension; the charges against John Brown were based on a reprinting of the 1788 letter to Muter; and the accusation against Harry Innes was based purely on hearsay. Though these articles were built on little evidence, they now seem remarkably acute. Marshall acknowledged authorship in a letter to Harry Innes, Sept. 1, 1810, Innes Papers, XXII, Library of Congress.

Littell, William. *Political Transactions in and concerning Kentucky, from the First Settlement Thereof, Until It Became an Independent State, in June, 1792*. Frankfort, 1806. Reprinted, with an introduction by Temple Bodley, as Filson Club Publication No. 31, Louisville, 1926. The Republicans maintained a discreet silence on the question of the Spanish conspiracy for many years, but Humphrey Marshall's 1806 charges finally induced them to speak. John Brown, Harry Innes, Caleb Wallace, Thomas Todd (a supporter of theirs), and perhaps Benjamin Sebastian commissioned William Littell, a rising young lawyer, to write an account of the statehood conventions proclaiming their innocence. Littell's account was based largely on the journals of the statehood conventions; he used the journal of the seventh convention (November 1788) to show that no motion had been made for separating Kentucky from Virginia absolutely, as Marshall had charged. Overlooking such a motion made in the sixth convention (July 1788), he did not reprint the complete journal for the sixth convention. Brown, Innes, Wallace, and Todd each paid the printer fifty-eight dollars for the publication of this book,[14] thus demonstrating that it was no impartial work written for the love of history alone.

Marshall, Humphrey. *The History of Kentucky, Including an Account of the Discovery, Settlement, Progressive Improvement, Political and Military Events, and Present State of the Country.* Frankfort, 1812. Here Marshall amplified the charges he had made in 1806. His work, with its unbelievably bad punctuation, is based on his own and Thomas Marshall's notes from the statehood conventions, and presumably on conversations with others who had witnessed those events. In the 1812 edition he only went up to 1792, but in 1824 he republished the 1812 volume with revisions, adding a second one that carried the history of Kentucky to 1811. For the second volume he used the legislative journals as a major source, in addition to his personal recollections and manuscripts. Marshall's history is an impressive study, but it does not pretend to be impartial. Both 1812 and 1824 were, after all, critical years for his Federalist Party.

Butler, Mann. *A History of the Commonwealth of Kentucky.* Louisville, 1834. By 1834 John Brown was the only surviving member of the Spanish cabal. Butler, writing in defense of his friend Brown, used Littell and Marshall as sources and added the recollections of more early settlers. His major contribution was a letter from the aged James Madison, printed in the second edition (1836), confirming Brown's contention that he had discussed Gardoqui's proposal with Madison.

Brown, John Mason. *The Political Beginnings of Kentucky: A Narrative of Public Events Bearing on the History*

14. Depositions of William Hunter and William Littell, *Innes* v. *Marshall,* 75, 117, Durrett Coll.; Marshall, *Kentucky,* II, 399.

of that State up to the Time of Its Admission into the American Union. Filson Club Publications, No. 6. Louisville, 1889. John Brown's grandson provoked the second round of the Spanish controversy with a treatise that exonerated all the Republicans except James Wilkinson, even Benjamin Sebastian, and that made a countercharge of British conspiracy against Thomas Marshall. When John Mason Brown wrote, he had at his disposal as fine a collection of sources as any historian could desire. He had, in fact, every important item that is available today, and some materials that have since vanished. From the members of his family he collected the papers of John Brown; his friends Harry I. Todd and Thomas Speed proffered the papers of Harry Innes, Thomas Todd, and the Political Club; from Madrid he gathered copies of papers in the Spanish archives there; in Louisville Reuben T. Durrett opened his extensive library of Kentuckiana. The letters of Washington, Jefferson, and Madison had been published; many of Wilkinson's letters were printed in Gayarré's *History of Louisiana;* and Force's *American Archives* and the *Calendar of Virginia State Papers* offered other choice items. In Harrodsburg Brown read the depositions in the case of *Innes* v. *Marshall,* and in Washington he saw the secret and public journals of the Continental Congress. Even his friend Theodore Roosevelt contributed a petition that he had found in the papers of the Continental Congress. With all of this material at his disposal, and with most of it collected in his home town of Louisville, Brown produced a history that is admirable chiefly for the beauty of its style. Even a friend said that he "evidently had only a superficial knowledge of his subject, and his treatment of it was both timid and very vulnerable to severe criticism." [15] It seems apparent either that Brown deliberately suppressed information or, more probably, that he did not read his sources, for his defense of his

15. Bodley, "Introduction," *Reprints of Littell's Political Transactions,* cxvi.

grandfather was despite three implicating letters in the
Gardoqui Papers he had acquired from Madrid.

Green, Thomas Marshall. *The Spanish Conspiracy: A Review of Early Spanish Movements in the South-West.*
. . . Cincinnati, 1891. If John Mason Brown's gentle
and uncomprehending soul seems remarkably like that of
his grandfather, so was Thomas Marshall Green as logical and as volatile as his grandfather Humphrey Marshall. It is easy to imagine that if Humphrey Marshall
had still been living he would have drawn up the argument in *The Spanish Conspiracy.* Even though Green had
access only to the printed sources that Brown had used
and to the depositions in *Innes* v. *Marshall,* by examining them carefully he was able to tear Brown's conclusions to shreds. Interpreting the phrase "separate and
independent state" as treason (which is, in fact, the correct interpretation), printing in toto letters which Brown
had offered in part, and pointing out one non sequitur
after another, Green concluded that John Brown, Harry
Innes, Caleb Wallace, and Benjamin Sebastian were im-
plicated in the Spanish conspiracy along with James Wilkinson. He also managed, by a more thorough examination
of Brown's sources, to show that Wilkinson was as involved as Thomas Marshall in the "British conspiracy"
and thus by implication to free his great-grandfather of
guilt. Green's work is based on a textual examination of
documents more similar to biblical research than to conventional historical study; consequently his argument is
more involuted than any his grandfather ever created, and
his style is as strained as Brown's is clear. Brown's friend
said that "for misapprehension of facts and wholly un-
warranted inferences, Green's book is more often vulnerable than Brown's, and is rivaled in errors by few others
professing to be history." [16] This statement, however, must
be understood as a part of the controversy rather than an
unbiased opinion, although it is true that Green made some

16. *Ibid., cxvii.*

serious mistakes. Yet, in spite of his errors, it is Green rather than Brown who has been accepted by non-Kentucky historians. Although his conclusions lack definitive proof, his argument is followed by writers as eminent as Samuel Flagg Bemis and Thomas Perkins Abernethy.

Bodley, Temple. "Introduction" to *Reprints of Littell's Political Transactions in and concerning Kentucky, and Letter of George Nicholas to his Friend in Virginia, also General Wilkinson's Memorial.* Filson Club Publications, No. 31. Louisville, 1926. A grandson of Harry Innes's ended the second round of the Spanish controversy with a reprinting of Littell's *Political Transactions* that served as a vehicle for an introduction far exceeding it in length. Temple Bodley brought to the controversy some new material, the most notable being an English translation of Wilkinson's first memorial and his expatriation declaration. Both of these he published in full. Like his friend John Mason Brown, Bodley defended the Republicans; unlike Brown he understood his sources and quoted them accurately. Bodley's major conclusion is, however, as undocumented as Green's. He uses a textual argument to show that Wilkinson was the author of all the documents ordinarily used to build a case against George Rogers Clark for drunkenness and incompetence in 1786, and from this he argues that even Wilkinson was not involved in a Spanish conspiracy but was instead plotting to usurp Clark's position as commissioner of Indian Affairs. This textual argument is extremely acute, and it may be valid, but it is not any better substantiated than anything else written during the second round of the Spanish controversy.

Thus the Spanish controversy in both its phases has been notable more for the heat than for the light it has generated. All those who have written on it have worked from a prior conviction of the innocence or guilt of those they wrote about; their writings suggest that no amount of evidence would have led them to another conclusion. But in fact their evidence is scanty. Except for the massive number of Wilkinson's letters to the Spanish officials in New Orleans—which no one, not even Thomas Marshall Green, has been quite willing to accept—there is very little evidence on the Spanish conspiracy. New authors have brought little new material to the topic. All of these writers have reached new conclusions merely by the reexamination of old evidence.

Three articles by authors who were not Kentuckians have added little to the controversy.

Shepherd, William R. "Wilkinson and the Beginnings of the Spanish Conspiracy." *American Historical Review,* IX (1903–1904), 490–506. Here Shepherd establishes, by publishing long excerpts from Wilkinson's first memorial, his expatriation declaration, and the report of Miro and Navarro to the authorities in Spain, that the first suggestions of a formal connection between Kentucky and Spain came from Wilkinson rather than from the Spanish. Shepherd in effect documents the hearsay charges made by Humphrey Marshall, but in fact the charges had already been substantiated by the letters of Wilkinson published in Gayarré, *History of Louisiana.*

Warren, Elizabeth. "Benjamin Sebastian and the Spanish Conspiracy in Kentucky." *Filson Club History Quarterly,* XX (1946), 107–130. Miss Warren convicts Sebastian on the basis of Wilkinson's letters published in Gayarré, *History of Louisiana,* and Sebastian's own letter to Wilkinson, Jan. 5, 1790, also published in Gayarré. She adds no new material.

Warren, Elizabeth. "Senator John Brown's Role in the Kentucky Spanish Conspiracy." *Filson Club History Quarterly,* XXXVI (1962), 158–176. Here Miss Warren exonerates John Brown because there is no evidence against him except that in Wilkinson's letters. In other words, she refuses to use the very letters that she did use in her article on Sebastian. She brings no new material to the discussion; like other authors she misses Brown's three letters to Gardoqui in the Gardoqui Papers, Durrett Collection, University of Chicago.

It is perhaps fitting that a Kentuckian, even though un-related to the major combatants, should have the last word to date on the Spanish conspiracy.

Watlington, Patricia. "John Brown and the Spanish Con-spiracy." *Virginia Magazine of History and Biography,* LXXV (1967), 52–68. In this article I tentatively charge John Brown of involvement in the conspiracy, on the basis of his three letters to Gardoqui and many previously unnoticed letters to other friends.

V. POLITICAL PARTIES

My use of the term "party" for the political groupings in Kentucky before 1792 requires some discussion. Julian P. Boyd has written to me,

It is only the historians who have invented the notion that "parties" did not begin until the mid-1790's. By defining parties largely in terms of organization and discipline, they have made this seem a plausible thesis. But Adams, Jefferson, and I suppose every other lit-erate political figure—perhaps illiterate as well—knew that parties existed in a real sense before that time. The Revolution could scarcely have come about if there had not been partisan divisions—and indeed some rather effective organization both within the individual states and on a continental scale.

I agree with you that we need more study of state politics, but not in order to demolish this theory of the historians. About that I think one could say what John Adams said about Jefferson's effort to disprove Buf-fon's theory concerning the degeneration of life in America. He said, in effect, that Jefferson might have spent his time to better advantage than in belaboring an inherently absurd proposition.[17]

17. Julian P. Boyd to Patricia Watlington, Mar. 10, 1969. The letter is in possession of the recipient.

I fully agree that the idea that parties did not exist before the 1790s is "an inherently absurd proposition." Yet this aspect of my work has received more criticism than anything else I have done. Consequently I feel obliged to justify my use of the term "party." I would like to do it by looking at some of the definitions historians have given for the term.

The number of political historians who have failed to define themselves is surprising. Wilfred E. Binkley undertook his ambitious survey of all the major American political parties, *American Political Parties: Their Natural History* (New York, 1943), without a word of definition and without any evident feeling of a need for one. Joseph Charles discussed *The Origins of the American Party System* (Chapel Hill, 1956) without a definition and on the national level alone, apparently assuming that if firm political divisions in Congress could be shown it would be conclusive evidence that national parties existed. There is some evidence that, had Charles lived to complete the study, he would have gone into an investigation of parties on the state level, but it is apparent that he thought the congressional evidence was the foremost and determining factor.[18] Noble E. Cunningham likewise undertook a study of *The Jeffersonian Republicans: The Formation of a Party Organization, 1789–1801* (Chapel Hill, 1957) without a definition, but not without an oblique apology. "No attempt," he explained, "has been made to determine whether at any given moment the political organisms under examination conform to any preconceived definition of political parties" (p. viii). Not a single study of political activity on the state level which includes a definition of either "faction" or "party" has come to my attention.

Four recent historians, however, have made an effort to come to grips with the problem of definition. One is Roy F. Nichols, who says in *The Invention of the American Political Parties* (New York, 1967), "American parties are

18. See the outline of projected work in the index of Joseph Charles, The Party Origins of Jeffersonian Democracy (unpubl. Ph.D. diss., Harvard University, 1942).

now really competing trade associations of professionals who operate highly organized groups which are federal, that is, they work on state and national levels. Their central organization of salaried staff deals with well-organized, independent, and often tough-minded locals" (p. 214). A second attempt at definition—or at avoiding definition— is made by Richard P. McCormick in *The Second American Party System: Party Formation in the Jacksonian Era* (Chapel Hill, 1966). "Rather than attempting at this point a definition of what a party *is,* I shall merely set forth those conditions I have taken to be indicative of the existence of a party or parties," he explains. "Where I have found that votes cast in an election were concentrated behind a slate of candidates nominated by some agency, formal or informal, and when such evidence of leadership and voter cohesion was manifested in successive elections I have concluded that a party existed. The minimum requisites of a party, then, would be leadership and voter identification with that leadership and with the candidates put forward by the leaders" (pp. 9–10). The most recent effort by a historian at defining political parties is that of Richard Hofstadter in his essay on "Political Parties," published in C. Vann Woodward, ed., *The Comparative Approach to American History* (New York, 1968). He calls parties "broadly based social structures that mediate between public opinion and the processes of parliamentary decision-making in a fairly regular manner" (p. 206).

The most nearly satisfactory definition of political parties is the one given by William N. Chambers in his *Political Parties in a New Nation: The American Experience, 1776–1809* (New York, 1963). "First, there is the matter of structure," he says.

Structure as the mark of party exists as a relatively durable or regularized relationship between leaders and followers. . . . Next, parties contribute continuing procedures for performing certain key political functions. At a minimum, these functions include nominating candidates and campaigning in the electoral arena, and readiness to undertake management or the general con-

duct of public business in the governmental arena. . . .
To the two aspects of party as structure and functions,
a third aspect may be added: range, density, and stability
of support. . . . Finally a party in the full sense entails
a distinguishable set of perspectives, or ideology, with
emotional overtones (pp. 45–48).

This definition Chambers has since modified in his essay
"Party Development and the American Mainstream," published in a book which he edited jointly with Walter D.
Burnham, *The American Party Systems: Stages of Political
Development* (New York, 1967). "Stated broadly," he now
says, " a political party in the modern sense may be thought
of as a relatively durable social formation which seeks offices
of power in government, exhibits a structure or organization
which links leaders at the centers of government to a significant popular following in the political arena and its local en-
claves, and generates in-group perspectives or at least symbols
of identification or loyalty" (p. 5).

Richard Hofstadter has recently added greatly to our
understanding of the development of American political
parties in *The Idea of a Party System* (Berkeley and Los
Angeles, 1969). While not attempting a further definition
of party, he suggests that a fully developed party system
does not exist until people recognize "that parties are not
only inevitable but necessary and, on balance, good" (p.
29). It is, he implies, only in a preparty system that politicians believe their opponents have no right to exist and try
to suppress them altogether; in a party system groups ac-
knowledge the existence of the opposition and simply try
to win power over it because of differences in views. It appears to me that the situation in Kentucky prior to statehood, although it came much earlier than the examples
Hofstadter gives, resembled an actual party system more
closely than a preparty system. It is true that both court
and country parties believed partisans should not organize
politically. In a society as unsuppressed as that of Kentucky, the right of partisans to political self-expression
could not be denied publicly, yet it is clear that privately
members of both sides of the old articulate center thought it

would be beneficial if the third party could be destroyed. But the court party and the country party could not deny each other's right to existence, and there is no hint that such a thing was ever insinuated. Both groups were composed of former Virginians, men who stood high in society, who were colleagues, often who were relatives. Social pressures forced them to recognize each other, and they did. Even when in 1806 Humphrey Marshall attacked the Republicans for having held treasonous views in 1788, he was only attempting to win power over them and never denied their right to exist.

Likewise, by three of the four definitions of party given by historians, the pre-1792 Kentucky groupings can be considered parties. Only Nichols's definition excludes them, and his definition in fact excludes the Federalists and Republicans of the early Republic in general. The Kentucky situation often included slates of candidates with clearly defined views nominated by an agency; the fact that the nominating power was usually a family or social group does not make it the less an "agency." There was certainly leadership in the Kentucky situation, and except between 1786 and 1790 there is some evidence of voter cohesion, although it is difficult to get at that information. The groups contributed "continuing procedures for performing certain key political functions"—making the specific decision about independence and the type of independence it would be, and the more general decision about the relationship of Kentucky to the eastern states—and the groups, each of them, certainly offered "a distinguishable set of perspectives, or ideology, with emotional overtones." Indeed, the overtones were often highly emotional, but never to the point where the perspectives were lost. Thus it seems to me that, by the definitions of the only people who have tried to determine what a party is, the pre-1792 Kentucky groups must be considered parties. It also appears to me that this is true of the groupings in several other colonies and early states; Connecticut and New York in particular come to mind. By their own definitions the national historians have made these state groups "parties."

INDEX

268 INDEX

Danville, 73, 95, 139–140; as
site of district court, 55,
108; stores begun at, 71; as
site of statehood meetings,
76, 77, 117, 119, 122; as
home of Political Club, 118
Delaware, 48
Democratic Societies, 224
District court, 26–27, 61, 76,
92, 97; Floyd appointed
chief justice of, 37; articulate center strengthened by,
53; initial problems of, 54;
planter bias of, 54–55;
composition of, 55–58; located at Danville, 55; political importance of, 58;
Kentuckians distressed
with, 73–74; salaries of
members, 81; and court
party, 83. *See also* Land,
lawsuits over; Court party
Dunn, Isaac, 142, 143, 144,
147, 180

E

Eades (schoolmaster), 61
Edwards, John, 166–167, 178,
203, 217
England, 31, 35, 52, 120, 121,
140

F

Falls of Ohio, 25, 51, 96
Fayette County, 39; fort-
dwelling in, 29; Marshalls
surveyors in, 38, 42; pe-
titions in, 66; partisan
stronghold, 94; delegation
at first, second statehood
conventions, 98, 99, 101,
102; election in, 113
Federalist Party, 231–234

Fleming, William, 56, 77, 222
Florida, West, 32
Floyd, Jenny, 36, 37, 38
Floyd, John, 56, 63; surveyor
of Kentucky County, 19;
experience and personality
of, 35–36; frontier discomforts, death of, 36–37; as
chief justice, 37, 55; in
articulate center, 43; on
separation, 53; on John
Brown, 80
Fowler, John, 87, 135, 153,
156, 174, 186, 204; back-
ground of, 82–83; in court
party, 83, 84; at fifth statehood convention, 129;
aware of Spanish plan, 143;
hosts Wilkinson, 146; op-
poses federal constitution,
148, 156
France, 35, 45
Frankfort, 139, 140, 146
Franklin (Tennessee), 68, 121
Froman, Jacob, 217

G

Galloway (partisan leader),
66, 67
Gardoqui, Diego de, 118,
160–165, 175, 177–181;
negotiates with Jay, 118
Germany, 45

H

Hamilton, Alexander, 229–
232
Harris, Jordan, 152–154
Holder, John, 32
Honoré, Jean A., 45n

I

Indians, 9, 25, 36, 37, 57, 96,
117, 130; as danger to Ky.

Wallace, Caleb (*continued*)
sixth statehood convention, 159
Wallace, Rosanna, 53, 56
Washington, George, 38
Wilkinson, Ann Biddle, 86, 139, 190
Wilkinson, James, 96, 101, 104, 135, 137–138, 139, 157, 166, 174, 193, 204, 208–209, 228; personality and experience of, 85–89, 86n, 88n; writes Ky. independence declaration, 102; at third statehood convention, 103–104; on closing of Miss. trade, 106; center of court party, 111; on public apathy, 113; runs for fourth convention, 113–114; at fourth statehood convention, 117; on British aid to Ky., 120–121; goes to New Orleans, 124–125, 140–142; returns to Kentucky, 133–134; attitude of, toward manufactures, 138; confides in friends about

Wilkinson, James (*continued*)
Spanish plan, 139–140, 142–143, 144n; presents Spanish program, 143–145, 147; expansive style of, 145–146; motives of, 146–147; attitude of, toward federal constitution, 147–148; elected to sixth statehood convention, 159; quarrels with Humphrey Marshall, 151–155; writes "A Whig" letter in *Ky. Gaz.*, 171–172; at seventh statehood convention, 175–179; petitions for Spanish land grant, 180–181; receives Spanish douceur, 186–187; accused of being in service of Spain, 196–197; plans for a Spanish connection thwarted, 196–197; leaves Ky., 201–202
William and Mary, College of, 80, 199, 205
Williamsburg, 33

PATRICIA WATLINGTON

A native Kentuckian, Patricia Watlington received her B.A. from the University of Kentucky and her M.A. and Ph.D. degrees from Yale University. She is Assistant Professor of History at Quinnipiac College in Hamden, Connecticut.